Unity in Diversity:
Embracing the spirit of group work

Proceedings of the XXXVI International Symposium
on Social Work with Groups
Calgary, Alberta, Canada, June 5-8, 2014

Unity in Diversity:
Embracing the Spirit of Group Work

Edited by

William Pelech
Karen Ring
Sarah LaRocque

w&b

MMXV

© Whiting & Birch Ltd 2015
Published by Whiting & Birch Ltd,
Forest Hill, London SE23 3HZ

ISBN 9781861771384

Printed in England and the United States by Lightning Source

CONTENTS

Acknowledgements

International Association for Social Work with Groups (IASWG)
XXXVI Annual International Symposium
Calgary, Alberta, Canada, June 5–8, 2014

Symposium International Honoree
Ann M. Bergart

Symposium Local Honorees
Jane Matheson
Rochelle (Robbie) Babins-Wagner
Ryan Geake

Symposium Cochairs
William Pelech
Karen Ring
Sarah Larocque

We gratefully acknowledge the diverse contributions of each of the authors in this year's symposium proceedings publication, *Unity in Diversity, Embracing the Spirit of Group Work*. From the initial call for papers that heralded the possibility of an exciting and unique IASWG Symposium in Calgary, the contributors' willingness and enthusiasm to be part of the event have certainly shone through in their scholarly writings and captivating chapters. These contributions were critiqued and reviewed by a talented and experienced cadre of behind-the-scenes social work academics and practitioners. These reviewers, who generously contributed their expertise and time, included Jen Clements, Mark Doel, Jennie Fleming, Rhonda Hudson, Jared Kant, Olga Molina, Reineth Prinsloo, Mamadou Seck, Mark Smith, and Greg Tully. We truly appreciate each of them and the responsive and vital part they played in this process.

Dr. Greg Tully, president, IASWG, was bestowed with a good old western welcome to Calgary with a white hat ceremony at the symposium. We would never have successfully achieved our tasks as editors or symposium cochairs without the support of this good guy in the white hat, who was always available and knowledgeable, with encouraging and supportive words, and wise counsel on which direction to take. Thanks to Greg Tully for his hard work over the years as president of the association and for his work with us. We cannot thank him enough for the way he believed in and trusted our abilities to produce a successful symposium and publication.

Gratitude is due to our publisher Whiting & Birch Ltd., and specifically David Whiting. David has not only been accessible to us in guiding this publication to press, but his consistent support of the Association and repeated presence at our yearly symposia over the years are noteworthy and greatly appreciated. As well, we appreciate the keen eye of Karen Crosby of Editarians, who undertook the final copyedit of the manuscript.

These proceedings could not have happened without a symposium. The 2014 IASWG Symposium could not have taken place without the enormous support from the University of Calgary, Faculty of Social Work faculty and staff, Hotel Alma, symposium cosponsors and contributors, organizational members, presenters, students, volunteers, exhibitors, and attendees. Our thanks to everyone once again who embraced the spirit of group work in Calgary. We also wish to acknowledge the generous support provided by the Social Sciences and Research Council of Canada (SSHRC).

And finally, we give our thanks to the IASWG Calgary 2014 Symposium Planning Committee members and the IASWG board members for their guidance, support, and encouragement from the first notions of a symposium in Calgary to the publication of these proceedings.

Tribute

Dr. Norma Caroline Lang (1927–2012)

Anna Nosko, Nancy Sullivan, & Joanne Sulman

Dr. Norma Lang's career was rooted solidly in social work practice, teaching, generating theories for social work with groups, consulting with practitioners in the field, and mentoring students and professionals who worked with groups. As stated by Nancy Sullivan, she was the "quintessential academic."

Norma made landmark contributions to our profession in the application of qualitative research methodology to social group work theory. Her doctoral dissertation, completed in 1972 at Case Western Reserve University in Cleveland, Ohio, gave us the broad-range model in group work, which demonstrated her exemplary skills in conceptualizing human phenomena. This model became central to Katy Papell and Beulah Rothman in their development of the mainstream model of social work with groups.

Norma continued to build group work practice theory in her development of collectivity theory, which looked at different social forms across social group work practices. Norma's differentiation of the social forms provided a theoretical understanding of the features that characterize fully formed "groups" and lesser developed collectivities while indicating the beneficial uses of each. A special 1986 issue of the journal *Social Work with Groups* was devoted to "Collectivity in Social Group Work: Concepts and Practice," coedited by Norma and Joanne Sulman.

The crowning point of Norma's career was the publication of her book, *Group Work Practice to Advance Social Competence: A Specialized Methodology for Social Work,* published in 2010 by Columbia Press. Norma was particularly pleased to have been invited to present the essence of her book at the prestigious international Grace Coyle Lecture Series at Case Western University School of Social Work. Norma's book offers a model for group workers who are working with populations needing particular professional intervention to benefit from social group work experience. As with all of her work, the book is a singularly brilliant example of her ability to conceptualize human phenomena and to teach knowledge for social work practice with groups.

As one of the founders of the Association for the Advancement of Social Work with Groups (AASWG), Norma was invited to give the keynote address on the opening night at the first symposium in 1979 in Cleveland. However, since she and I (Anna) were caught up in a terrible snowstorm in her car in the ditch en route to Cleveland, Dr. Ben Zion Shapiro stepped in to read it on her behalf. Fortunately, we did arrive the next day to attend this astonishing and seminal group work gathering that became a turning point in the resurgence of social group work. Norma attended and presented at almost every symposium until 2012.

Norma chaired the Fourth Annual AASWG Symposium "Patterns in the Mosaic" held in Toronto in 1982. Her attention to the minutest details and her high standards made the event a huge success. She suggested to the planning committee that we continue to meet under the name Toronto Group Workers Network, with Norma at the helm, our founder and chairperson. This network became a formal chapter of the AASWG in 1988. She maintained involvement in the Toronto chapter to the end. She was known for nurturing and mentoring students and practitioners, connecting them with one another through the chapter and beyond. She encouraged and assisted practitioners to write about their field work and to present it at the AASWG symposia. Norma gave countless workshops and courses for the Toronto Group Workers Network and in continuing education at the University of Toronto, promoting social group work theory and its application in practice. In 2000, Toronto hosted a second symposium, "Social Justice Through Social Work With Groups," for which, with her expertise and experience, Norma was the unmistakable leader.

Many who knew her academically have described her as a superb conceptualizer (Ester Blum); a giant in our field (Dominique Moyse Steinberg), who has made a unique contribution to social group work theory; a brilliant mind, having an unbiased eye as an editor who looked for conceptual clarity (Bob Basso); having intellectual integrity (Alex Gitterman); and generous in her encouragement towards newer group workers and a brilliant thinker (Greg Tully). She did have a huge influence in the teaching practice and contribution of theoretical knowledge of social work with groups both internationally, nationally, and locally in Toronto (Nancy Sullivan).

What many do not know is that despite Norma's careful attention to detail, she was wonderfully creative, intuitive, and artistic. She used these gifts to create yet another extremely important theoretical contribution to social group work: nondeliberative practice theory.

Nondeliberative describes practice that enables problem-solving in ways other than verbal and cognitive. These activity-based helping modalities activate analogic experiences. Nondeliberative ways of problem-solving include play, art, games, action, music, dance, drama, role-play, rehearsal, intuitive thinking, and other activities. By combining verbal and nonverbal components, the worker helps the group operationalize experiential forms of problem-solving.

Although Norma died before completing her book on nondeliberative theory, a special issue of the journal *Social Work with Groups* is being compiled to make her nondeliberative practice theory available to the social work community and the group work literature.

As Canadians we are extremely proud of Norma Lang's innovative and stellar work: her teaching, her theory building, her writing, her advancing all aspects of social work with groups, her caring, and her compassion. It is only fitting that she be given a grateful tribute in these proceeding of the IASWG Symposium in Calgary. She was there in spirit with all of us.

Norma would have approved.

References

Lang, N. C. (2010). *Group work practice to advance social competence: A specialized methodology for social work.* New York, NY: Columbia University Press.

Lang, N. C., & Sulman, J. (Guest Eds.). (1986). Special edition: Collectivity in social group work: Concepts and practice. *Social Work With Groups, 9*(4).

About the Editors

Dr. William Pelech currently holds an appointment as full professor and associate dean (academic) in the Faculty of Social Work at the University of Calgary. Dr. Pelech has conducted research and practice group work and currently holds a major national Tri-Council grant; his research focuses on how practitioners use diversity in their group work practice. He has been a coprincipal investigator on a major Canadian Institutes of Health Research grant relating to intergenerational trauma among First Nations people as well as a national research project, which developed a virtual community of practice for practitioners and caregivers for individuals who experience fetal alcohol spectrum disorder. Dr. Pelech also pioneered the Bachelor of Social Work (BSW) Virtual Learning Circle, a blended BSW program, and was presented the Killam Award for Innovation in Education for this work.

Karen A. Ring is a licensed clinical social worker (LCSW), group worker, trainer, and transformational consultant in Barbados. She was a lecturer in social work at The University of the West Indies, Barbados (1996–2012), an adjunct professor at Florida State University College of Social Work, Tallahassee, Florida (1991–1996), and a visiting scholar at the University of Calgary, Alberta, Canada (2011). She has conducted professional training and group work throughout the Caribbean as a volunteer with the Florida Association for Volunteer Action in the Caribbean and the Americas. She has published on disaster research in the Caribbean, conducted a work force study on the social work profession in Barbados, and contributed as a team member on the Global Group Work Project, funded by the International Association of Schools of Social Work (IASSW). Her clinical practice areas include personal empowerment, spiritual development, dream work, retreat facilitation, counselling training, and clinical supervision. She is currently writing a book about dreams and dream groups for personal and spiritual transformation.

Sarah LaRocque is a clinician, field instructor, and PhD candidate in the Faculty of Social Work, University of Calgary. Sarah specializes in group work in private practice and is clinical director of a dialectical behaviour therapy program. She provides group training for mental health practitioners in psychoeducational, support, and process-oriented groups. She is past president of the Calgary Section of the Canadian Group Psychotherapy Association and has served as secretary on the national executive. She has published on group work and has developed a group training framework for use in field education, currently the subject of the dissertation.

The Contributors

Mari Alschuler, PhD, LISW-S, is an assistant professor of social work at Youngstown State University. She teaches in the BSW and MSW programs, and starting in 2015 will be the MSW program coordinator. Her research areas of interest are student veteran success, reflective journaling, mindfulness meditation, poetry therapy, and LGBTQI issues. Email: mlalschuler@ysu.edu

Stephanie Baird, MSW, RSW, is a PhD student in the Factor-Inwentash Faculty of Social Work at the University of Toronto. Her social work practice experience has been in providing individual, family, and group counselling services at community-based counselling centres. Much of this experience, as well as her research focus, has been specifically dedicated to social work services for women who have experienced abuse or trauma. Email: stephanie.baird@mail.utoronto.ca

Betty Bastien, PhD is a member of the Piikani First Nation and Associate Professor at the University of Calgary, Faculty of Social Work. Her Traditional knowledge is situated in the Brave Dog Society and Thunder Pipes of the Blackfoot. Some of her works include research and publications on Indigenous science, cultural and language re-vitalization, colonization and intergenerational trauma, and Aboriginal Child Welfare. She has presented in Peru, New Zealand, Australia and China. Dr. Bastien's recognitions include: Women of Distinction Award; Esquao Awards from the Institute for the Advancement of Aboriginal Women; Member Alumni Honor Society, University of Lethbridge in recognition of Outstanding Achievement and Contribution to the Community; and the John Hutton Memorial Award for Social Action and Policy. Email: bastien@ucalgary.ca

Ginette Berteau a toujours eu la passion du travail social de groupe. Après l'avoir pratiqué, elle a formé et supervisé plusieurs intervenants et étudiants, a réalisé un doctorat sur les habiletés spécifiques à l'intervention de groupe. Elle est professeure en travail social de groupe à l'UQAM, Montréal, depuis 15 ans. Email : berteau.ginette@uqam.ca

Sylvie Cameron, MSW, est responsable de la formation pratique depuis 2003 à l'École de travail social (UQAM), et elle a enseigné le travail social en milieux collégial et universitaire. Elle a participé à plusieurs recherches dont une sur les conditions de supervision et a oeuvré au développement et à l'implantation de projets en prévention/promotion. Email: cameron.sylvie@uqam.ca.

Carol S. Cohen, DSW, LMSW, is an associate professor at Adelphi University School of Social Work, in Garden City, NY. Carol focuses on social group work, community-based practice, international social work, and professional education. Committed to collaborative participatory research, she has a strong network of international partners and extensive publication record. Carol is a Fulbright Scholar, founder of the Global Group Work Project, and cochair of IASWG Commission. Email: cohen5@adelphi.edu

Reg Crowshoe is a ceremonialist and teacher within the oral Blackfoot Piikani system from which he finds strength. His Blackfoot name is Awakaaseena, and he is from the Piikani Nation in Southern Alberta. He attended St. Cypriot Anglican Residential School on the Peigan Reserve and the University of Calgary, where he eventually developed cultural courses and was awarded an honorary degree. He co-authored a book, Akak'stiman, and other publications on justice and sentencing circles, and co-authored a book with the University of Colorado; its title is "Science in the Native Community". His passion is cultural preservation, cultural protection and cultural renewal.

David Delay, PhD(c) MSW, RSW, is a sessional lecturer and a PhD candidate in social work at the Factor-Inwestash Faculty of Social Work, University of Toronto. His research interests include group-based intimate partner violence interventions for men, traumatic brain injury and violence, mindfulness-based trauma counselling, and the teaching of group work practice. Mindfulness has a welcome daily presence in his life. Email: david.delay@utoronto.ca

Mark Doel, PhD, MA (Oxon), CQSW, is a professor emeritus of social work. His principal interests are groupwork, social work methods (especially task-centred work), field and practicum social work, international social work, and service user (client) involvement. He has 20 years of experience as a social worker, with subsequent experience as social work teacher, trainer, manager, researcher, and author. Email: doel@waitrose.com

Joan Farkas, MSW, RSW, has 20 years' experience in community development; much of her work has focused on women's issues, poverty reduction, and policy change. Joan has presented at numerous conferences and facilitated a range of workshops on social justice, comedy and social action, and the skills of advocacy.

Jayleen Galarza, PhD, received her Master in Clinical Social Work, Master in Education, and PhD in Human Sexuality from Widener University (Chester, PA). She is also a licensed clinical social worker (LCSW) in Pennsylvania as well as a certified sex therapist through the American Association of Sexuality Educators, Counselors, and Therapists (AASECT). Dr. Galarza is currently an assistant professor in the Social Work & Gerontology Department at Shippensburg University in Shippensburg, PA. Her clinical and research interests include intersectionality, Latina sexuality, sexual/gender identities and experiences, empowerment, sexuality social justice, narrative therapy, and feminist therapy. The focus of her work is on exploring empowering approaches to working with oppressed communities as well as raising awareness of such issues. Email: jgalarza@ship.edu

Charles Garvin, PhD, LCSW, is a professor emeritus of social work at the University of Michigan, where he was on the faculty from 1965 until 2002. During that period he taught group work, interpersonal practice, community organization, research, and administration at the master's level and group work, individual work, and multicultural work at the doctoral level. He was director of the doctoral program in social work and social science in the 1990s. He was one of the first chairs of what is now called the International Association for Social Work With Groups (IASWG). He has directed or participated in research projects on the Work Inventive Program (WIN), Task-Centered Group Work, and client directed programs for people with severe mental illness. He is the author or coauthor of such texts as *Contemporary Group Work, Interpersonal Practice in Social Work*, and *Social Work in Contemporary Society,* and the coeditor of *Handbook of Social Work With Groups.* He has written over 50 articles or book chapters on such topics as group work, direct practice, the concept of "levels" in social work, research, teaching social work, and social justice. His email address is charlesg@umich.edu.

Sadie Goddard-Durant, MSc, is a Canadian Certified Counselor who holds a Master of Science degree in Clinical Mental Health Counselling. Currently a consultant in Barbados, Sadie develops and implements culturally relevant, trauma-informed mental health services using groups and expressive art therapies to facilitate healing in community settings. She also teaches and trains psychology and counselling students. This practice-based knowledge informs her contributions to research on Caribbean Mental Health. Email: sgoddarddurant@gmail.com

Étienne Guay est un travailleur social en pratique privée et étudiant au doctorat en sociologie. Il agit à titre de superviseur au Centre de Thérapie Caplan. Il est aussi engagé dans la formation en travail social de groupe comme chargé de cours et superviseur de stage à la maîtrise (UQAM, Montréal). Email: guay.etienne@uqam.ca

Alice Home, MSW, PhD, is professor emeritus of social work at the University of Ottawa. Her teaching focuses on group work and research while her practice centres on empowerment, mutual aid, and self-help groups. Her research explores groups for parents of children with hidden disabilities, parents of adopted children with special needs, and employed mothers raising children with disabilities. She has published widely on these topics. E-mail: ahome@uottawa.ca

Liza Lorenzetti, PhD(c), MSW, RSW, is an instructor, researcher, and PhD candidate in the Faculty of Social Work at the University of Calgary. Her practice, activism, and research in the areas of gender-based violence, anti-racism, peace, and social justice informs the perspective that solutions lie in systemic change and social transformation. Email: lizalorenzetti@gmail.com

Nicole Lynch, MA, received her Master of Arts in Counselling Psychology with a specialisation in School Counselling in 2009. She is currently a Registered Counselling Psychologist in Barbados. Her professional activities focus on child and youth mental health and education reform. Primary areas of her work include advocacy for improved psychosocial environments for children and adolescents in the Caribbean and the development of culturally relevant group interventions for this population. E-mail: Nicolenlynch12@gmail.com

Jennifer Martin, MSW, PhD, is an assistant professor in the School of Child and Youth Care at Ryerson University. Her research examines trauma and online child exploitation and victimization. She integrates mindfulness practices into the "helping" classroom with students to enhance the development of their professional self-awareness, professional practices and interventions, and self-care. Email: jjmartin@ryerson.ca

Jane Matheson, PhD, RSW, is CEO of Wood's Homes, in Calgary, Alberta, and an adjunct professor at the University of Calgary Faculty of Social Work. Jane has been working at Wood's Homes and teaching for 30 years in online education, supervision, practical leadership, and children's mental health. Her interest in research was stimulated by her PhD, resulting in a research department at Wood's Homes and the recent announcement of the Wood's Homes Chair in Children's Mental Health. Email: jane.matheson@woodshomes.ca

Linda McArdle, LISW-S, is a senior instructor in the School of Social Work, University of Akron, where she teaches BSW and MSW courses including micro and mezzo practice, groupwork, ethics, social work in health care, and field seminars. She is the chapter development chair of the Executive Committee of IASWG. Email: Linda15@uakron.edu

Dawn Lorraine McBride, PhD, is a registered psychologist and an associate professor in the counsellor education program at the University of Lethbridge. She is an international speaker, researcher, and writer. Her specialty areas include supervision practices, professional ethics, cultural competencies, online education, group therapies, and complex emotional (mental health) challenges. Email: dawn.mcbride@uleth.ca

Kyle McGee is a licensed social worker with nearly 20 years of experience in the field as agency clinician, supervisor, educator, and trainer. He is currently employed by FEGS Health and Human Services in New York City as a clinical coordination specialist. Kyle is a PhD student at the School of Social Work, Adelphi University, and has served as an adjunct faculty teaching group work practice courses at both Adelphi University and the Silberman School of Social Work at Hunter College. Kyle's practice has focused on mental health treatment with youth and adults living with mental illness and chemical dependency. His research interests include the provision of group work services to individuals residing in homeless shelters. He has also incorporated the use of music and drumming into his practice with therapeutic groups. Email: kylem.mcgee@gmail.com

Barbara Muskat, PhD, RSW, is the director of social work at the Hospital for Sick Children and an assistant professor (status-only) at The University of Toronto Factor-Inwentash Faculty of Social Work. Dr. Muskat's many years of experience are in direct clinical work, clinical supervision, community consultation, and organizational management. Her areas of expertise are direct clinical practice and group work, with a focus on children with developmental needs. Email: barbara.muskat@sickkids.ca

Anna Nosko, MSW, RSW, Diploma in Social Work Research, is a social worker at Family Service Toronto. She teaches for TAPE (Toronto Advanced Professional Education) which serves clinicians and social group workers with various organizations. She is a consultant to group workers in a Toronto youth organization and is presently chair of the Toronto Region Groupworkers' Network.

Rachael Pascoe MSW, RSW, works as a therapist at Bellwood Health Service in Toronto, Ontario, facilitating residential process groups for individuals coping with addiction and concurrent disorders. Rachael received clinical supervision facilitating first stage concurrent trauma and addiction groups in a hospital setting and has extensive experience working with individuals facing systemic barriers and marginalization in drop-in centres, shelters, and transitional housing programs. She has published in the area of addiction services and has presented at conferences on topics such as group work practice, post-traumatic stress disorder, wait times for addiction services, and concurrent mental health and addiction care. She can be contacted at rpascoe@bellwood.ca.

Reineth (CE) Prinsloo, DPhil (Social Work), RSW, is an associate professor in the Department of Social Work and Criminology, University of Pretoria, South Africa. Reineth teaches family development and guidance and social work with groups, and has been involved with the integration of theory and practice in social work for more than 20 years. She specialises in teaching sensitivity to diversity, marriage, and family preservation, as well as in growth groups, based on a strength perspective. Email: reineth.prinsloo@up.ac.za

Tomasz Michal Rapacki, MC, is a registered provisional psychologist who is active in the fields of rehabilitation and clinical/counselling psychology. He has lived extensively in Poland, Canada, and China, and has focused much of his research on cross-cultural psychology and cultural competencies. His academic interests include culture, learning, cognition, personality, psychometrics, and cognitive linguistics. Email: tomrapacki@culturedpsychology.com

Jorune Vysniauskyte Rimkiene, MSW, PhD, is a lecturer in the Department of Social Work at Vytautas Magnus University in Kaunas, Lithuania. She has practiced group work for 20 years in several practice areas, including children and adolescent groups, school and kindergarten teachers, parent groups for hearing and deaf parents, social work practitioners, and interdisciplinary teamwork. She has taught group work for six years at the MSW level. Email: j.rimkiene@sgi.vdu.lt

Rachel Seed, MSW, is a recent MSW graduate from Loyola University of Chicago. She is currently the psychiatric rehabilitation services director at Park View Rehab Center, a long-term care facility in Chicago. Rachel has focused much of her interest and practice on mindfulness-based interventions. Currently, she concentrates her clinical work and research on individuals living with serious mental illness. Email: rachelseed@outlook.com

Thelma Silver, MSW, PhD, LISW-S, LICDC, is currently a professor in the Department of Social Work at Youngstown State University in Ohio. She teaches groupwork in both the BSW and MSW programs, and also is a field work supervisor. Her areas of interest in research and practice are focused on mental health, chemical dependency, and groupwork. Email: tsilver@ysu.edu

Nancy E. Sullivan, MSW, PhD, is a retired faculty member of the School of Social Work, Memorial University, of Newfoundland, Canada. She is a founding member of the Toronto Region Groupworkers' Network (Toronto Chapter of IASWG) and past president of the IASWG.

Joanne Sulman, MSW, RSW, is a qualitative research and group work consultant; research analyst in the Division of Thoracic Surgery, Toronto General Hospital; and an adjunct lecturer at the Factor-Inwentash Faculty of Social Work, University of Toronto. Her research interests include collectivity theory, single session groups for persons with inflammatory bowel disease, nondeliberative groupwork skills in focus groups, quality of life in esophageal cancer, diversity and human rights in the workplace, and adverse childhood experiences and illness.

Samantha Swift, MSW, graduated from California State University, Long Beach, in May 2015. Her social work and group work interests are in mental health, substance use, and spirituality. Email: Sswift318@gmail.com

Rebecca Witheridge recently earned her MSW from Loyola University Chicago in Illinois. For her internships, she ran a restorative justice program at a high school and provided individual, group, and family therapy for adolescent boys at a residential facility. Rebecca was privileged to receive the President's Medallion for the School of Social Work and was also inducted into the Alpha Sigma Nu honor society. In the future, she hopes to help develop and run arts- or activities-based programming for at-risk/trauma-affected youth, supported by neuroscience research on developmental trauma. She can be reached at rebecca.e.witheridge@gmail.com.

Introduction

Our theme for the 36th Annual Symposium was inspired in part by Helen Phillips, a noted social group theorist in the 1940s and 1950s. In her seminal book, *Essentials of Group Work Skill*, Phillips (1957) cited the work of John Dewey to describe how the complex interrelationships present in a group can come together to form a unity that can bring about change. One could say that a group that forms in this way is a beautiful thing. In speaking of these aesthetics, the pragmatist, John Dewey, who contributed to group work the process of problem-solving, once stated,

There is an old formula for beauty in nature and art: Unity in variety. . . . The formula has meaning only when its terms are understood to concern only a relation of energies. There is no fullness, no many parts, without distinctive differentiations. But they have esthetic quality, as in the fullness of a musical phrase, only when distinctions depend upon reciprocal resistances. There is unity only when the resistances create a suspense that is resolved through cooperative interaction of the opposed energies. (Dewey, 1934, p. 167)

One way of looking at diversity may be to regard it as something that occurs in the space between us. It offers an opportunity for learning and growth. How people respond to diversity will ultimately determine whether they benefit from this opportunity. If people respond with fear and judgment, it can become a space of violence. If people respond with appreciation, openness, and vulnerability, it can become a space for transformation.

Our collective histories are rife with examples of where religion has been used to condemn, oppress, and marginalize those who adopt different beliefs. In many countries such as Canada, we have witnessed many atrocities committed by religious orders. In Canada, we continue to experience the tragic legacy of residential schools, which allowed for cultural genocide under the guise of educating Indigenous children. However, spirituality can make a difference. Our belief in a power greater than ourselves, and the commitment to serving others, is an ethic that is espoused by many religious traditions. Moreover, it is something that all group workers understand. It is through our work with groups that we can transform scared spaces into sacred spaces. It is a place where, if we do our work well, we realize the power of the group to bring about change that transforms its members and the world.

The symposium is a meeting space where people with diverse ideas, perspectives, and identities can meet to share, learn, and grow. Valuing diversity and recognizing the power of groups contribute to the spirit of group work. For those who participated in the Calgary symposium, perhaps one of many enduring experiences was the bringing together of students, educators, and practitioners from across the globe to a large circle, and with the beat of the drums we all moved together. Over time, while we each moved in unique ways, we for a moment once again experienced that beautiful sense of unity in diversity that Dewey spoke of 80 years ago, which is the spirit of group work.

Just as the elder at the opening ceremony turned to honor the four planetary directions, these proceedings are organized into four parts, which contain a diverse series of chapters. In keeping with our respect for the theme of diversity, you will find that we have not attempted to standardize the text. In these proceedings, you will find portions that are written in both of Canada's two official languages: English (including U.S., Canadian, and British spellings) and French. In Part 1: Global Group Work Plenary you will find a variety of international perspectives that share a common interest and concern relating to the future of social group work. The Calgary symposium opened and closed with indigenous ceremonies, which honoured the indigenous traditions and people of the region. For this reason, we are pleased to include a summary of a plenary address given by Dr. Betty Bastien on sacred circles. Next, in Part 2: Invitationals, you will find summaries of three invitational addresses. The Robert Salmon Invitational, presented by a major academic voice in social group work, Charles Garvin, summarizes the literature to date and poses some vitally important questions about mutual aid. We also offer a transcript of the University of California Invitational given by Jane Matheson, wherein she summarizes 10 keys for working with organizational groups. Part 2 closes with a paper presented at the inaugural Social Justice Invitational by Liza Lorenzetti and Joan Farkas. This paper outlines a unique presentation process named Pechakucha, which involves a six-step journey of individual reflection and group sharing.

In keeping with our symposium theme, in Part 3: Sessional Papers you will find a diverse array of papers that collectively come together to address diversity and spirituality in group work practice. David Delay and Jennifer Martin describe how they integrated mindfulness into the classroom. Rachael Pascoe outlines trauma-informed care among diverse populations and its implications for group work practice. Karen

Ring describes the use of dream work in professional self-care. Sadie Goddard-Durant and Nicole Lynch describe a model of culturally informed group work practice with Barbadian youth. Jayleen Galarza explores the intersection of queer Latina experiences and identities along with group work Latina(o)s. Ginette Berteau, Sylvie Cameron, and Etienne Guay critically appraise their experiences in supervising graduate group work students. Alice Home presents findings from two qualitative studies, including one focusing on groups for caregivers of children with disabilities. Tomasz Rapaki and Dawn Martin describe the development of a scale measuring culturally responsive mental health services with an emphasis on group work practice. Marie Alschuler, Linda McArdle, and Thelma Silver offer a paper which focuses on strength-based group supervision.

A distinctive feature of these proceedings is Part 4: Student Voices, which offers mini-papers by four future group work scholars. Samantha Swift shares her experiences as a neophyte group worker. Stephanie Baird poses some key questions about professional responses to the diverse needs of survivors of intimate partner violence. Kyle McGee offers a brief paper, which examines how two models of group development informed his experience as an instructor. Rebecca Witheridge outlines the chrysalis model of peer jury program design. Finally, Rachel Seed offers an interesting discussion about the mind-body connection in group work.

We hope you find that these proceedings reflect the aesthetic quality that Dewey spoke about so long ago. Like the XXXVI Annual Symposium, which brought together so many diverse voices from across the globe to the land where two rivers and many cultures meet in Calgary, we hope that you will find beauty in the unity and diversity present in this work. For it is through the bringing together of diverse voices that something quite remarkable arises, which is, and will always be, the spirit of group work.

References

Dewey, J. (1934). *Art as experience*. New York, NY: G. P. Putnam's Sons.

Phillips, H. (1957). *Essentials of social group work skill*. New York, NY: Association Press.

Part 1
Plenaries

Global Group Work Plenary: The Future of Social Group Work

Introduction by Mark Doel, Sheffield, United Kingdom
Elder Reg Crowshoe, First Nations, Canada (oral contribution)
Barbara Muskat, Toronto, Canada
Ginette Berteau, Montréal, Canada
Jorune Vysniauskyte Rimkiene, Vilnius, Lithuania
Reineth Prinsloo, Pretoria, South Africa
Carol Cohen, New York, United States

With acknowledgements to Karen Ring, Barbados, for inviting this session and for her help in framing it.

Introduction

Each of the six contributors to the panel was asked to offer thoughts on the status of groupwork in their region and to consider current trends that contribute to or hinder group practice. Of course, these are personal views from a serendipitous collection of countries and cultures; taken together they add to our understanding of the commonalities and differences in groupwork practice and, indeed, the meaning of groupwork across the globe. Readers should note that the style of this article reflects the conversational nature of the original panel presentations and, accordingly, the pieces that comprise this article are not referenced in the usual way. Indeed, Elder Crowshoe's presentation was in the oral tradition and therefore is not included in written form here. This article incorporates two languages, again reflecting the languages at the original presentation. We hope this decision demonstrates the pressing need for greater linguistic diversity, both generally and in our own groupwork community. Our presenters were asked to reflect on the practice of groupwork and groupwork education, with some thoughts about the International Association of Social Work With Groups' (IASWG) role in supporting global groupwork.

Practice of Groupwork

Where is groupwork practised? The responses from the panel suggest that its reach is generally great, but that there are variations in its nature. For example, Berteau noted that the more dynamic and original forms of groupwork in Québec are to be found in community settings, with more of a struggle in the service sector, where an outcome-based mentality is proving to be a strait-jacket for innovative groupwork. Also in the Canadian context, Muskat noted the worrying trend for "individual work in groups," often led by people without groupwork training.

Countries like Lithuania are in a more pioneering stage of development, and Vysniauskyte Rimkiene noted the importance of individual enthusiasm—champions, one might say—in the promotion of groupwork. This resonates with Cohen's notion of legacy, her remembrances of the mentors and the significance of such individuals in passing on the flame of groupwork, and her call for support for "emerging leaders." As readers will see in more detail later, South Africa seems differently positioned, along with Elder Crowshoe's account of his First Nations community, as Prinsloo highlighted the universal experience of group in her country. For South Africans, the question, "Where is groupwork practised?" is rather like asking, "Where do people breathe?"

As group workers, we see, recurringly, the significance of social and political contexts. Perhaps this is most stark in Lithuania, where the shadow of Soviet rule still affects people's abilities to trust—not just other people, but themselves, too. This underscores a basic truth: that good groupwork relies on belief and trust. For others, the immediate social climate is affected by the willingness of the public purse to fund groupwork through agencies (state or otherwise) that want to promote it, but also by the degree to which the accountability that accompanies this funding becomes burdensome—"He who pays the piper calls the tune?" The funding for groupwork, whether state-financed, insurance-based, or funded very little at all, indirectly reflects the different histories of statehood from nation to nation. And group workers cannot, nor should they, escape the bread and butter issues, literally in the case of South Africa, where incentives such as food and housing might be offered to attract people to groups: what Cohen has described as "integral" groupwork.

Education for Groupwork

Opportunities for groupwork education vary in the extent of university-based learning and also the availability of supervision in groupwork in the field. Aside from South Africa, there is a universal sense that education for groupwork in schools of social work is "dimming," to use Muskat's phrase, though the picture in Québec is brighter, with Berteau recording 50% of students opting for groupwork placements at one university. And, though the situation in Lithuania is one of a groupwork drought, Vysniauskyte Rimkiene has optimistically noted that this at least means there is much to be done and much exciting new ground to broken.

Post-qualifying, Muskat's notion of groupworker networks is important wherever groupworkers practise, to refresh their enthusiasm and skills as keepers of the flame. Cohen's four concepts—critical, integral, responsible and personal—are applied to the U.S. context but are universal ones that can be transferred across national and cultural borders to help "index" the state of groupwork.

In brief, then, Berteau's description of groupwork in Québec—"une certaine vivacité, mais sa situation reste fragile [a certain vivacity but the situation remains fragile]"—has a near-universal truth. Juxtaposed to this, however, is Prinsloo's insight that in the African context most things happen in a group context, so groupwork is already the lifeblood rather than an emergency transfusion. The challenge in the South African context is how to join with existing groups rather than expecting communities to regroup in social workers' offices and clinics. "How fractured is your community?" could perhaps be a litmus test question. It could be a way to consider whether as a groupworker the challenge is primarily to regroup people where groups have shattered and are no longer present or whether it is how best to shake hands with existing groups in the community, perhaps to help them become more accessible to those who are marginalised and to help give them a voice to be heard by the rest of society, in particular the powers that control resources and policy.

IASWG already plays an important part in the development of cross-national and cross-cultural understandings of groups and groupwork. As an organization, it questions the dominance of Western paradigms of groupwork, though there remains much still to be done. A number of presenters noted IASWG's Standards for Groupwork as a way to secure ethical and effective practice across borders, in what Cohen described as responsible groupwork. Her plea for more of the personal in groupwork is universal for the West, but already present in South Africa. Above all, the main message from these varied presentations (written and oral) is that practitioners have so very much to learn about groupwork from one another.

Canada (English-Speaking)

Thank you for inviting me to offer thoughts on the status and future of social group work in my region as well as on current trends that contribute to and hinder group practice. I am going to offer reflections on social group work practice as well as education.

The Calgary symposium has highlighted the beautiful mosaic that comprises Canada, the many individuals who identify across categories of language, culture, religion, gender, sexuality, and location, as well across theoretical approaches to group work. This requires me to name my own social location, as what I am writing is very much situated in my experience as a female Anglophone based in a large, urban, English-speaking location, which is filled with individuals who are privileged as well as those highly impacted by the social determinants of health. Group work is alive in the city of Toronto, a city noted for its embracing of diversity. But whether social group work is thriving is less certain.

Toronto is fortunate in that various levels of government provide financial support to a diverse array of organizations and agencies that offer health and mental health care, support, therapy, and social services. This allows greater access to services but also requires due diligence to demonstrate the effectiveness of these services for participants. Organizations are looking for evidence that services are efficient, effective, and worth the cost of running them. There are an ever-growing number of short-term, problem-focused groups taking place that are based in a specific methodology (e.g., groups offering cognitive behavioural training), in delivering information (e.g., psychoeducational approaches), or in a manualized treatment (e.g., social skill teaching) and that are often facilitated by individuals who have not been trained to facilitate social work groups. Thus, group processes are not emphasized, the group as a whole is not a concern, and empowerment and democratic values are not specifically considered in the group's facilitation. However, these programs have been based on methods that have demonstrated effectiveness and are attractive to funders.

There are also a number of psychotherapy groups offered in this city, generally embedded in adult mental health and addiction programs. In these, the emphasis is on curative and therapeutic factors and the goal is individual healing. While some psychotherapy groups are held in hospitals, others are facilitated by individuals in private practice. When led by a psychiatrist, fees are covered by health insurance. Social work services are rarely covered by Canadian private insurance programs.

There are an ever-growing number of grassroots organizations, which have been established to support the many newcomers to the country and the city, and where the emphasis may be on both learning about Canadian culture and preservation of traditional practices. These agencies generally exist on very small budgets and are staffed by individuals who speak the language and share the culture of the participants and not necessarily by individuals with training in social group work. The work of these centres probably most closely resembles the work of original settlement houses, although the focus is now on ensuring legal immigration status, legal rights, and securing of affordable housing and economic support. Some group work takes place, primarily for children and teens, as well as for women who are parenting on their own.

Longer-term support groups are still present in the city, especially for chronic health or mental health conditions. Some of these groups are facilitated as self-help groups, run by volunteer group facilitators out of grassroots organizations. While it is encouraging that there are still opportunities for member-to-member support, agendas set by members, and development of helping systems, availability of these groups is decreasing on the whole.

There are a growing number of online support group programs taking place, particularly in the health community. While social work academics and staff at a long-established centre serving seniors developed an excellent model of online support for caregivers of individuals with dementia, which was found to be effective and demonstrated a well-developed model for delivery, others do not seem to consider this model when developing similar online group programs.

In the area of social group work education, there are ample potential opportunities for training in social group work. Three local universities operate Master of Social Work (MSW) programs, with three more MSW programs within a close commute. Group work courses are likely offered in the universities; however, they are often taught by individuals with limited group work experience. I am not aware of a group work specialization available in any of the schools. And while group work skills are taught, I am not certain that social group work principles are emphasized. Furthermore, new practitioners would likely have difficulty finding supervision or mentoring in social group work, as there are so few social group work specialists. New practitioners would most likely be asked to develop and/or facilitate groups on their own with no additional supports, thus further eroding high quality group work practice.

Returning to the focus of this presentation, I believe that social group work is still alive in Toronto; however, it is certainly less available and dimming in stature. The future of social group work depends on what social group work practitioners and academics do to champion this approach. To begin with, social work practitioners tend to proudly focus their efforts on direct individual encounters with their clients. I do not wish to negate the importance of individual work, but it is incumbent upon our practitioners to examine their work and demonstrate its effectiveness. The IASWG Standards for Practice have emphasized the importance of evaluation. This provides an opportunity that has the potential to enhance social group work practice and continuity.

The Toronto Region Group Workers Network, which is the Toronto chapter of IASWG, is a keeper of the flame for social group work in Toronto. The network offers workshops and opportunities for mentorship. Members of the network are engaged in a variety of strategies, such as bringing in participants from other professions, reaching out to grassroots organizations, and teaching in group work classes, as ways to sustain this modality. It is equally important to draw in students and new practitioners if social group work is to survive. In summary, I believe that social group work is still alive in Toronto and could survive if those who practice it, teach about it, and believe in it consider how to go beyond our passion for it and demonstrate its effectiveness for those who are isolated, marginalized, oppressed, and struggling to cope.

Canada (langue française)
Présentation de la situation du travail social de groupe au Québec

Le point suivant donne un aperçu de la situation du travail social de groupe au Québec. Rappelons que cette province est d'abord francophone et que la francophonie représente 30% de la population canadienne.

Formation des étudiants

À l'instar de nos voisins américains, l'enseignement du travail social de groupe a été négligé pendant longtemps, mais depuis quelques années, la situation s'améliore dans les Écoles du Québec. Dans chacune des huit écoles, il y a au moins au baccalauréat, un cours obligatoire de 45 heures sur le travail social de groupe ; cinq écoles exigent que chaque étudiant suive 90 heures de cours et une école offre une possibilité de 135 heures de cours sur le travail social de groupe. Selon un sondage effectué en 2011 et 2012 auprès de deux cohortes de l'Université du Québec à Montréal (UQAM) portant sur les freins et les leviers pour développer une culture de travail social de groupe chez les étudiants, ces derniers disent apprécier cette formation. Dans certaines universités, plusieurs choisiront le travail social de groupe lors de leur stage pratique.

Du côté de la maîtrise en travail social, deux universités offrent une formation complémentaire de 45 heures à ses étudiants. Nous observons un fort engouement des étudiants de ce niveau pour le travail social de groupe. À titre d'exemple, à UQAM, chez les étudiants qui choisissent l'option stage et essai, 50% d'entre eux opteront pour expérimenter le travail social de groupe.

Par contre, s'il y a des avancées du côté de la formation des étudiants, les résultats du sondage cité précédemment met aussi en évidence que les étudiants interrogés perçoivent que le travail social de groupe n'est pas assez intégré à l'ensemble de leur cursus. Cela devient un cours parmi d'autres et ils considèrent avoir de la difficulté à réinvestir leurs acquis.

Une explication possible à ce résultat réside dans le fait que plusieurs professeurs au sein des Écoles de travail social ne sont pas très sensibles au travail social de groupe et que cette méthode n'est pas reconnue à sa juste valeur. Pour plusieurs, le travail social de groupe correspond au travail d'équipe, à l'animation de rencontres ou de groupes de rencontre. À cause de cette méconnaissance, il est parfois difficile de promouvoir le travail social de groupe. Il arrive encore que certains professeurs soient engagés pour l'enseignement du travail social de groupe sans avoir de véritable formation. Mentionnons à cet égard, que peu de personnes ayant un doctorat sont aussi formés au travail social de groupe. Ajoutons enfin à ce portrait, que, tout comme l'indique la littérature, il y a peu de superviseurs de stage formés au travail social de groupe au Québec, ce qui n'est pas pour aider les étudiants à s'investir dans le travail de groupe en début de carrière.

La pratique

Au Québec, le travail social de groupe est pratiqué autant dans les services sociaux en milieu institutionnel que dans les organismes communautaires. La situation est nettement plus dynamique dans le secteur des organismes communautaires. Le travail de groupe y occupe une place importante. Il est souvent initié à partir d'initiatives citoyennes et/ou à partir des besoins de la population. Il y a donc place pour une pratique de groupe y est variée et originale.

Dans le secteur institutionnel, la situation est plus nuancée. Dans certains milieux le travail social de groupe est de plus en plus intégré comme le cadre de référence de la pratique de groupe. C'est le cas pour les Centres de réadaptation en dépendance où 95% des services sont dispensés via le travail de groupe. Des travailleurs sociaux chevronnés et formés en travail social de groupe font actuellement de la formation continue avec les intervenants de ce secteur qui avaient été jusqu'à maintenant très peu initiés au travail de groupe. Déjà, 4 centres sur 11 ont reçu une formation sur le travail social de groupe. Des postes clés sont aussi occupés par des travailleurs sociaux de groupe assurant ainsi la vitalité et la pérennité de cette méthode d'intervention.

D'autres secteurs tels le travail social en milieu scolaire ont développé des pratiques innovantes (ex sport et travail social de groupe) et ont un rayonnement international du côté de la francophonie.

Par contre, dans certains milieux tels les Centres de santé et de services sociaux, la situation est plus difficile. Le travail social de groupe y est pratiqué, mais souvent sans que les travailleurs sociaux aient une formation et dans des conditions qui ne respectent pas les principes du travail social de groupe. La pratique dans ces milieux est sous l'égide d'une gestion basée sur les résultats et la productivité. Le groupe n'est pas une priorité et lorsqu'il l'est, c'est pour des raisons économiques. Ceux qui font du groupe se plaignent qu'ils ne peuvent comptabiliser leur intervention dans les statistiques. Il n'y a pas de place de prévu pour le travail de groupe.

Dans l'ensemble, les travailleurs sociaux sont préoccupés par la situation du travail de groupe au Québec. Cela se traduit par des efforts de publications dans les revues en français, par la tenue occasionnelle de journées québécoises de formation sur le sujet et par des initiatives telles que la création des communautés de pratiques sur le sujet.

Bref, le travail social de groupe au Québec a une certaine vivacité, mais sa situation reste fragile. Que pourrait faire pour nous l'IASWG ? Inclure davantage la diversité culturelle et linguistique dans ses diverses actions afin de soutenir les efforts de tous et chacun dans la consolidation du travail social de groupe. Ce soutien permettrait de se sentir appuyé et de continuer ce travail de consolidation qui est de longue haleine.

Lithuania

Analyzing the current trends contributing to and hindering group practice in the region, I can share mostly the experience of Lithuania, which links with other post-Soviet counties and mostly Baltic states. Starting with the trends that contribute to group work, it is important to take account of the fact that the social work profession is very young in this country. Twenty-two years ago, the first master's degree study program was started, and this was the beginning of social work education. A positive influence on this education was social capital from foreign countries. It made possible the new social work profession to meet European and global standards of education. Good relations with foreign professors and practitioners and with national psychologists helped to hasten the development of new methods of social work implementation into practice. Existing international rating systems of study programs in every university and college prove that social work programs are well developed. Other positive influences on group work are good practices by social work practitioners working with groups that are shared in the field. Analysing how group work is implemented in practice, one can notice that it is mostly built on the individual enthusiasm of the group leader—and that leader's interest in working with the group. This experience demonstrantes that a lot can be done, but it also shows that there is not enough understanding and support from agencies to use group work practice. Trying to list what is hindering group practice in the country, the list becomes long. First of all, group work it is not a popular social work method, and its worth is still not recognised among social work practitioners. The reasons for this are different. Even after more than 20 years of independence, there exist post-Soviet relics such as lack of trust in oneself and others. This factor makes people feel unsafe participating in formal groups. For this reason, the culture of participating in groups is very low. People prefer to communicate in informal groups, mostly formed from close networks, so these informal groups are popular. As well, practitioners are more likely to choose to work with individual cases to solve social problems. One of the explanations for this choice can be that few social work schools provide a curriculum that includes social work with groups. So, there is still a lack of professionals who have the knowledge and skills to work with groups. Practice shows that in a lot of cases practitioners use a class format and adopt the instructor role, delivering lectures in the group, rather than working with the group as a group. Literature analysis shows that there is almost no research in social work with groups in Lithuania, so another obstacle to using group work professionally is the lack of textbooks and journals in our national language. It is important to bear in mind that colleagues from different fields (e.g., medicine, education, policing) in a lot of cases are not aware that social workers are able to use group work.

All of the aforementioned reasons demonstrate that group work is still not used enough in social work and is only a niche for researchers, social work instructors, and some practitioners. Nonetheless, the future of of social work with groups is promising. Various channels spreading the value of this social work method need to be used: new textbooks, research, practical seminars, and scientific conferences. Social workers need to find their own indentity as group workers. The role of IASWG in developing group work in Lithuania can become very important. IASWG international events, professional group work journals, the opportunity to learn new methods and experience the newest trends in group work, and to get support, can encourage the growth of group work practice in Lithuania.

South Africa

South Africa is fortunate in many ways. The African concept of ubuntu, roughly translated as "human kindness," "humanity towards others," and "a person is a person through other people," encompasses everything that group work stands for. In Africa, life happens in groups with a universal bond of sharing and caring. The African way is not individualistic. Daily living, rituals, survival, celebrations, support: it all happens in group contexts.

Another advantage is that group work as an intervention method in social work is taught in all schools of social work, both as theory and as a practice component. In the schools of social work, the specific use of groups is slowly expanding. HIV and AIDS support groups, luncheon groups for women in rural and semiurban areas, support groups for grandparent-headed households, and formal programs used in offender care and rehabilitation contexts are but some of the uniquely South African examples.

Yet, South Africa also experiences numerous challenges. Social workers are responsible for thousands of statutory cases in child protection services. Foster care applications, supervision, and reunification services, with the accompanying administrative expectations of reports, draw away from creative thinking. Social workers are pressed to meet targets. The remedial model of solving problems and providing resources often takes priority over the strength and developmental model. People often still depend on the state for survival, and an extensive social security system affects expectations. Social workers report that people will come to groups if incentives such as food and housing are offered.

With cuts in government subsidies, welfare organisations have to deal with the challenge of not having the funds to appoint enough social workers for the demand. With caseloads of up to 150 cases per month, which often require crisis intervention, social workers in the field feel overwhelmed and experience burnout. Because of the geographical context of South Africa, service users often live in remote areas. A lack of resources such as transport opportunities and available venues for both the social workers and the people to be served result in missing many opportunities.

The answer to the challenges may lie in the advantages. South Africa has both Western and traditional contexts. Groups are natural and common contexts in African daily functioning. Should the future of group work in South Africa not lie in using traditional group processes? Should social workers not go to the existing groups and not expect people to come to the social workers and their offices? I personally regard the established and functional African group contexts as an opportunity for action research and through the research contribute to existing group work knowledge.

Practitioners should also remember that groups are prevalent in organisational contexts, in management areas, in family functioning, and in religious and political contexts, to name but a few. The theoretical foundations, research, and knowledge base of social work with groups can be used in training programmes focused on small group functioning and group dynamics. Based upon our knowledge of human functioning, our sensitivity to diversity, our group leadership skills, and our use of theories and approaches for changing thoughts, feelings, and behaviour, we as practitioners have much to offer.

The future of group work does not look grim. It does, however, ask for thinking creatively and allowing for paradigm shifts, moving away from the conventional way of conducting groups. As group workers, we do not have to discard anything; mutual aid is so important in human relationships, even more so in current times where individuals live in a world of less personal contact and more electronic communication. Ideas and inspirations—let us go to the people, learn from them, and be inspired to act upon the lived experiences of those we want to serve.

United States

Thank you for inviting me to join this panel on global group work. Without question, it is a great honor and opportunity. I am learning from my fellow panelists' reports, as they illuminate contextual and cultural variations in group work practices around the world. My understanding of social group work in the United States resonates with the challenges and advances being shared. Through this experience, I am reminded that while our approaches to group work may vary, we are united in an intense belief in the restorative, energizing, and empowering potential of group membership. This symposium and the IASWG embodies this passion for groups, fostering participants' sense of belonging in a group flexible enough to weave together diverse needs and contributions.

Elder Crowshoe has inspired me to recall and acknowledge two people who helped me join a highly formative workplace group (some might say family) many years ago, at Catholic Charities in Brooklyn, New York. Al Cowles, the brilliant, empathic founder of an early project to reunite young fathers with their estranged children, was a beacon for community members who sought his counsel to launch a range of supportive groups. Marianne Chierchio, our masterful, straight-talking administrator, responded with agency sanction, encouragement, and resources to make such initiatives possible. Al and Marianne left an indelible mark within me and in the communities they served. Part of their legacy is a thriving program that continues to support grandparents raising their grandchildren and great-grandchildren, the Grandmothers as Mothers Again group. First documented in 1995, this group serves as an exemplar for four key indicators of successful practice, in which groups are critical, integral, responsible, and personal. I will use these concepts to frame my remarks on concerns and opportunities in contemporary group work practice.

Group Work as Critical

As widely reported, the number of group-based interventions is growing across service areas and client populations in the United States. In the workplace, teams have become an integral part of organizational life across institutions with a wide variety of goals. Educational programs have been expanding attention to learning communities and championing team projects, cohort, and dialogue group approaches as high-impact practices for student and institutional success. Families, now defined more inclusively, are seen as vital to well-being, and peer-led groups are growing exponentially to meet a wide range of community needs and concerns. Taken together, this appears to be a consensus that groups are critical in virtually all aspects of life.

However, group workers must look deeply at this phenomenon before celebrating. The study of the Grandmothers as Mothers Again group proposed that to be considered critical, groups must directly address and meet important needs of members and their communities. In this regard, group work in the United States is falling short. For example, while groups are expanding in human service programs, they appear less likely to be organized and led by workers with social group work expertise, and more likely to be narrowly proscribed for compliance. If some of the growth of group interventions comes from calls for efficiency and sole reliance on highly researched models, without fully considering clients' needs and practice effectiveness, we as group workers must wonder if increased group interventions are likely to fade as groups do not deliver their expected savings. We can have some impact on this trend by promoting evaluation, disseminating practice informed models, and increasing our capacity and study of group work practice to build evidence-based practice. Our social group work literature provides extensive critique, support, and guidance in pursuing these critical activities.

The accreditation standards of the U.S. Council on Social Work Education (CSWE) require that all undergraduate and graduate students develop competence in working with groups before graduation, although without guidance on implementation. One sees a parallel between the social work education and practice arena, in that both identify groups as critical but do not fully support the achievement of competence in group leadership focused on members' outcomes. As more social workers graduate without strong skills and knowledge in group work this deficit is magnified, leading to a diminished cadre of expert group work practitioners, advocates, educators, and scholars. In a similar vein, there is recognition of how groups are at the core of family and community systems. However, there appears to be insufficient respect for the self-organizing capacities of groups. As attention to empowerment in groups diminishes, natural and peer-developed groups become targets of intervention, rather than potential collaborators.

Trends in education, agency-based practice, and community practice suggest that there is still work to be done to achieve the goal of group work as critical. While the sheer volume of groups provides opportunities, we group workers need to highlight the good work that is being done and further promote groups and partnerships designed around the interests of clients and communities.

Group Work as Integral

The Grandmothers as Mothers Again experience taught me that groups have the best chance of success when they are closely linked with the primary interests of their organizational auspice. While groups may be common, they are vulnerable to easy cancellation or manipulation if not integrated into their sponsor's core purposes. To achieve this goal, group work interventions need strong advocates who will promote and maintain group work practice as central to meeting organizational, client, and constituent needs. In the United States as elsewhere, there is widespread hiring of leaders who do not have social work or related practice-focused degrees, training, or experience. Professionals with group work expertise need to be in key positions to demonstrate group skills in organizational leadership, promote effective group work interventions, and provide mentorship and support for emerging leaders.

In social work education, the integral nature of group work has been an ongoing topic of discussion. Over the last 40 years, social group workers have been in the forefront of developing integrative, generalist social work practice approaches, as well as advocating for robust specialist education in group work. Presently, CSWE requires a generalist foundation for all baccalaureate and master's degree programs, articulated through required competencies that include group work practice. At the advanced practice level, MSW students are expected to demonstrate sustained or deepened competency in group work. Many of the group work scholars who helped frame the generalist model have subsequently critiqued its adverse impact on group work, as well as other areas besides individually focused practice.

Today, group work educators can engage the largest number of social work students in the generalist foundation through insuring true integration of content and learning in group work education. This often requires assertive roles in curriculum design, support for group work educators to teach foundation practice, and assistance for colleagues without such expertise with mentoring and training. Concurrently, educators must ensure that specific group work knowledge and skills are learned through a range of method, population, and field of practice based courses and learning opportunities.

The growing demand for groups in practice settings suggest that now is a time of opportunity for renewal of group work's position in the academic organization. In addition to classroom courses, group work educators can advocate further assignment and supervision of students' group work practice in field education, as well as broaden field instructors' supervisory expertise and corresponding development of practice skills. Today's climate also provides opportunities for group work training and research, which can raise the level of practice and attention to member needs, thus strengthening the connection of group interventions with agency mission and goals.

Group Work as Responsible

Unfortunately, there are many instances of irresponsible group work in the United States, when practice is neither skillful nor ethical, and has little chance of success. Goal displacement, when the organization's bottom line takes priority over client and community needs, appears across human service sectors to varying degrees. When social work educational programs fail to support student achievement of competence with groups, they become complicit in this trend. Group interventions that are narrowly defined to clinically address members' deficits can foreclose options to promote well-being and justice. Clearly, it is not enough to promote and implement groups regardless of whether workers are sufficiently skilled in facilitating groups that can effectively serve their members and their environments.

Group workers across disciplines should be well trained, supervised, and supported in their organizations. Ethically, no worker should be providing services beyond his or her level of expertise, suggesting the need to realign the qualifications for group leadership with a competency framework. The IASWG Standards for Social Work Practice with Groups is the member guide to ethical and competent practice. The standards have been found useful, comprehensive, and relevant in a wide range of group work practice settings, as well as in administrative practice and community-based approaches. Current efforts to enhance the standards' cross-cultural and cross-regional application will be valuable in the diverse United States. Progress has been made in raising awareness and in incorporating the standards in social work education, practice, and research. Yet, there is still room for IASWG members to expand these efforts, beginning with becoming more familiar with them, using them, and sharing them with staff, students, and colleagues.

IASWG has brought greater attention to the need for responsible group work practice. Some member efforts, such as partnerships with CSWE and other organizations, have increased visibility and interest in group work education and practice. Further collaboration within the United States and internationally will enhance IASWG's ability to impact practice and education. The IASWG's stance on inclusion and nonoppressive practice within the organization serves as an important model for the organizations in which members operate. The IASWG maintains its commitment to the advancement of social work practice with groups through its chapter events, international symposia, and group work camps; encouragement of member innovation through the Special

Projects Application Review Committee (SPARC) project; and service as a critical arena for building networks of group work scholars and practitioners. We see some fruits of its efforts to position groups as critical and integral in practice, and continue to promote greater commitment to reach high quality, responsible practice.

Group Work as Personal

The final indicator emerging from the Grandmothers as Mothers Again program often surprises. In the United States, many practitioners were told by early supervisors and peers not to take things personally and to find ways to isolate the feelings we experienced when facilitating groups in order to avoid counter transference and subversion of the group to meet our own needs. In contrast, making group work personal has a number of positive dimensions. First, it honors the personhood and contribution of group members who join and participate in groups. Second, it acknowledges the need to understand one's own motivations and connections with members and groups, and then marshal this awareness in the professional use of self for effective practice. Disconnection of the personal nature of social group work practice can lead to abandoning beliefs in the power of effective groups, disrespecting the expertise of members, elevating efficiency above all else, and validating irresponsible approaches. In other words, we need more of the personal in social group work in the United States.

I hope that I have presented a picture of social group work in the United States that highlights key trends, challenges, and opportunities through the use of four key principles. My perspectives are my own, developed through a range of experiences. I am grateful for the wisdom of my colleagues, including those who I consulted in preparing for this panel.

I would like to conclude with a final personal dimension of group work. I began my remarks with honoring Al Cowles and Marianne Chierchio for their legacies. Their contributions and those of the members of the Grandmothers as Mothers Again group endure in the people and communities they touched, including me and my passion for social work with groups. I suggest that as practitioners we all have people and touchstones from our persistent efforts in the face of many challenges. Bringing these powerful connections into consciousness can enrich our investment and promotion of group work, our enjoyment in the process, and the achievements of groups and members we serve.

Sacred Science of Circles: An Inclusive Approach to Social Work Practice

Betty Bastien

The continuing impacts of colonialism, constructed and perpetuated by the domination of Eurocentric worldviews, are the root causes of current conditions experienced by Canada's Indigenous peoples. These conditions include relentless colonial violence and intergenerational trauma. The causes of these conditions are obscured by Eurocentric worldviews that deny the ongoing colonial experience of Indigenous peoples. At this juncture, the conceptual frameworks underlying the healing practices provided for Canada's Indigenous peoples are premised on a Eurocentric paradigm consisting of fragmented theoretical orientations, research methodologies, and worldviews, which deny the holistic nature of Indigenous modalities. An Indigenous healing framework is needed if social workers are to successfully address the social, personal, and community disruptions that intergenerational trauma has produced in contemporary Indigenous society in Canada (Lederman, 1999).

This paper is based on a study funded by the Canadian Institutes of Health Research (CIHR), which focused on the affirmation of the Indigenous identity of First Nation peoples and the recovery of Indigenous conceptual frameworks through their stories of surviving colonial violence. To that end, I relate the lived experiences of the participants and their understanding of these experiences. Moreover, I identify appropriate healing and empowerment strategies that support a conceptual framework as well as report on the participants' evaluated effectiveness of the sacred circles.

The project was funded for two years and adopted a participatory Indigenous methodology. Research activities were guided by community elders and incorporated Indigenous ways of knowledge building intended to formulate a culturally based healing framework with empowerment strategies. Sacred Circles were the principal source of information gathering and assessment used for the pilot testing of this healing framework conducted in collaboration with a First Nation health centre. The research was a concerted effort between the

Bachelor of Social Work Access Division of the Faculty of Social Work at the University of Calgary and First Nations health and educational organizations.

I address the use of Sacred Circles as the method for collaborating and for pilot testing the data gathered with a group of students. I provide a contextual view of circles and their relationship to the Siksikaitsitapi's (Blackfoot people's) way of creating and maintaining balance. I also focus on the ontological responsibilities of Siksikaitsitapi, which are synchronized with the natural and cosmic alignment of balance and harmony. These methods are the primary means of the Siksikaitsitapi affirming their spiritual connections with the cosmologies, and thus, renewing meaningful responsibilities, which provide a context for being and a schema for participating with the world.

Circles Are Wholeness and Healing

Colonial violence against Indigenous peoples and trauma experienced by First Nation peoples has been addressed by many disciplines in academia; however, the conceptual tools most readily adopted are from the social sciences. The literature on colonial violence and oppression has addressed some of the psychological effects (Adams, 1995; Bastien, Kremer, Kuokkanen, & Vickers, 2003; Battiste & Youngblood Henderson, 2000; Davis & Zannis, 1973; Duran & Duran, 1995; Fanon, 1963; Frideres, 1974; Ralston, 2014; E. Ross, 2014), but this research has largely been developed from the Eurocentric ontological perspective. Specifically, it has served an agenda through which the colonizer has maintained control of Indigenous populations through the production of knowledge about them (Waldram, 2004, p. 10). This pattern is reflected in academia, including social work education, which has failed to provide a narrative that is located in the Indigenous paradigm, a narrative that can examine the process of colonialism from an Indigenous lens.

Within an Indigenous paradigm, the discourse would include using Indigenous philosophical and relational perspectives of Indigenous experiences. However, the discourse continues with interpretations and conceptual frameworks that have had a detrimental impact on the perception and treatment of Indigenous peoples, primarily because of the colonial narrative that is embedded in the approach. This approach is located in the fragmentation of the Cartesian paradigm. Most harmful for Indigenous people is the suggestion by Descartes that the body works like a machine, with the material properties of extension and motion, and that it follows the laws of physics. The mind (or soul), on the other hand, was described as a nonmaterial entity, and does not follow the laws of physics. Furthermore, Descartes extended his mechanistic view of matter to living organisms. Plants and animals were considered simply machines. Human beings were inhibited by a rational soul that was connected with the body through the pineal gland in the center of the brain, but the human body was indistinguishable from an animal-machine (Capra, 1982). Subsequently, rationality has denied the spiritual nature of knowledge and sacrifices the wholeness of human beings (Ani, 1994, p. 32).

A conceptual framework premised on the fragmentation of Indigenous identity and relationships severs the connections of the wholeness of reality. The elders have expressed this process as the major issue contributing to the impact of colonization and the subsequent 500 years of violence directed at Indigenous peoples, their way of life, and their environment. The severing and fragmenting of the peoples from their source of life and ways of knowing is described as *iipono'taksskowawa*, which literally refers to separation from spirit connections. The following is a breaking down of the morphemes: *ii/* has been + *pon/* parted ways with + *[m]o'ta'k/* Spirit + *sskowaw/* chased (Duane Mistaken Chief, personal communication, October 2007). Severe and long-term trauma results in severing relationships with the sacred or source of life; severing nourishing relationships that support strengthening spirit, subsequently nourishing all Indigenous collective consciousness which included all that is in existence.

The violent history of subjection to totalitarian control over a prolonged period is reflected in the apparent denial and absence of any authentic response to the trauma experienced by Indigenous peoples. These experiences have been the legacy of Indigenous peoples through the apartheid system of the Indian Act, residential schools, child welfare, poverty, racism, etc., which continue without reprieve simply because of the denial of violence against this group. The genocidal experiences of First Nations are an anomaly because they are living with the processes of expanding colonization at the same time as they live alongside the colonizer. As a result, they must observe, experience, and witness their own destruction, which is the continuous construction of their dependencies cloaked in the illusion and deception of support. Moreover, instability is constructed in their lives and their environments through the lens of an individualistic ideology founded on personal lifestyle choices, all continuing to obscure the systemic forces of racial violence and collective spiritual trauma.

These approaches are born out of a fragmented reality that constructs perspectives that negate the existence of holism in humanity, pathologize the impact and consequences of this violence, and support the illusion of separation between victims and victimizers. This reality uses person-blame approaches and racism, which blame and shame the victims in the process of destruction referred to in the policy as assimilation. Theses perspectives have created processes, identified below, which continue to demoralize First Nation peoples, and which deny, reject, and destroy their natural adaptive human and cultural resources for recovery and health.

First, any response to the systemic violence against Indigenous peoples that serves to pathologize and psychologize them continues to support an industry of victim making. The following quote illustrates such an analysis of deficiency, which has been prevalent in Eurocentric clinical approaches focusing on individual pathology:

> The effects of genocide are quickly personalized and pathologed by our profession via the diagnosing and labeling tools designed for this purpose. If the labeling and diagnosing process is to have any historical truth, it should incorporate a diagnostic category that reflects the effects of genocide. Such a diagnosis would be "acute and/or chronic reaction to colonialism." In this sense, diagnostic policy imposes a structure of normality based in part on the belief in the moral legitimacy and universality of state institutions. (Duran & Duran, 1995, p. 6)

From a Eurocentric view, trauma and violence resulting from oppression and colonization are classified as pathological, therefore requiring control and alteration in the form of clinical treatment. The concept of personalization is part of "blaming the victim." Although pathologizing supports the idea of the need to alter and adjust the victim to European-style norms, the analysis includes neither societal forces nor an Indigenous interpretation. Rather, the theory of deficiency can be readily illustrated:

> "The 'residential school syndrome" is a term coined by psychologists who have noticed among those who have shared the residential school

experience a set of symptoms comparable to the grief cycle characteristic of a person losing a close relative. (York, 1990, p. 37)

Second, Eurocentric perspectives have created and maintained a cycle of victims and victimizers. The concepts of victim and victimization are born from a colonial interpretation of Indigenous peoples' experiences and are characteristic of a particular type of psychology used for ideological control. The use of these terms facilitates the consciousness of powerlessness or victimry. The idea of victimization can be found in much of the social science literature (Boldt, 1993; Davis & Zannis, 1973).

Third, theories and research become primarily reactionary responses, often supporting the existing power relationships inherent in such hierarchical worldview. The solutions proposed from such a hierarchical perspective become part of the relationships of the colonized. The solutions proposed for the colonized are subsequently based on the constructs of power, domination, and control. They are created from the Eurocentric paradigm of fragmentation and disconnection, and are the perspectives that maintain the thought structures embedded in colonial consciousness. Therefore, the theoretical analysis of colonialism itself is hegemonic unless done outside the perpetual lens that constructs the colonial cognitive system of domination and control. Moreover, these cognitive systems legitimize the social control exercised by state institutions and are perceived by the dominant society as acceptable, perhaps even humanitarian (Bolaria, 1991, pp. 128–130).

> The person-blame approach enables the authorities to control deviants under the guise of being helpful. Another social control function of the person-blame approach is that it allows deviant individuals and groups to be controlled in a publicly acceptable manner. Deviants—whether they are criminals or social protesters—are incarcerated in social institutions and administered a wide variety of therapies. In the end, a person-blame approach requires the individual to change, not the structure of society that is causing the problem. (Bolaria, 1991, p. 129)

The systemic policy of assimilation has been a complete failure for First Nations because it is has been a cloak for racism. In respect to colonial racism, Battiste (1998) identified four related racist strategies used to maintain colonial power over Indigenous people:

(a) stressing real or imaginary differences between the racist and the victim; (b) assigning values to these differences to the advantage of the racist and detriment of the victim; (c) trying to make these values absolutes by generalizing from them and claiming that they are final; and (d) using these values to justify any present or possible aggression or privilege. (p. 21)

Racism has been used primarily to control and subjugate the colonized populations. Residential schools systematically impacted generations of children, who were dehumanized and inculcated with inferior beliefs about themselves. As an example, according to Littlewood and Lipsedge (1997, as quoted in Waldram, 2004),

> psychiatry was deployed extensively during the nineteenth and twentieth centuries to justify what we may term internal colonisation of American Indians and African-Americans, as an instrument of colonialism and or the product of the same mind-set that led Europeans to believe that Aboriginal peoples were emotionally and intellectually childlike and inferior provided the rationalization for control. (p. 106)

First Nations people have always been in the constant struggle of reconstructing their Indigenous paradigms, cultures, and identities. Without the development of a paradigm grounded in their own knowledge and science, tribal people will remain the hostages of a colonial consciousness that inherently ascribes to them deficiencies in character and abilities. Duran and Duran (1995) proposed the following framework:

> A post-colonial paradigm would accept knowledge from differing cosmologies as valid in their own right, without their having to adhere to a separate cultural body for legitimacy. Frantz Fanon felt that the third world should not define itself in the terms of European values. Instead, Fanon thought that everything needs to be reformed and thought anew, and that if colonized peoples aren't willing to do this we should leave the destiny of our communities to the European mind-set. (p. 6)

By redefining the humanity of Niitsitapi (Indigenous peoples) within Eurocentric concepts, the ultimate power of European imperialism consisted not only in altering physical reality, but also in subsequently changing Niitsitapi views of the nature of humanity. If the realities of genocide are to change, there must be stories of survivance, a body of knowledge that embodies restoration. Survivance is the activity of reclaiming and recovering Indigenous peoples' own interpretations of the experience and their own sense of truth. Ultimately, Indigenous peoples must affirm and renew their holistic practices and use their conceptual frameworks in their stories of surviving colonial violence and subsequent intergenerational trauma.

Sacred Circles Conceptual Framework

Sacred Circles are perceived as metaphors for infinity, holism, and timelessness. They are the essential properties of Indigenous worldviews; they give rise to their purpose for existence, renewal, and transformation through cycles and rhythms.

> Even the seasons form a great circle in their changing, and always come back again to where they were. The life of a man is a circle from childhood to childhood, and so it is in everything where power moves. (Neihardt, 1961, pp. 194–195)

It understood that Niitsitapi have a culture founded on the interconnection with all life; human beings are part of an indivisible whole. Consequently, the essence of human existence is our relationship with *ihtsipaitapiiyo'pa* (Source of Life), the universal intelligence. This relationship is the source of renewal through a way of life (*kiipaitapiiyssinnooni*) that is based on balance and harmony. Through this unified consciousness comes the collective strength and survival of existence through *ihtsipaitapiiyo'pa*. In a connection and experiences of unified consciousness, an understanding gives rise to way of being with the universe that is referred to as ontological responsibilities (Bastien, 2004). This understanding is reflected in the following quote:

> You have noticed that everything an Indian does is in a circle, and that is because the power of the world always works in circles, and everything tries to be round. . . . The sky is round, and I have heard that the earth is round like a ball, and so are all the stars. The wind, in its greatest power,

whirls. Birds make their nests in circles. (Neihardt, 1961, pp. 194–195)

Circles are the methods used for Indigenous gatherings, emulating the interconnectivity of life and the connection with greater world and cosmos. In contemporary quantum mechanics, interconnectivity is understood as the intelligence that binds atoms to molecules and molecules into structures. After 50 replications, one fertilized ovum cell can produce one hundred thousand billion cells, and each cell does a few billion things per second and knows what every other cell is doing (Chopra, 2003).

Through the natural process of sharing and giving, reciprocity is the continuous transfer of intelligence and responsibilities through which the balance of creation is renewed and restored. The practice of reciprocity involves continuous engagement and interaction with the cosmic world, all the while understanding the processes of natural rhythms and coherent electromagnetic fields. As an example, one million things happen in the body if its sugar levels go up, and the body must bring them down (Chopra, 2003, pp. 65–66). From the understanding that reciprocity maintains balance, Indigenous people understand and experience a simultaneous and intricate connection to the cycles and rhythms of a universal intelligence. These connections place Indigenous people in the sacred circle of life, aligned with ihtsipaitapiiyo'pa, the source of the power of life. In this context, "spirit" is understood as the intricate embodiment of the source of life and expressed as the universal consciousness. From this vantage point, an integrated holistic framework would include the universal consciousness as expressed and experienced through narratives or stories, language, land, and ceremony. Indigenous cultures provide such a framework. They offer an approach that focuses on the renewal of wholeness, a journey of returning to oneself while fully engaged in the universe.

Sacred Circles Are Cosmic Laws of Creation and Renewal

The interconnections of relationships in a cosmic world are the basis of life, reality, and truth; they give rise to the responsibilities of Niitsitapi.

In addition to knowing how these alliances are formed, knowing simultaneously the processes of being are distinguished as ontological responsibilities. These ontological responsibilities synchronize with the rhythms of the alliances, and correspondingly with nature's way of maintaining balance and harmony. Without the celebration and affirmation of interweaving relationships through these alliances, the means of cultural reproduction are severed. The processes of circles and rhythms are the ways in which the knower and knowing become one, and knowledge is transferred. These processes are the sources of transformation.

Sacred Circles have been the approach for integrating knowing, knower, and knowledge as one; an experience of wholeness. Connections with the universal intelligence align human beings with the natural rhythms of the cosmic order, a way of knowing that potentiality can continuously transform the quality human consciousness. Harrod (1992) observed that as long as the people retain their connection to the source of life, they will retain their connection to transformational ways of being. As described in the old stories, the people will continue to renew their responsibilities as instructed in the original *pommaksin*, through transfers from cosmic and natural alliances. *Pommaksin* is where song, prayer, dance, and other mimetic movements were given, and they embody the vibrational patterns by which the power of the alliances can be transferred to *Siksikaitsitapi* (Harrod, 1992, pp. 67–71).

Circles are the processes that source the transformation of *Niitsitapi*, the natural process of creation. They structure everything in the Indigenous worldview, including social organization, and frame the ontological responsibilities and group value systems. Indigenous peoples synchronize to regular patterns of seasons such as the migration of animals and astronomical movements, which reflect the constant change of the universe. *Aipommotsspist* (we are transferred, it was given, or passed on) are ways of becoming one with the universe. They are the connections to all time, the ancestors and ancients. They ensure the continuance of *Siksikaitsitapi*. As one ceremonialist said, "Our life is transferred to us. Transfer is the way knowledge is passed on; it is the way to maintain balance among all your relations. The ceremony maintains the connection with ihtsipaitapiiyo'pa, Source of Life" (as quoted in Bastien, 2004, pp. 140–141). Human beings from an Indigenous paradigm emulate the cosmic nature of affinity and compassion by aligning themselves with natural laws of reciprocity through ceremony, language, and ways of knowing. Reciprocity, the expression of an integrative whole, the vibrational energy of sound and music (languages) promotes wholeness. Advances of science in neuroplasticity have revealed genes are not deterministic, and telomeres change through emotional experiences and attitudes of loving kindness. And finally, timelessness is the experience of being present to the wholeness of spirit. Aligned with natural energy of wholeness, the experience is embodied aistomatop (a concept referring to the integration and embodiment of knowledge) and is integrated through ceremony. These experiences renew relationships that are embodied in a holistic way of being and are similar to the instantaneous biocommunication mentioned earlier. They are demonstrated by changes in the cellular activity in human bodies to changes in any of its organs or systems. With every thought, movement, and word spoken, each breath taken and exhaled, there is an exchange; each movement and thought influences the physical world in which we live. These systems of exchanges and transfers of embodied kinship relationships hold the balance of the natural cosmic world. There is no separation; the oneness of the circle is experienced.

Circles Are Spirits of Healing and Transformation

In the study, eight circles with themes integrated story and language while supporting the connections with source of life and the renewal of the participants' understanding of and relationships to their ontological responsibilities. This article illustrates this integration through the cultural hero Pawaksski (Scarface) and the term for invoking the delicate balance, aatsimoyihkanni, generally referred to as ceremony. However, first I discuss the transformational nature and implications of sacred circles.

The interdependence of the cosmos is experienced through a network of kinship responsibilities in a sea of motion consisting of spiritual energy, where all existence is transforming in death and birth or deformation and restoration; the essence of existence is renewal. In this dance with spirit, transformation is integral to wholeness and is achieved in the changing of relationships between what is known and who is the knower. The shifting perception changes one's relationship to self and to one's experience of consciousness. In a real sense, there is no difference between oneself and the cosmic world: This connection with spirit literally changes the molecular structure as it nourishes and balances the body. The relationship between existence and consciousness becomes translucent.

Science has understood this transformation to be a change in one's circumstances without going through the necessary space to make the change. Quantum change occurs when one's circumstances change to another set of circumstances without passing through the circumstances in between (Chopra, 2003). This principle supports the notion of *unbroken wholeness*, which denies classical analysis of the world into separate and independent existent parts (Dossey, 1989, p. 158). Healing is reclaiming and regaining the unbroken wholeness for Indigenous peoples; it is the process of generating ways of knowing and restoring the responsibilities to life itself. Learning the responsibilities of traditional alliances is the path of coming to know one's purpose in life and of learning the sacred knowledge that can address adversity experienced by contemporary Niitsitapi (Bastien, 2004, p. 109). With this knowing, the study used sacred circles to provide a medium for the participants to connect with the sacred power of life, and, through sharing their stories and making meaning from their own context, a forum for personal transformation.

The participants understood that the sacred power of the universe is pervasive and reveals itself through all of creation, including thoughts, objects, speech, and actions. It speaks through rocks and animals, and may take the form of an animal that transforms into a person, or it may begin with a person who transforms into an animal (Harrod, 1992, p. 23). As part of the transcendent or transformational power of the universe, people migrate regularly into what Harrod (1992) described as dream worlds. These migrations provide the meaning and knowledge sought and acquired by Siksikaitsitapi. In fact, all human beings, according to the Plains cultures, transcend beyond the limits of their embodiment through these dreamworld migrations. They are considered normative experiences, which means that they are interpreted as ordinary experience (Bastien, 2004; Harrod, 1992). The participants shared stories of an ancient epoch, while making meaning of their experiences, and these experiences were affirmed in the context of wholeness.

Circle Are Affirming Identify

The nature of human beings must be revisited, a sentiment that Kolbert (2014) has suggested. The existing understanding of humanity has been described as living from the reptilian brain. One of its primary functions is fight or flight, creating a consciousness that is focused on control and domination, which are both violent acts (Chopra, 2009). On the other hand, the cosmic and human consciousness of the Plains Indigenous social structures is organized by clans forming a web of kinship systems. The journey of becoming whole was transferred to the People, *kipaitapiiwahssinooni*. *Kipaitapiiwahssinooni* refers to our life: *ki/* our collective + *pai/* vertical + *tapi/ (matapi* = root word) essence of our human existence (Duane Mistaken Chief, personal communication, March 20, 2015). Connections to the ancestors imply relationships which constitute the human journey based on raising the collective consciousness for collective well-being. These ways of being and becoming are held in their ontological perspective.

The basic ontological responsibility, *kiitomohpiipotokoi* (way of being), refers to the ways of life given to the people as ways of being and relating. One of the ontological responsibilities is generosity; giving, sharing, and gifting are the expression of the cosmic order. These actions of sharing and giving are consistent with the natural order of the universe. They are understood to be transferred by the universal intelligence, and through one's relationship with the natural world are demonstrated by giving and sharing through life cycles and ceremonies. These actions promote reciprocity, which is necessary for maintaining balance.

Siksikaitsitapi has a term, *aipommotsp*, which means we are transferred, it was given, or it passed on. The word depicts reciprocal responsibilities or the exchange of responsibilities and teachings among all of existence. The natural law of reciprocity is not limited to ceremony only (Bastien, 2004). It is extended by Siksikaitsitapi to their daily customs and practice of living. The understanding of cosmic consciousness is demonstrated through the Plains Indigenous social structures, wherein clans form a web of kinship relationships that locate them in their local ecologies and seasonal conditions.

These ways of being among Siksikaitsitapi known as holistic ways of being, or responsibilities, are understood as *kiitomohpiipotokoi aatsimoyihkanni, isspomotsisinni*. These concepts refer to the collective and unifying consciousness, which maintains balance and good relations, as well as renews the delicate balance of the dynamic power of the universe. Being one with life and the life source constitutes integrity and living for the goodness and well-being of all.

Language: Sacred Way of Speaking

Using *niitsi'powahsinni*, or Indigenous speaking, is integral to the healing process. Indigenous languages are spiritual languages that originate in an organic holistic universe. Their vibrational patterns call the world into alignment with sacred processes of becoming whole. Their words provide the context for intricate interrelationships of being, including an awareness of being, meaning, purpose, intentions, connections, responsibilities, and consequences; all providing the context for daily activities and lifelong learning simultaneously. The terms embody the collective consciousness that is necessary to strive for the delicate balance of life, and the life source. They align the ways of being with nurturing the spirit of the universe, creating supporting, nurturing, and renewing connections.

Aatsimoyihkaan requires the good heart, which is a harmonious way of being that supports one's connection to the source of life. It is inclusive and demonstrates a collective philosophy; cultural and structural balance. Describing this and other terms has been the work of Duane Mistaken Chief, an eminent scholar of the Blackfoot language. Each term is separated into its morphemic components, then a list of similar terms containing the morpheme is assembled. The terms are examined in terms of their usage, which means referring to their context in stories. Finally, a detailed examination of the morphemes is undertaken; the sum of those morphemes transmits the meaning of the terms. For example, in the Blackfoot language, aatsimoyihkaan, defined in English terms by Christian missionaries, has today come to be understood in terms of Christian conventions. Today, when Blackfoot speakers hear *aatsimoyihkaan*, they immediately think of Christianity. However, this is out of integrity with the true meaning of the word, which is "verbally tending to the delicate state of harmony in the Blackfoot world including relationships." *Aatsim* comes from *aatsimapi*, the delicate state of harmony. The second morpheme, *oyihk*, is an "oral/verbal expression." The third, aan, simply refers that is a "product/result" of that act. The sum of those three morphemes are the expression of the cultural meaning for the purpose of relationships; they embody values, behaviors, identity, responsibilities, health, and survival knowledge. Language unfolds reality; words are the maps to navigate within a world of energies and powers (Peat, 1994).

Through their language and ceremonies, Siksikaitsitapi reveal an intricate understanding of interrelationships of their world, an understanding that the universe works in a collective or organic manner. Isspomotsisinni, the collective sharing, supports and strengthens the unity consciousness, from which all existence is manifested, and contributes to the general balance and harmony of life. It is a way of being that involves service to others, manifesting in the collective well-being of Indigenous families and communities. Collective support is seen as providing strength to the powers of the universe and is understood to be the source of well-being and harmony. Culture and social organization are premised on strengthening these relations so that all can live. For example, being stewards of the land and participating in ceremonies such as the Sundance are ways that share the organization of collective efforts and resources that were respected by everyone. The sacred circles provide a structure and process for the opportunity to be of service to everyone through sharing and receiving. The reciprocity and generosity inherently contribute to the understanding of knowledge that balances the lives of the participants.

Circles Are Stories of Timelessness

Siksikaitsitapi's conceptualization of knowledge is found in the sacred stories; they are the guiding archetypes for daily experiences, and subsequently, the living knowledge of the people. The knowledge they contain is alive simply because they frame the motifs for existence. They guide the understanding of reality (Ralston, 2014). Each generation, however, must listen carefully so that they can adapt the lessons and wisdom to apply to their present circumstances. The ways of knowing, of acquiring knowledge and truth, are dependent upon skills of observation known as kakyosin, which includes the knowledge that has been accumulated in the retelling of stories over time and by applying that knowledge to the present. Knowledge lives in the process of observing, in reflecting on connections among observations, and in applying the experiences of akaitapiwa, or ancestors (Bastien, 2004).

Both stories (narratives) and Sacred Circles are processes of Niitsitapi epistemologies, which connect the group to an ever-present, infinite, and all-encompassing moment, where the story is relived and experienced in its timeless nature. The story of Pawaksski (Scarface) and his Journey to the Sun Lodge is an illustration of the wholeness of Indigenous practices, where the alliances of the natural and cosmic continuously are blending seamlessly with the intelligence of the universe; the experience of unity consciousness of Siksikaitsitapi. The hero's journey lives on through the challenges facing humanity, a journey that leads to the potentiality of illumination and transformation, and more important, the need for Indigenous peoples to pursue alternative interpretations and meaningful experiences as they navigate through a system of colonial violence.

Paawaksski had been born with a terrible scar on his face—hence his name. He sought to marry a beautiful woman, who asked him to find the Sun's Lodge and ask to have his scar removed by Naatosi (the Sun), the greatest manifestation of the source of life known to the people. Upon the counsel of an old man, he was told to seek and ask for guidance and support from natural alliances as he walked on the earth, especially in times of grave challenges, such as in deep disappointment, despair, and fear. After encountering many challenges, starvation, despair, and defeat, Paawaksski found the Sun's Lodge, with the support of many natural alliances including the bear, the swan, and the wolverine, to mention a few. On his arrival, he met Morning Star, who he saved from great danger, from which he received an invitation to the Sun's Lodge. As a result of his gratitude, Sun transferred the Sweat Lodge to him, and many other gifts for the people's well-being and survival. Sun conducted four sweat lodges to remove Paawaksski's scar. After each sweat, Sun asked Moon to point to Paawaksski each time. On the last sweat, when asked, she pointed to Paawaksski and the scar had completely disappeared. As a result, he is also known as Pahtsiipissowaasi (Mistaken Morning Star). After Sun gave him the sweat lodge, he showed him the short route home, which was through the Wolf's Trail known as the Milky Way.

The story of Paawaksski demonstrates the transformational consciousness and practices of the sweat lodge. The ultimate challenge of transformation is giving yourself up to something higher or to another. It begins with connecting to the source of life, by the way of service, compassion, and gratitude; a process in which one moves from the ordinary existence to the extraordinary or transcendent. Service for others comes from an awareness that one is living in an indivisible whole, where there is no separation. Furthermore, a form of death occurs which shifts the location of consciousness away from material or physical reality, resulting in the loss of a sense of individual identity and the creation of a spiritual existence of wholeness and inclusiveness. The lived experience is one of compassion, affinity, and joy to be a part of the wholeness of creation. The ability to transform experiences by overcoming challenges demonstrates illuminated revelations of wholeness. These revelations are experiences that transcend the separated and fragmentary relationship of self to align with the source of life. Ceremonial practices such as the sweat lodge create a space–time for transformation. Wholeness is a journey of returning to oneness while fully engaged in the universe. To move out of the conventional safety of life and undertake transformation has been the people's quest in being and becoming Siksikaitsitapi.

The Circle Process

Each Sacred Circle includes the integration of story and language supporting the renewal of the participants' understanding and relationships to their ontological responsibilities for restoring balance in their relationships. The power of circles are recognized and easily observed in healing and talking circles. Groups in a Sacred Circle are aligned with the natural forces of interdependence, interconnection, reciprocity, and reverence in creating balance. Groups renew the organic nature of circles through the connections of ceremony (ancestors), language, stories (knowledge), and integration. The integrity of the circle is the source of the healing powers that are co-created among the participants. They create wholeness through the divine attributes embodied in their spiritual essence including honesty, truthfulness, present time awareness, and listening with affirmation and support. The participants through these ways of being experience their soul connection with the source of life, and through this connection experience the illuminations of healing. The circles correlate with cosmic and natural forces, which have been the source of the ancient way of knowing of Siksikaitsitapi. The participants share their challenges, pain, despair, and fears as they have experienced them, while the process strengthens their soul connection the source of life. Through this process, through the support they receive from other participants collectively, and through unity consciousness, participants experience insights, illuminations, and an understanding of how to move forward. Creative ideas, deeper spirit connections, stronger alliances, deeper reflections, and more accountability for change are the forces which support the healing and talking circle process.

Participants sit in a circle, and the circle process is guided by protocol, commencing with a smudge ceremony by a person who has been transferred the rites (through their initiation to ceremonial practices) through protocol. The process of the circle moves clockwise, beginning and ending at the east end. The opening at the east end is for entering and exiting the circle. Each participant embraces an ancestor, a rock, one of the oldest ancestors which embodies wisdom. According to R. Ross (1996), "Rules govern how each person is required to participate in such circles, for they are integral parts of the healing strategy" (p. 36). Protocols in the circle include respect and awareness of the sacred space of ceremony, connections to the ancestors and alliances, and listening for others who are speaking.

Stories or narratives are shared through mini-lectures, which are designed to create an awareness of the healing, knowing, and practices held in the language and transferred through story. These experiences of story and language reveal inner challenges and support the search for truth, meaning, identity, belonging, and acceptance. The participants cannot but engage in deep self-reflection, which is the source of empowerment of insight and peak spiritual connections. These changes promote practical skills into one's own spiritual and natural resourcefulness, which support the self in its process for well-being. In sum, the circles are processes for integrating the themes of stories, language, identity, responsibilities, and balance: the elements for well-being.

Participant Response to the Circle Process

I highlight the benefits of the sacred circles for the participants; however, it is not my intent to discuss the study findings. The participants first clearly expressed an understanding of the processes of colonization and its continuing destructive impact, including an understanding of the fragmentation of generations of kinship systems arising from their parents' residential school experience and their own connections with the child welfare system. They began to understand the long-term destructive policies and practices which impact their lives on a daily basis. The collective soul trauma of their First Nation was understood, which serves to alleviate personal blame and the stigma associated with this trauma, and alters the intergenerational cycle of abuse in the community. They understood that healing can occur only through their recovery of family and Indigenous responsibilities and well-being. They also realized that kinship is a foundational institution, which has been the target of attack for more than 100 years. They also realized that they must begin to mend these wounded relationships.

Second, participants expressed a shift in consciousness, one of being victim to one of transformation. They understood that they would have to take responsibility for their recovery and begin connecting to their Indigenous science and practices. The renewal of ceremony was consistent: returning to smudging, face painting, helping with ceremonies, speaking the language, and learning the stories were some of the practices mentioned. Most important, participants connected to their identity through their ancestors, finding a place for themselves in the cosmic world through their Indigenous names and stories. These insights into understanding the collective soul wound, the destruction of meaningful relationships, pointed to the kinship system as a network to begin the reconciliation process with the journey of being Siksikaitsitapi. Through these relationships and processes experiences become meaningful, and thus create the potential for the illumination of hope and a future built upon the authenticity of being Siksikaitsitapi.

Implications for Social Work Practice

The time and need to examine the continuing violence against Indigenous people and to change the narrative that has been constructed to support and legitimize this violence has long passed. Each national crisis that society has experienced in regard to First Nation peoples has had its day in the press, courts, and House of Commons. However, for the most part, the violence continues without any reprieve. Society has taken a solid approach of denial, supported by a political ideology of evolution, progress, and race, which justifies and constructs "organized racism" (Ralston, 2014, p. 9). Furthermore, the continuing power of these narratives in universities provides a context for social functioning and the appearance that these narratives are universal and absolute. The educational system is full of these absurdities, which primarily justify global expansion of imperialism (Ralston, 2014, pp. 10–11). Presently, Indigenous peoples' way of life, or kiipaitapiiyssinnooni, has demonstrated its environmental sustainability, while the colonizer must understand that the narrative constructed for domination and control has outlived its usefulness. Simply stated, it threatens sustainability of the planet.

Social work must change its narrative from a helping profession to a change agent. Knowledge and practices under the ideological umbrella and social structure of colonial history have been transplanted in First Nations and continue to create trauma, victims, and dependency. They continue to preserve a reality in which the colonizer has maintained control of Indigenous populations through the production of knowledge about them (Waldram, 2004, p. 10). Social work must be equipped with practices that provide an alternative narrative and a forum to construct new meaning to human experience and the potentiality of human coexistence. It can begin with constructs and integrative practices for holistic and community health practices derived from Indigenous practices.

Conclusion

Indigenous ways of being and knowing have sustained the Blackfoot for over 10,000 years, evidence by the carbon dating of stone flint found at Head-Smashed-In Buffalo Jump. This finding predates the Neolithic period of Stonehenge and the Egyptian pyramids, and consequently provides irrefutable evidence of the sustainability of Indigenous science for survival and well-being. The science of Indigenous circles offers processes aligned with the cosmic energy of nurturance and sustainability, which continue the renewal of life. The strength of this narrative is founded on nonlocal reality and is synchronized with the natural energy of the universe. Undoubtedly, this is the power that has supported Indigenous consciousness and survival. The hope is that it is not too late for a shift in colonial consciousness and a new trajectory towards planetary survival.

References

Adams, H. (1995). *A tortured people. The politics of colonization*. Penticton, British Columbia: Theytus Books.

Ani, M. (1994). *Yurugu: An African-centered critique of European cultural thought and behaviour*. Trenton, NJ: Africa World Press.

Bastien, B. (2004). *Blackfoot ways of knowing*. Calgary, Alberta: University of Calgary Press.

Bastien, B., Kremer, J., Kuokkanen, R., & Vickers, P. (2003). Healing the impact of colonization, genocide, and racism on indigenous populations. In S. Kripper and T. McIntyre (Eds.), *The psychological impact of war trauma on civilians: An international perspective* (pp. 25–37). Westport, CT: Praeger.

Battiste, M. (1998). Enabling the autumn seed: Toward a declonized approach to Aborginal knowledge, language, and education. *Canandian Journal of Native Education, 22*(1), 16–27.

Battiste, M., & Youngblood Henderson, J. [Sa'ke'j]. (2000). Decolonizing cognitive imperialism in education. In M. Battiste & Youngblood Henderson, J. [Sa'ke'j] (Eds.), *Protecting indigenous knowledge and heritage: A global challenge* (pp. 86–96). Saskatoon, Saskatchewan: Purich Publishing.

Bolaria, B. S. (1991). *Social issues and contradictions in Canadian society.* Toronto, Ontario: Harcourt Brace Jovanovich.

Boldt, M. (1993). *Surviving as Indians: The challenge of self-government.* Toronto, Ontario: University of Toronto Press.

Capra, F. (1982). *The turning point: Science, society and the rising culture.* New York, NY: Bantam Books.

Chopra, D. (2003). *The spontaneous fulfillment of desire.* New York, NY: Three Rivers Press.

Chopra, D. (2009). *Reinventing the body, resurrecting the soul.* New York, NY: Harmony Books.

Davis, R., & Zannis, M. (1973). *The genocide machine.* Montreal, Quebec: Black Rose Books.

Dossey, L. (1989). *Recovering the soul space, time, and medicine.* Boston, MA: Shambhala.

Duran, E., & Duran, B. (1995). *Native American post colonial psychology.* Albany, NY: University of New York Press.

Fanon, F. (1963). *The wretched of the earth.* New York, NY: Random House.

Frideres, J. S. (1974). *Canada's Indians: Contemporary conflicts.* Scarborough, ON: Prentice Hall of Canada.

Harrod, H. L. (1992). *Renewing the world.* Tucson, AZ: University of Arizona Press.

Kolbert, E. (2104). *The sixth extinction.* New York, NY: Henry Holt and Company.

Lederman, J. (1999). Trauma and healing in Aboriginal families and communities. *Native Social Work Journal, 2*(1), 59–90. Retrieved from https://zone.biblio.laurentian.ca/dspace /handle/10219/378

Neihardt, J. G. (1961). *Black elk speaks.* Lincoln, NB: University of Nebraska Press.

Peat, D. (1994). *Lighting the seventh fire.* Secaucus, NJ: Carol Publishing.

Ralston, S. J. (2014). *The comeback.* Toronto, Ontario: Penguin Books Canada.

Ross, E. (2014). *Indigenous healing: Exploring traditional paths.* London, England: Penguin Group.

Ross, R. (1996). *Return to the teachings: Exploring Aboriginal justice.* London, England: Penguin.

Waldram, J. B. (2004). *Revenge of the Windigo: The construction of the mind and mental health of North American Aboriginal peoples.* Toronto, Ontario: University of Toronto Press.

York, G. (1990). *The dispossessed: Life and death in native Canada.* London, England: Vintage U.K.

Part 2
Invitationals

Next Steps in the Investigation of Mutual Aid Processes

Charles Garvin

This paper reports on presentations at the last two symposia of the International Association of Social Work With Groups (IASWG) that sought to clarify the concept of mutual aid and to suggest next steps in the investigation of processes of mutual aid in groups. These previous presentations involved reporting work done on this by myself, Mark Macgowan, William Pelech, Barbara Muskat, and Carol Cohen, who are here today as a panel to discuss these next steps with you.

Definitions[1]

In the previous presentations at symposia of IASWG by the above named individuals, we have noted as a beginning point the classic writings of Peter Kropotkin (1904) that have formed the basis for group workers' use of the term *mutual aid*. Kropotkin developed this concept and challenged the social Darwinist and laissez-faire capitalist conceptualization of competition and "survival of the fittest" as the basis of evolution. Almost all writings by group workers down to the present day have emphasized the importance of developing mutual aid in groups.

Schwartz (1961/1994) is credited with much of the current emphasis on the processes of mutual aid in group work. His classic statement follows:

> The group is an enterprise in mutual aid, an alliance of individuals who need each other, in varying degrees, to work on certain common problems. The important fact is that this is a helping system in which the clients need each other as well as the worker. This need to use each other, to create not one but many helping relationships, is a vital ingredient of

the group's process and constitutes a common need over and above the specific tasks for which the group was formed. (p. 18)

Particularly in the writings of Shulman (1986), Gitterman (1989), and Steinberg (2010), the processes of mutual aid have been clarified and illustrated and many case examples have been presented. These authors have referred to their model as the mutual aid model (Gitterman, 2004), although most other group work authors such as myself (Garvin, 1997, p. 1) have indicated that developing and maintaining mutual aid is one of the central propositions for social work practice with groups.

There have been other definitions of mutual aid. Lindsay, Roy, Mountainy, Turcotte, and Genest-Default (2008) have defined it as "the reciprocal helping relationships among members of a group, which are essential for the achievement of individual and group goals" (p. 256). Steinberg (2010) has indicated it is "various forms of help that people can offer one another (process) or experience together (result)" (p.55). Garvin (1997) stated, "We join with other group work theorists in emphasizing how the group worker helps the members help one another achieve their individual and collective aspirations" (p. 4). Gitterman (2004) referred to Schwartz in stating,

> His "reciprocal model" is referred to as "the interactional model" and more recently as the "mutual aid model." The idea of reciprocal captures the mutually [emphasis added] dependent relationship that exists among members within a group and between the group and its social environment. (p. 95)

Cicchetti (2009), in his dissertation on mutual aid processes in treatment groups for people with substance abuse disorders, cited Gitterman as declaring that "the mutual aid processes that unfold help group members 'to experience their concerns as universal,' to 'reduce isolation and stigma,' to 'offer and receive help from each other' and 'to learn from each other's views, suggestions and challenges'" (p. 93).

I believe that we have reached a point at which the concept of mutual aid should be more systematically clarified and investigated in field settings. This would include answers to the following questions, and we will indicate after each question to what degree I have found that the literature answers these questions. Finally, I shall discuss some types of investigation that might be conducted to find answers to these questions. In preparing for this invitational, I identified 89 papers published between 2000 and 2014 through the use of the

Psychoinfo database. I also had available a literature review prepared at the University of Calgary (LaRocque, 2013). LaRocque used three databases: Social Services Abstracts, Social Work Abstracr Plus, and Google Scholar. Her search yielded 151, 81, and 352 citations respectively.

Questions About Mutual Aid

What Are the Members' Understandings of Mutual Aid?

How do group workers know what this understanding is? I have found no literature that systematically investigates this issue.

How Are Understandings Achieved?

How did members achieve this understanding? Did some or all of the members have this understanding when they entered the group? Did the members obtain this understanding through specific discussions in the group of mutual aid? What was the nature of such discussions and how did the worker know, as well as contribute to, what members took from these discussions?

Most of the literature indicates that the worker should teach the members how to engage in mutual aid, and the worker should stress this as an important part of the way the group should function. The workers do this, in part, by modelling ways of interacting with members (e.g., offering support, questioning for clarification) but also by reinforcing examples of mutual aid that occur among members. I have not found, however, any investigation as to the effectiveness of various ways of teaching about mutual aid.

What Are the Similarities and Differences in Understandings?

Do all of the members have similar views of mutual aid, or do some have views that differ from others? What is the variance in the group regarding an understanding of mutual aid? I have found no explorations of this topic.

How Are Understandings Used?

How do members employ their understanding of mutual aid in their interactions in the group? This implies that there has been some clarification of the linkage between explicit understanding and member behavior. It is assumed that the linkage exists when the behavior is manifested but this issue requires further investigation.

What Are the Indications of Mutual Aid?

What are the kinds of interactions in the group that indicate a process of mutual aid is taking place? In what ways was mutual aid taking place, such as through expressions of empathy or support, concrete suggestions in response to a member or in a problem-solving process, or in what other ways?

Shulman (1986) has done a great deal of work on this question, and he indicates that there are nine processes through which members engage in mutual aid.

1. Sharing data: "Group members are able to provide each other with ideas, facts, beliefs, resources, which they have found helpful in coping with similar problems" (Shulman, 1986, p. 51).
2. The dialectical process: This "consists of one or more members advancing a thesis, other members countering with an antithesis, and the group members attempting to develop their own synthesis" (Shulman, 1986, p. 51).
3. Exploring taboo subjects. Shulman saw this as occurring in a group when one or more members have the courage to begin discussion of a topic that other members are fearful of discussing.

4. The "all in the same boat phenomenon" (Shulman, 1986, p. 53). Shulman saw this as occurring as members discover that they are not the only ones who have a problem.
5. Emotional support. Members can bring empathic support to an individual who is "in difficulty, or has experienced a trauma, . . . or is revealing painful feelings" (Shulman, 1986, p. 53).
6. Mutual demand. Shulman described situations in which members confront one another, and such confrontations are accepted in areas that the worker hesitates to confront.
7. Helping with specific problems. Shulman saw this as occurring when members help an individual engage in problem solving that also is relevant to them.
8. Rehearsal. Shulman identified this as "a form of role play in the group [that] can help the mother [Shulman is giving an example] find the words and feelings for a follow-up discussion with her daughter" (1986, p. 54).
9. Strength in numbers. Shulman summed this up with the idea that "in unity there is strength" (1986, p. 54). This idea has also been stated by Breton (1989, 2004) and Lee et al. (2009).

There has been some research on how often members employ the above principles. Wilke, Randolph, and Vinten (2009) engaged in research on five of the above mutual aid processes in a web-based social work class. They found that 56% of comments reflected data sharing, and this was the most common mutual aid process; 25.3% of the comments showed mutual support; 16.5% showed dialectic process; and 2.2% showed all in the same boat.

What Is the Variance in Members' Practice?

How many members (a few members, many members, all the members) showed mutual aid behavior in a given interaction? Does mutual aid take place when all members seek to provide it while other members are not connected to or aware of this process? I have not found any explorations of this issue.

How Appropriate Are Expressions of Mutual Aid?

How appropriate (and/or helpful) were these expressions of mutual aid, and how do practitioners know this? Again, I have not found any explorations of this issue.

What Are the Outcomes?

What were the immediate outcomes for a member or all of the members of these expressions of mutual aid (e.g., cohesiveness, satisfaction with process, advance in seeking solutions to problems)? Although evidence is not offered, Kelly (1999) asserted that the presence of mutual aid restores diminished self-confidence in members and, for the group, members are more ready to share concerns, take risks, feel less isolated and stigmatized, experience themselves as helpers, invest in others' well-being, and accept and give feedback to others. Various authors (Gitterman, 1989; Gitterman & Shulman, 2005; Steinberg, 2010) have stated members learn how to give and receive feedback. Many authors have asserted that this takes place (Shulman, 1986; Steinberg, 2003, 2010), but this has not been systematically demonstrated.

What Is the Impact?

What impact did these expressions of mutual aid have over time on some or all of the members, and how do practitioners know this (e.g., through examination of these processes by members or in the worker's reflection on these processes)? Or how else? Again, I have not found an examination of this question.

What Barriers Exist?

What are barriers in the group to expressions of mutual aid? Breton (2004) saw competition in the group as compatible and even supportive of the mutual aid process. Gitterman (1989), Gitterman and Shulman

(2005), and Steinberg (2010) noted the following as barriers to mutual aid: scapegoating, subgrouping, poor attendance, avoidance of group conflict, lack of group rules, lack of readiness or social skills in group members to address conflict, fear of intimacy (disclosing taboo subjects), conflict with authority figures, and group workers struggling with mediating functions. These ideas about barriers are a good beginning in the investigation of this topic, yet explorations might be conducted that look at the existence of barriers, the efforts to remove the barriers, and the effects of these efforts.

What Are Workers' Roles?

What are the ways in which workers respond to the above aspects of mutual aid? Steinberg (2003) has stressed that workers should help members learn the norms of mutual aid. Gitterman (1989), Kelly (1999), and Lee et al. (2009) have indicated that workers should help members find commonalities in order to engage in the process of mutual aid. These authors have also asserted that mutual agreement on goals, rules, and member roles and responsibilities support the processes of mutual aid.

Breton (2004) has asserted that the worker facilitates mutual aid by modelling respectful communication, helping members discover strengths, and facilitating the process of member-to-member helping. Gitterman (1989) stated that the following worker actions facilitate mutual aid: directing members' transactions to each other, inviting members to build on each other's contributions, reinforcing mutual support, clarifying members' tasks and role responsibilities, reaching for discrepant perceptions and opinions, inviting members to participate, and helping create emotional and physical space for individual members. The worker helps members find connections, emphasized by Gitterman (1989), Kelly (1999), and Lee et al. (2009). I recommend that group workers continue to examine various worker actions related to mutual aid and the effects of such actions.

What Variations in the Mutual Aid Processes Are Related to Culture, Time, and Place?

Steinberg (2000) has written a very thought-provoking article about the impact of time and place on mutual aid processes, especially focusing on mutual aid processes in short-term groups. Among the many excellent points she made are the greater role of the worker compared to long-term groups and the specific activities of the worker during the phases of the group's development. There also are articles that have dealt with mutual aid processes in cultures other than those found in North America. Illustrative of these is an article by Liu (2002) on mutual aid groups in Chinese society. She pointed out that in Hong Kong she found that members in that society were reluctant to give personal information, confront one another, or query each other on personal issues. The field needs more such examinations of how the mutual aid processes evolve in other societies.

Another set of issues is presented in work with such populations as persons who suffer from mental illness. An example of this is an excellent paper by Kelly (1999) dealing with mutual aid groups with mentally ill older adults. In this paper, Kelly closely examined a group of such members. He presented how the group developed and provided detailed process examples of the group as it faced various developmental issues such as approach-avoidance during the first stage of the group. He was particularly interested in identifying how the issues faced by such persons differ from those of other types of members. His paper is similar to many others in that as close a scrutiny does not take place with respect to how mutual aid is manifested.

Recommendations

In the previous section, I indicated many issues that require further investigation. It is not my intention here to make recommendations about each issue but rather to suggest some strategies that might be employed to further group workers' empirical knowledge of mutual aid processes.

Qualitative Approaches

There are many qualitative approaches that will be useful for this task. One is to do content analyses of case records. There are many such case illustrations in the literature, but these are often summary statements of the process presented by the author, and it is hard to tell how the author may have colored these as is inevitable in narratives (although it is a strength of a narrative if that is the approach used). While it is an expensive process, the most objective way is either to transcribe and then analyze a process, or to use one of the means available to do an analysis of an audio-visual recording. There are a number of good programs, such as N-vivo, to code and then analyze interactions, and these programs also do some of the work of organizing the findings.

Another approach that can be used is interviews with members. This would be especially appropriate when one is seeking to learn what the members know about mutual aid and how they observed it in the group. This approach would also reveal differences among members on these issues, which is one of the questions I raised above. One might also trust observers of the process if one uses several observers and can compare the observations in order to determine reliability.

Quantitative Approaches

A very important research study on mutual aid processes was done by Cicchetti (2009), who, for his doctoral dissertation, looked at treatment groups for people with substance abuse disorders. He developed a scale, the mutual aid process scale (MAPS), comprised of 30 mutual aid processes. He surveyed 484 workers in such groups and found that the most frequently used processes were mutual support, all-in-the-same-boat phenomenon, and installation of hope. This latter variable is problematic to me, however, as I do not see it as a mutual aid process but rather one of the so-called curative factors (Yalom & Leszcz, 2005). There seems to be some confusion between these two concepts, and I do not see the curative factors as a whole as a typology of mutual aid except in the most abstract sense.

There is a role for the use of quantitative instruments. These might be one way, although there are qualitative ways as well, of determining what workers or members know about mutual aid and what kinds of variation exist within and between these groups. Quantitative approaches might also be used to assess outcomes of groups in which defined mutual aid processes were present, partially present, or absent. As one can tell, in the conduct of mutual aid investigations, I see a role for a mixed-method approach in which quantitative and qualitative methods are both used, as appropriate, in various stages of the research.

Note

1   In this section of the paper, as well as in other sections, I used a literature review by Sarah LaRocque (2013) prepared for Dr. William Pelech entitled "Literature Review: Mutual Aid in Social Work Groups."

References

Breton, M. (1989). The need for mutual-aid groups in a drop-in for homeless women. *Social Work With Groups, 11*(4), 47–61.

Breton, M. (2004). Competition as a factor in mutual-aid and the pursuit of social justice. *Social Work, 27*(4), 5–16.

Cicchetti, A. (2009). *Mutual aid processes in treatment groups for people with substance use disorders: A survey of group practitioners* (Doctoral dissertation). Available from Proquest Dissertations and Theses database. (UMI No. 3344964)

Garvin, C. (1997). *Contemporary group work* (3rd ed.). New York, NY: Allyn and Bacon.

Gitterman, A. (1989). Building mutual support in groups. *Social Work With Groups, 12*(2), 5–21.

Gitterman A. (2004). The mutual aid model. In C. D. Garvin, L. M. Gutiⓧrrez, & M. J. Galinsky (Eds.), *Handbook of social work with groups* (pp. 93–110). New York, NY: Guilford.

Gitterman, A., & Shulman, L. (2005). *Mutual aid groups, vulnerable populations, and the life cycle* (3rd ed.). New York, NY: Columbia University Press.

Kelly, T. B. (1999). Mutual aid groups with mentally ill older adults. *Social Work With Groups, 21*(4), 63–80.

Kropotkin, P. (1904). *Mutual aid: A factor in evolution.* New York, NY: McClure Phillips.

LaRocque, S. (2013). *Literature review: Mutual aid in social work groups.* Unpublished manuscript, Faculty of Social Work, University of Calgary, Calgary, Alberta.

Lee, C. D., del Carmen Montiel, E., Atchison, J., Flory, P., Liza, J., & Valenzuela, J. (2009). An innovative approach to support social groupwork: A university groupwork club. *Groupwork, 19*(3), 11–26.

Lindsay, J., Roy, V., Mountainy, L., Turcotte, D., & Genest-Default, S. (2008). The emergence and the effects of therapeutic factors in groups. *Social Work With Groups, 31*(3-4), 255–271.

Liu, F. L. (2002). Closing a cultural divide: Enhancing mutual aid while working with groups in Hong Kong. *Groupwork, 13*(2), 272–292.

Schwartz, W. (1994). The social worker in the group. In T. Berman-Rossi (Ed.), *Social work: The collected writings of William Schwartz* (pp. 309–323). Itaska, IL: Peacock Publishers. (Original work published 1961)

Shulman, L (1986). The dynamics of mutual aid. *Social Work With Groups, 8*(4), 51–60.

Steinberg, D. M. (2000). The impact of time and place on mutual-aid practice with short-term groups. *Social Work With Groups, 22*(3), 101–118.

Steinberg, D. M. (2003). The magic of mutual aid. *Social Work With Groups, 25*(1-2), 31–38.

Steinberg, D. M. (2010). Mutual aid: A contribution to best-practice social work. *Social Work With Groups, 33*(4), 53–68.

Wilke, D. J., Randolph, K. A., & Vinten, L. (2009). Enhancing web-based courses through mutual aid framework. *Journal of Teaching in Social Work, 29*(1), 18–31.

Yalom, I., & Leszcz, M. (2005). *The theory and practice of group psychotherapy* (5th ed.). New York, NY: Basic Books.

Cat's Cradle:

Managing and (Maybe Even) Enhancing the Complexities and Diversity of Groups in Human Service Organizations

Jane Matheson

This presentation and resulting paper is based on experience; based simply on what I have learned from working in groups in many types in human service organizations over the past almost 40 years. These organizations and the people in them—clients and staff, board members and bosses—have taught me such a great deal. I owe them many thanks because learning how to be a team member and how to use groups for powerful collective decision-making is worth its weight in gold. It is the power of getting your hands dirty with the work and the accompanying and inevitable mistakes that make us better. And of course, learning how to prove that clients benefit from all this "working together": that is the best result.

I offer here a collection of 10 lessons learned or strategies used to get results in working with groups. These results have been mostly happy staff, a good reputation in the community, growth in the organization, and client care—just to name a few. And all of them have resulted from mistakes reframed, in most cases, as opportunities.

This paper is called "Cat's Cradle" based on a seemingly simple children's game played with string first written about in 1754. You may have even played it years ago. The designs for cat's cradles are seemingly endless. The designs are connections—string to string, string to fingers, strings in knots, or strings wound around other strings. A cat's cradle can turn from simple to complicated in one turn and back again. It can also mess you up. It is interesting to note that a cat's cradle is also defined as "something intricate, complicated, or elaborate" ("Cat's cradle," n.d., para. 2). This part of the definition speaks to the way the game works but also to the metaphor of creating something complex. It occurred to me that these descriptions—the game and the metaphor both—capture my experience of working and living with groups of people in social work over the past four decades. Cat's cradles are like organizations and departments: complicated, detailed, elaborate, aggravating, and also fun. Hence, the title.

Cat's cradles in organizations can be described as the powerful connections between people and programs or just as easily be interpreted as a "strings attached" culture. This is where groups and their existence are inherently linked with both the leaders and the group members: their styles, values, and standpoints, not just the work to be done. And these factors together create organizational climate and culture—whether people realize it or not. The permutations and combinations are endless.

To further complicate matters, the way we see ourselves as leaders or members in groups is often not the way we are seen by others in the group or in the organization. Perception is key: of those cat's cradles created by a myriad of communication networks and also of what they represent when they are created. For example, trust (or the lack thereof), the management of shame and mistakes, forgiveness and ethical standpoints, and the enhancement of things such as quality service to clients, staff and stakeholder turnover, and satisfaction—all of these topics addressed in organizations today are dependent on good communication and then the wild card: perception.

Successful groups demand something from each leader or member: responsibility for oneself is key; self-awareness is demanded; skill in appreciating, not just tolerating, difference is required; and that is just a start. There are high standards for everyone, not just leaders. It is also necessary to remember that there is always a lot going on in any organization—on the surface, below the surface, and also in someone's mind. It is human nature to get together in groups and talk about it all!

A Short Context

I stumbled into social work when I was 23 and needed a job. In doing so, I discovered two new worlds: the scary and mystifying world of children with serious problems in residential treatment and the world of groups in a therapeutic milieu. Without the latter, I would not have understood the former, discovered my own capabilities with them, nor made it through those days without those coworkers. The people who hired me asked me questions, supported and reassured me, taught me, laughed at me and with me, confronted my naiveté boldly and swiftly, and without a thought helped me develop a little thicker skin that still allowed my vulnerabilities to show through. And all of that happened inside the structure of some kind of group and in front of many.

Looking back, I experienced a profound shaping experience. I lived and breathed groups—of coworkers and kids with very big troubles and in any combination you can think of. I knew almost nothing about group theory but by doing it every day, I learned about listening; how to combine the straightforward with the kind; how groups develop strength and how they fall apart; how collective decision-making works; the power of vulnerabilities; the messages in behaviour; the importance of not jumping to conclusions without facts; and how to think straight by using emotions like fear and shame instead of hiding them.

So, time has passed. I have more education now and have been a supervisor, leader, mentor, manager, CEO, and teacher for about 40 years. Today, I am the CEO of Wood's Homes, a large, nonprofit children's mental health centre located in Calgary that has been helping children and families for 100 years. Today, Wood's Homes offers 35 different programs in Alberta and the Northwest Territories. Most of the work done by these programs is done in a group of some kind. It is the nature of the work and its complexities for sure, but it is also our preference, too.

This paper is not about group theory and/or any kind of deliberate research on group activity in a human service organization. It is about practicalities and experience, accompanied by stories and a great deal of risk-taking.

So, What Have We Learned?

1. Know That the Leader Is Important

In all organizations, leaders are important. The concept of leadership overall is, in and of itself, another entire presentation, but leading groups is a skill not all leaders have or even feel is important. Leaders have a tendency to rely on what works for them—what is tried and true, and of course, no leader is perfect. Each one excels in particular areas and often avoids or delegates others. For example, I am fond of saying about myself that given two choices, behind one door is one person I have to ask for $1 million and behind the other sit 100 angry people, I would choose the 100 people. I am no less nervous, but I know I have more skill in one area than in the other. Experience tells me this. Others who work with me fear large groups of people attacking them and struggle with the idea that being in charge means people should obey and agree! Each to his own!

So, for this first item, let me give one caveat: everything I have learned about groups, I have learned from being responsible for groups of adolescents who did not want to do what I was suggesting, what they needed to do, or what needed to be done right away. I had to develop (and quickly!) powers of persuasion, creativity, and quick thinking, and an ability not to take myself too seriously. I also learned from this audience that some sense of structure is required, though it will never be requested. However, it must be a structure that offers a lot of freedom—and an open door over there in the corner, but only slightly open; one they would have to squeeze through with difficulty or be really strong to open!

In those early days, I doubt I was the leader of anything. I was following the lead of these singularly fascinating young people, listening, watching, and trying to figure out what to do. As a result, I happened upon the importance of a leader.

At Wood's Homes there are about 50 leaders now. Some have been in leadership positions for over 20 years and others are brand new, enthusiastic puppies who aspire to be good leaders but have no clue about the demands of the job or the challenges of supervising people and their worries. The management group at Wood's Homes is committed to teaching people how to be leaders, and as a result, we have eagle eyes about who will shape themselves and the positions they hold and who will not. And as groups are so important to the organization and how it runs, leading them and building teams is a big part of the job.

Leaders are very important in groups: this is so regardless of one's desire for a flat organizational system or a hierarchy. And this has nothing to do with ego or being all-powerful. It is about those things I mentioned earlier: structure, an open door, a sense of humour, a bit of self-deprecation, an ability to fall into an abyss, get yourself out, and keep your eye on the task at hand and the light at the end of tunnel or the prize.

If there is no designated leader, one will emerge, trying. And when there is a leader but said leader is weak or indecisive, someone else will step up and may take the group in a direction that is not planned or wanted. This can be a real problem when a group has a task to complete and little to no decision-making occurs. But most important, human service organizations are not just think tanks; they have to do something and do it well in order to survive. We who teach leaders must help them with concrete ideas for their back pockets. Lately, I have three favorite pieces of advice for leaders. First, The 3 Secrets of Leadership Success by Fidler (1995), and it applies very well for group leaders, too:

1. Humbly show up.
2. Tell the truth with compassion.
3. Give up trying to control the outcome.

My second piece of advice is that a leader's power does not really lie in a list of strengths he or she possesses, but in the ability to transform those weaknesses or vulnerabilities. Third, people want to be inspired to something bigger than themselves. Leaders show us that possibility.

Leaders also have plans for the future, favorite causes, strengths, idiosyncrasies, and weaknesses. Using all of these attributes, leaders set a tone for the way any group in their organization will operate. Unspoken rules are understood by what leaders say and do; what they like and dislike; how they handle conflict, mistakes, and crises; or even how they give compliments.

Leadership style and group process thus go hand in hand. And regardless of style—collaborative or nonhierarchical—it is how one is the leader that matters. We, the followers, are watching. This is not rocket science. It is just human nature.

2. Grasp Something Bigger Than Yourself

When an organization is mission-driven and appeals to people's emotions, it draws them into the work of making a difference in a person or situation and somehow touches them in a visceral place. Wood's Homes is like that. Our little motto—"We never give up, we never say no and we never turn anyone away"—started out just because a few people thought that abandoning or giving up on exasperating children was simply unacceptable. In those early days, we sometimes did not know exactly what we were going to do with that very troubled child, but with figuring it out we developed a good deal of ability in the risk assessment and clinical knowledge areas. However, we faced major criticism for years for this standpoint. We were called "bleeding hearts"; we were harming children by protecting them too much; and even—we had psychological problems of our own. It was hard to stand alone.

However, 25 years later this philosophy is depended upon and copied by many. And inside the organization people are proud of this history, from board members throughout. The board members say one "gets sucked into the vortex of Wood's Homes and never wants to leave." Leaders of program groups tell stories of staying the course to inspire their group members to do the right thing, take a risk for kids and families, advocate for the good and right thing to do, go that extra step. Employees leave for greener pastures and then come back because they like being part of never giving up.

3. Please Set Context!

It never ceases to amaze me. Someone gathers a whole collection of people together for a really good reason (a task force, a team meeting) and then starts in the middle of the story, in the middle of what she wants people to do: somewhere between the reason she asked everyone to come, the thinking she has been doing, the challenges she faces, and what she needs.

What happens without fail (if there is no saviour in the room) is everyone sits quietly, trying to figure out what she wants, what she is talking about, and what she might want. Then they all start to guess. They want to contribute, to help. They offer suggestions about what they have decided she is talking about and she, in turn, tries to counterbalance these guesses with information and background to refute these ideas. If the issue is contentious, defensiveness is rampant on both sides. This goes on for some time and pretty soon, the meeting deteriorates; the initiator may even have forgotten the original purpose and feels most certainly like a failure. The members are wound up, may be worried about "what is really going on," and have a bad taste in their mouths. They are, for sure, talking amongst themselves later.

All for the want of a good context setting! And some idea we have that people can read our mind. Instead, wait for everyone to be seated.

Thank them for coming. Plan beforehand to tell a story about what led up to this meeting, why you called them together, what you want from them, where you want to go. Draw your story out a bit (yet succinctly) and ask for any questions, ensuring people understand what you are hoping to gain and how the conversation might unfold.

This problem is a lot more usual than you might think. We all think we set context, but as leaders or even members of groups, we get so excited about where we want to go and our perception of need. Of course, this means we are starting where we are at, and perhaps that is not the same place as our neighbour. We assume people can read our minds and catch up with us, and they, in turn, suffer from what Taylor, Chait, and Holland (1996) called dysfunctional politeness. There are few people in groups who have the courage to say: "I have no idea what you are talking about. Can you please start at the beginning?" We do not want to feel like we are the only one in the room who does not know. Context fixes a lot of problems before they begin.

4. Mattering Matters

Sally Helgesen (2006) coined this title, and I am borrowing it here, as it describes a key facet of group membership and the desire to belong. Belonging is important in any group and can be as easy or difficult as making a connection with one person who makes you feel like you have worth or interest. Many of us may have attended a class or group where we felt like an outsider, wanting to be noticed and welcomed, to belong. Helgesen has made the point that people want their work to matter. I posit that this concept of working for something bigger than yourself goes hand in hand with the other side of the coin: People want to matter to the workplace, too. People who are working in groups of any kind at all want to know their place; they want to feel that they can offer something, do it well, and know their offering to the work is recognized and matters to the overall product. Leaders have a tendency to forget this.

In these days of working in partnership or collaboratively, many diverse groups are formed, bringing people from various sectors together for a common purpose. One person usually has the idea and contacts particular people to join this "common purpose." Very often, the purpose of the group is clearly related to your main job or to your organization; but sometimes that is not so clear. You may not really know why they asked you to attend, but you go anyway. When you arrive at the first group meeting, you see people you know so you feel like you have a leg up on "belonging." But time passes and beyond the group appreciation of thanks for coming, you do not know what your particular contribution is going to be, and this does not become anymore clear as subsequent meetings occur. So, you stop going. Why? Because you know what you do well and what contributions you can make. You want someone to tell you that you matter to the bigger issue and then give you a job to do that would use those skills.

A board of directors is an excellent example. Board members join boards because they are interested in the mission of the nonprofit, they know someone, or both. They matter to someone who takes them under his or her wing, helping them understand things. Often this takes a surprisingly long time as organizations are complex; it is a steep learning curve. As a result, board members are often fearful of speaking up as their ideas may seem lame. And, indeed, they may be, as the board member is new and does not have knowledge of the past. However, we want new board members to feel that they matter to the work, that their skills and knowledge are appreciated, and that they are welcome to belong, so it is a delicate balance to listen, consider, and then adapt what they said or disagree without appearing to be dismissive.

I am not saying that people should wait around to be asked to get their ego stroked. What I mean is that group leaders and organizers need to ensure the people they invite matter to their idea, the work ahead, and the outcome. A leader should tell each person about that "mattering" in front of everyone else so there is a mattering cat's cradle, if you will, developing connections between people and encouraging them to work together. This is such an easy thing – paying attention to what matters. It is separate from the task at hand and yet solidifies the outcome almost effortlessly.

5. Have a Point and Be Able to Prove It

Who has not been a member of a group that seemed to be going nowhere? There are regular times to meet, and often for way longer than you have time for, but it feels like nothing is planned and no actions are taken, or if they are, they do not get accomplished by the next meeting. Soon, you are thinking up excuses to miss the meeting and feeling guilty. You find yourself complaining to others about the waste of time or dread getting up to attend a morning meeting with people who drive you crazy. You blame the leaders while you, yourself, have some responsibility.

Groups have stages as we all know. It takes time to coalesce and achieve commitment from everyone to a group process and regardless of how arduous this gelling may be, it is important. Some groups, like task forces, have a time frame and a precise topic and so time is of the essence; "getting to know you" needs to happen while work is being done. Others are ongoing groups—such as a weekly management meeting of an organization. This meeting might deal with issues on a regular basis, issues that change and need follow-up and attention in a different way. Still others are one-time groups where many people are called together, such as a Town Hall or training session. One of the most important considerations for any kind of group—large, small, new, old, spontaneous or regular—is that it has to have a point: a reason for people to get up, drive over, be on time for, and spend time to contribute something. Every group has to have a point that everyone who is attending understands and agrees with.

As well, there must be a sense of measuring success. How will people know that this group, this task force, this meeting, this Town Hall, this impromptu conflict resolution get-together is a success? How will we measure it? When you have a point and you are prepared to prove it, people are inspired to show up. They want to see what is going to happen next. They like the idea of an end result, being part of a successful outcome. Having a point and wanting to prove it provides structure, too. If members lose their way, they can always be drawn back by the point and the carrot at the end of the ride.

It is definitely more possible to do this with short-term or one-time groups, but not impossible with long-standing groups, too. You just have to be a bit more nimble, more able to think on your feet or change direction if the superficial reason for a discussion turns into something more serious and seemingly off-topic. Just keep in mind the ultimate goal while having a secondary and perhaps even more important goal—getting to know each other's point of view or resolving a disagreement, for example—front and centre and resolved before going back to the original plan. Often long-standing groups are places to get advice, agreement, plan new things, understand things, and settle disagreements. Some are meant to be places of support and confrontation as well as task centres or decision-making places. Balancing the needs of both and having meetings end with a feeling of accomplishment on both ends is a skill worth developing.

6. Groups Are Major Brain-Power Resources: Contribute to Them and Use Them

Once a group has been created and has formed a bond or tone, trust, role clarity, and expectations become clearer. A group is never perfect or static, as it is made up of human beings who are always changing. From one day to another, groups function in better or worse ways. People often show up to groups expecting something will happen to them, and they will then simply respond. And sometimes, attendees to groups just make reports, usually of good news, and while people are happy about that, they wonder about what really matters; did they contribute to the group? Was the point of the group attended to?

For many groups that have a point—as noted above, they are waiting with eagerness to sink their teeth into problems. Leaders should not fear bringing problems and asking for help, advice, or suggestions to make something better, fix a serious issue, or get new ideas for something that is making us stuck. The use of all that brain power is the point. Once leaders have crossed that line into the realm of admitting to mistakes or problems, listen. Do not explain or get defensive. Do not debate. Write things down. Consider everything carefully. Be in charge of your problem and see the members of the group as library books or the Internet—resources to plumb for ideas. Be clear about what you want and what you can do.

Of course some groups and some people sound as if they expect you to do what they say whether you like it or not. In some cases, a hierarchy may determine this is so. However, try to keep in mind that the problem is still yours and you can be in charge of what you need and hope for regardless of power systems. On the other side of the coin, people who are members of groups must see themselves as there for a reason. Each person contributes to this collective brain power and the brainstorming that most likely will occur; not contributing is the only problem. Sitting in silence is anathema to group process. Yes, people are shy. Yes, they have trouble speaking up in large groups as they are afraid. Yes, they might say something wrong and be humiliated. Leaders are watching for the silent ones and a good leader tries to draw each one out but the onus is also on the person who attends. Why come if you will not share your ideas? How can one call oneself a contributing member and squander resources?

The balance here is very hard to maintain and for leaders, it can be doubly hard to know what to do to balance too much–too little talking.

This is where the importance of all members must be reinforced. A group is only at its best level of success when all members contribute, all know they matter, and all take contributing as their own personal responsibility.

7. Be Patient; Change Takes Longer Than You Think

I am quick on my feet. I get an idea, and I want to do it right away. I can see the steps that need to be taken, and I can see the end result, too. I get excited about the potential, and I am ready to start! And I can actually get this together in a 15-minute ride to work! It's just my nature. Unfortunately, upon the presentation of my great idea, I often face a group of people who look at me askance. They are surprised, maybe angry, puzzled, or frightened, and they fall silent. They resist change; they think what I am suggesting will not work. They really don't want to tell me this and be seen as raining on my parade. But they must. If I truly stand behind one of my own elements of good advice, I need them to be devil's advocates, risk assessors, and cautionary tale-tellers. My 15 minutes in the car did not give me time enough to do all of that, and I must be able to make an argument that convinces all them wholeheartedly—otherwise, I am and they are irresponsible.

Here is an example. Ten years ago I presented my "very good idea" to become a "no-restraint agency" and only one person in a room of 25 managers thought it was a good idea. The rest thought I had lost my mind. It took a very long time to make change,. It took a lot longer than I imagined or wanted, and so many more things needed to happen that in my new idea fog I never even considered.

Today, Wood's Homes restrains children in distress only 13 times per year. Ten years ago, we restrained about 400 times. We provide more service to more children in our residential programs than we did in 2002, and yet, we have many fewer restraints. This is still not perfect, but every restraint is investigated, each one is reviewed; every one serves as a catalyst for change. I am grateful to the naysayers for ensuring we thought this change through more carefully. I am grateful for the lesson I learned that change takes time, a lot more time than I ever thought. This has been such a good lesson for many other similar situations where I wanted people to change or groups to get action happening faster or for understanding what stands in their way.

8. Use the Power of Surprise

When an organization has regular ongoing groups that are integral to the development and implementation of organizational plans and decisions, these get-togethers can get very stale and boring. I guess this is just human nature, too—same old, same old puts us to sleep. It is important to change it up every once and a while. Sometimes, yearly retreats or trainings can fulfill this need, especially if it takes the group out of its natural environment and allows members to focus on one topic and involves fun. Sometimes retreats and collective trainings are not well planned, however, and end up as holidays or an extra-long weekend with little action to show for it in the end. This has short-term benefit only.

I have found that surprise works best. First of all, I determine the need for surprise by my own barometer. If I am bored in the meeting, that probably means everyone is, too, and they are just being polite. Then, I look for something new and different. And then I plan how I am going to use it.

One time many years ago, our regular senior management meeting was falling into ennui. People were not speaking up in the meeting, no one had agenda items, arguments would happen over the slightest of things. This meant to me that something was needed. I found a book called The Five Dysfunctions of a Team by Patrick Lencioni (2002). This book is written as a story with a kind of "what will happen next?" style, accompanied by a model of team dysfunction, a graphic, and an assessment tool. The group completed the assessment tool, and then I read a chapter or two aloud at each weekly management meeting. What this did was change the tone and feeling of the management meeting completely. The management group listened to the story carefully, waiting with anticipation for what was next. They understood the not-so-hidden meaning. They reviewed the assessment results, found themselves on the pyramid graph, practiced conflict management, did a posttest with the same questionnaire, and in the end got to know each other better, developed trust, and, well, the meetings became so interesting, one member did not even want to miss one for a holiday! This little book served as a jumping off point for many future activities within the meeting: new agenda formats, the expectation of participation, and permission to confront one another. Spirited debate was encouraged. Senior managers found their voices and took charge of many components. This transformation—as that was what it was—kept up a pace for about three years and has since morphed into the use of many other leadership tools, and the use of world cafés on a regular basis, inviting Mr. Lencioni to come for a visit, and using his new book, The Advantage (Lencioni, 2012), to change the meetings once again.

There has also been a shift in responsibility. Managers now shape these meetings, presenting their ideas to an enthusiastic crowd while confidently managing the inevitable questions and anxieties noted in any new change—all on their own. It is never perfect, I might add. There are always the ones who drag behind, the ideas that flop, the meetings where conflict is not successfully managed, but the point is there and the expectation for all to be engaged is front and centre. Change and new ideas may be either a welcome or unwelcome surprise to folks, but in the end, the wonder is really with themselves—their enjoyment of the process and the new skills they acquire with being pushed gently towards change—while in tandem with the group.

9. Embrace Stories and Storytelling

When I undertook a PhD in the late 1990s, I researched the process of social work supervision. During the collection of data, the use of stories and storytelling emerged as a strong theme. The power of stories to humanize, inspire, encourage change, reframe difficult situations, educate, teach values, entertain, give advice, set context—the list goes on—was amazing. Stories told in groups of people can set the stage for understanding at a whole new level.

Wood's Homes is a story-making place. Every day we make stories by what we do, what we think, and the crazy, profound, kind, remarkable, scary, amazing things that people do—our clients and staff, board members, volunteers, even our neighbours. We use stories to understand things, encourage action, inspire the fearful, express emotions, and inculcate our values in people who wonder about our work. We tell the really meaningful ones over and over. We have learned about the value of good storytelling, too, and teach people that delivery is key! Wood's Homes has stories that are told over and over—ones that show how much we have learned or how strongly we are affected by something. One such story is the story about Miss Adventure:

> In the 1980s a 13-year-old girl came to one of our residential programs as she was acting out at home and school. Over time,

she could not (nor could we) get her behaviour under control; all of our efforts seemed to be failing. She eventually took to the streets. Her therapist devised a clinical intervention: the girl who ran away to the streets was called "Miss Adventure." The girl who stayed in the program was her real name. Periodically she would want to get rid of Miss Adventure, and we would bury her accoutrements in an orchestrated ritual in the back woods: her fur coat, high heels, black wig, false eyelashes, etc. But each time she would dig them up and off she would go again. It was a terrible time of frustration and fear.

Eventually she moved away and grew older, always keeping in touch with us and telling us how she was planning to go back to school, to settle down. Then one day she was murdered. It took a long time to come to grips with this event and our sense of responsibility. Remembering her was done with a simple plaque inscribed "Miss Adventure". But her life and death inspired us to create programs for girls and boys involved in the sex trade, homeless youth in need of a safe place, and opportunities for work and a future. These programs have been growing and expanding ever since.

We tell this story to kids, to board members, to staff for a whole variety of reasons. It is one that always shows the complexities of work at Wood's Homes.

10. Do Not Fear Anger, Upset, Disagreement, or Sadness; Encourage Them

My final lesson is a simple one—easy to say but hard to do. It might seem to you as just looking for trouble. But in fact, it is an excellent strategy that is disarming and teaches the doer, I think, a kind of mindfulness that opens up our senses to the universality of the human condition, reduces shame and defensiveness, and promotes deeper connection between people. For groups to function well, these are the ideal components, too.

Every day, I manage conflict, upset, worries, and fear. These are the problems that come to my door. Sometimes these issues are the issues of children and their parents but often staff, too. Their concerns arise from day-to-day interactions with others and are mostly based upon fear, misunderstandings, not asking enough questions, jumping to conclusions, allowing resentments to build, and having an unhealthy dose of either hubris or unforgiveness. I do a lot of listening to upset and try not to let it overwhelm me. I ask questions. I gather facts (and few people have many of these, may I say). I stay away from guessing games as much as possible and try to be nonjudgmental. I tell stories and encourage taking responsibility for oneself and the bigger picture. I lay the groundwork for forgiveness. I discourage mean-spiritedness or derogatory descriptions. I demand resolution quickly. Mostly I have success, I am happy to report. But not always. Sometimes people are just too afraid. But I do get to see changes when next the group may meet, and this gives me great pleasure as it is like a domino effect. It just takes a lot longer than I would like!

So, there you have it: my top 10 "best group making and sustaining practices" for human service organizations. These top 10 tips have helped me make cat's cradles inside organizations and even between them as well as helping me make sense of them, too. Thank you for the invitation to present this work and to the audience members for taking the time to listen to this presentation and consider its potential applicability for you.

References

Cat's cradle. (n.d.). In *Merriam-Webster's online dictionary*. Retrieved from http://www .merriam-webster.com/dictionary/cat's%20cradle

Fidler, M. (1995). Leading the association. *Association Management, 47*(1), L41–L42.

Helgesen, S. (1990). *The female advantage*. New York, NY: Doubleday.

Lencioni, P. (2002). *The five dysfunctions of a team*. San Francisco, CA: Jossey-Bass.

Lencioni, P. (2012). *The advantage*. San Francisco, CA: Jossey-Bass.

Taylor, B., Chait, R., & Holland, T. (1996, September–October). The new work of the nonprofit board. *Harvard Business Review*, 4–11.

How Did You Get Here? Engagement in Social Justice Journeys Through Pechakucha

Liza Lorenzetti & Joan Farkas

Social justice is a foundational element of social work theory, ethics, practice, and research. According to the International Federation of Social Workers (IFSW; 2014), social justice, and the work of human rights and liberation, can be viewed as defining features that separate the social work profession from other related disciplines. IFSW Europe (2010) has set specific standards to implement a human rights and social justice practice framework.

A key process to facilitate the integration of a social justice lens among social workers is the personalization of one's own journey to a necessary anti-oppressive paradigm (Lorenzetti, 2013). The concept of critical consciousness (conscientização) developed by Brazilian educator and activist Paolo Freire (1970), can be depicted as a self-journey to understand and challenge dominance thinking, which promotes collective silence and tacit approval within our profession to forms of outrageous injustice that permeate the lives of our clients. An important realization toward centralizing an anti-oppressive and collectivist voice within our profession is that power relations are a central feature of knowledge creation (L. Brown & Strega, 2005) and social arrangements, and that our humanity as social workers is a core feature of our existence, elevated beyond any professional standard or skill set (Lorenzetti, 2013).

An anti-oppression framework recognizes that fundamental changes are necessary in structures and social arrangements that marginalize targeted individuals and groups, and (re)produce relations of dominance (Baines, 2011; Dominelli, 2002; Mullaly, 2010; Strier, 2007). Doing one's own self-work in understanding oppression and uncloaking internalized dominance (Lorde, 1984) is a difficult task, but necessary in order to avoid "contribut[ing] to dominance in spite of our liberatory intentions" (Pease, 2002, p. 135).

Experiential group-work methods, from the lens of liberatory education (Freire, 1970), can be effective tools to move social work students, practitioners, and educators from passive observers of oppression to what Boal (1979), in his Theatre of the Oppressed, referred to as engaged actors. This paper discusses another approach to developing critical consciousness and personalizing an anti-oppressive or social justice stance within social work. Using a Pechakucha process to explore and share one's own social justice journey, facilitators and participants engage together in a journey of self-discovery and (re) commitment to the fundamental social justice aspirations of the social work profession. In this paper, we explain the Pechakucha method, discuss its use as a group method for liberatory education, and describe a process through which facilitators and participants can share in a powerful experiential learning method that engenders a passionate response toward becoming actors for social change. This process, sharing our journeys to social justice, can be adapted for diverse audiences and participant groups.

Context and Method

Liberatory Education and Social (Justice) Work

Although the international definition of social work (IFSW, 2014) and the various national and regional codes of ethics underscore a necessary a commitment to social justice (see, for example, Canadian Association of Social Workers [CASW], 2005), "narratives and movements for equity-based alternatives to a neo-conservative/neo-liberal charity model . . . [are] still marginal, [but] increasingly occupy a segment of popular social work discourse" (Lorenzetti, 2013, p. 54; see also Mullaly, 2002; Pease, 2002).

It is our view that modern social work, at least within the North American context, has been focused on enhancing and articulating a unique worldview, an evidence-based skill set, practice methods, research approaches, and legislative accountability (see, for instance, McLaughlin, Rothery, Babins-Wagner, & Schleifer, 2010; Shaw, 2007). These efforts have greatly assisted in the development of a social work discipline and identity, including protective mechanisms against the most evident forms of abuse and mistreatment of those who seek the support and services of social workers: see, for instance, the Government of Alberta's (2000) Health Professions Act. Social work education and practice as expressions of a liberatory praxis, however, continue to occupy a marginal space within social work, embraced by a limited number within the profession who often find themselves designated as a radical fringe.

The practice of conscientização as the key underpinning of liberatory education can also be defined as critical self-reflection or reflexivity, which are catalysts to understanding how experience and knowledge shape one's worldview and positioning (Carter & Little, 2007; Gilbert & Sliep, 2009). Given that reflectivity is an emerging concept within social justice work, a reflexive stance resonates with the codes of ethics, principles, and practice standards of the profession (CASW, 2005).

It is our view that experiential group learning based on the development of reflexivity and critical consciousness can be accomplished by using the tool of Pechakucha with a critical lens and a focus on personalizing one's own social justice. With the proper reflection and understanding of practitioners' places in the world and how key points in their journeys have influenced them, it is not possible for them to "implicitly adopt a theory of knowledge" (Carter & Little, 2007, p. 1319), but build the internal capacity to articulate and act on a social work framework which marks it as a profession of resistance (Leonard, 2001).

Pechakucha: Catalyst for Group Dialogue and Conscientização

Pechakucha is a fast-paced presentation style that was developed by architects Astrid Klein and Mark Dylan in 2003 (Lehtonen, 2011). With the aim of limiting the amount of "talk" in professional presentations, Pechakucha uses visual representations to articulate complex ideas (Lehtonen, 2011). The format of 20 slides of 20 seconds each, for a total of 6 minutes and 20 seconds, shifts the focus of traditional presentations from simply presenting ideas to developing new ideas through reflection and discussion with participants (Lehtonen, 2011). In contrast to traditional presentation styles such as PowerPoint, participants move from passive receivers of information to active contributors to knowledge creation. Pechakucha is more commonly used in corporate settings but has proven effective in many disciplines as a tool for brainstorming, training, and creating space for innovation (Lehtonen, 2011). Retention of visual images has proven to be stronger than in presentation styles such as PowerPoints (Beyer, Gaze, & Lazicki, 2012). In addition, the short length of time of the Pechakucha creates more opportunity for participants to reflect and deepen their understanding of key concepts. Through discussion, participants "situate the new knowledge in their existing context. This knowledge, then, can be used as a platform to start the process again" (Lehtonen, 2011, p. 468).

A search of the literature did not uncover evidence where the Pechakucha method was used in the context of social work or social work group methods. As a tool of communication, Pechakucha was noted as an effective tool for the retention of information (Beyer et al., 2012; Lehtonen, 2011) and for English language learners (Sukitkanaporn & Phoocharoensil, 2014).

Although Pechakucha is distinctly a presentation style, we have adapted and used this approach as the foundation for a group reflexivity process centered on personalizing one's social justice journey. As presented in the next section, the Pechakucha as a group process and vehicle for critical consciousness provides facilitators and participants a framework within which to explore and uncover various life-points that have led to the formation of values, beliefs, and actions/inactions with regards to social justice.

The Process: Our Journey to Social Justice Using the Pechakucha

The Pechakucha process that we developed is a 6-step journey of individual reflection and group sharing which can be viewed as a form of interrelational reflexivity (Gilbert & Sliep, 2009) and collective discovery. Interrelational reflectivity "recognizes the complexity of the interlinking relationships connected to historical and current power dynamics and positionality that impact individuals, groups, and institutions" (Gilbert & Sliep, 2009 p. 469); this concept is interwoven within the process as we viewed interrelational reflectivity as an underpinning of liberatory education.

As discussed in detail below, step 1 of our process centers on creating a safe climate for group interaction; step 2 is led by facilitators, who share their personal journeys (through the Pechakucha); step 3 is a debrief of facilitator-led Pechakucha through feedback and questions that connect with participant experiences; step 4 is the engagement of participants in documenting their own personal journeys and preparing their own presentations; and step 5 is an opportunity for participants to share their Pechakucha with others in the group. The final step, step 6, focuses on collective discoveries of content and process introduced in the Pechakucha through a group debrief. This final step brings forward the harvesting of views, beliefs, and commitments to social justice.

Step 1: Creating a Safe Climate for Group Interaction

Creating a welcoming environment for participants is a key component of group work settings and a context for meaningful conversations (D. Brown & Isaacs, 2005). Considerations of comfort, aesthetics, and seating arrangements that promote group cohesion among participants and the facilitators work in tandem to create an environment that fosters interrelational reflexivity. Placing seats in a circle serves several purposes. As a symbol of harmony, equality, and connectivity, the circle is highly symbolic, particularly among Indigenous populations, as a way to ritualize working and learning together as one unit (Lepp & Zorn, 2002). The circle formation allows for everyone to see one another, further emphasising the nonhierarchal nature of the group.

The provision of food, soft lighting, and tables placed around the room further creates a comfortable and relaxed setting. As participants enter the room, they are warmly greeted and invited to enjoy the refreshments and take their seats in the circle. The facilitators position themselves within the circle, standing in presentation style. A sense of drama is intentionally created in order to peak interest and anticipation. With no introduction, the Pechakucha begins.

Step 2: Facilitators Share Personal Journeys

The facilitators share their personal journeys to social justice through a

Pechakucha presentation. The sharing is presented through a lifespan approach. Recognizing that the process of conscientization is rooted in childhood and develops throughout maturity, it is critical to link early childhood messages and personal family histories to how a person may currently view the world—or alternatively, how one may have worked to refute damaging aspects of childhood conditioning (Berkowitz & Grych, 1998). An essential element of the facilitator-led sharing process is to invite participants, through role modeling, to uncover the impact of their own families of origin on the development of a social justice lens in both their personal and professional lives. Other points in the lifespan, as demonstrated below, are elemental to the exploration this process (please see the appendix for an example of our own personal journeys).

Roots, family, and childhood influences

The first slides of the Pechakucha presentation use the following one-word titles in a sequential format: Roots, Family, and Childhood Influences. Each facilitator chooses an image alongside the word to represent the message. As the title and image flash on the screen, each facilitator takes a turn to share a personal story within the brief timeframe allotted to that slide. For example, during one of our presentations, under the title "Childhood Influences," an image of three interlocking circles was displayed and was overlaid with the word "Integrity." While the image was in play, the facilitator articulated the following statement: "From my mother, I learned compassion, and from my father, the courage of taking a stand for what is fair and just. The social well-being and the collective far out-measured the individual. Family loyalty was paramount." The facilitators share their messages in sequential format in tandem with the changing of the slides.

In this segment of the presentation, the influence of families of origin and childhood messages are underscored as foundational to understanding how the social justice journey might begin. Lessons of compassion and community may be presented as well as the alternatives where fear or negative messaging hindered one's capacity to develop a social justice lens at that point in time (Berkowitz & Grych, 1998). As one of the facilitators demonstrated in a recent presentation, childhood teachings can include the intertwining of contradictory messages of love and kindness at the same time as biases and harsh judgment: "We were a traditional family. My mother was a soft place to fall. She was compassionate and kind. My dad, God love him, was authoritarian and very strict."

The emphasis on childhood and family is important, as practitioners must first know themselves if they want to be effective in supporting others. A logical beginning place lies with understanding the values, beliefs, assumptions, and biases of childhood, and then, through a process of reflection, these can be deconstructed and challenged.

Oppression and oppressors

The next slides focus first on one's experience of being oppressed, and then on the experience of being an oppressor. Self-discovery in social work must be guided by honesty and integrity. This section of the presentation reminds social workers to be mindful of the duality of life: experiencing oppression while simultaneously acting as oppressor (Bishop, 2002).

Mullaly (2010) underscored the need for critical self-reflection, which he defined as the "never-ending questioning of our social, economic, political, and cultural beliefs, assumptions, and actions" (p. 277). Practitioners, who are often members of privileged groups, risk reproducing the very systems, structures, and patterns of behavior that they seek to overcome if they fail to engage in critical reflection and action. Recognition of the unconscious and insidious ways in which practitioners have adopted oppressive attitudes and beliefs is essential. Working to "unlearn" internalized privilege must be the constant task of any practitioner, regardless of the setting. This is the dichotomy between oppression and oppressor of which every social work practitioner must be cognizant. The oppressor/oppression slides of the Pechakucha demonstrate this dynamic. Examples from our presentation include: "[Oppression] One in 3 girls will be assaulted prior to age 18. Despite my protection, I joined this statistic."

[Oppressor]: My first real job was with Aboriginal women who had been repeatedly victimized. I was angry. But I was young and too scared to rock the boat. Outside of my job, I didn't know how to challenge the racism that was everywhere. I was silent.

As shown in these examples, as women facilitators, we recognize our experience of sexism and its many challenges. The impact of systematic patriarchy, from internal messages of self-hatred to sexual violence, are expressed in ways that that allow participants to understand some of the contexts and social locations that have shaped the facilitators' experiences and, in turn, professional identities. Through this, intentional space is created for participants to reflect on the ways that they too experience oppression in its duality.

In our Pechakucha example, exploring the inherent oppression of dominant power structures in society is presented alongside the positional place of power and influence afforded to the facilitators, two white, middle class, educated women. Shields (1994) called this the dichotomy of "double lives" (p. 8), in reference to the lack of congruence that exists in those working toward social justice who also benefit from the very injustice they protest against. In one of the above slides, expressing solidarity with the survivors of colonization while at the same time acknowledging the reality of benefitting from the spoils of racism and classism, recognizes the tension that many social workers face. How do practitioners work and be in solidarity with those who are marginalized while privilege continues to reap its rewards? These are some of the questions and discussions which may emerge when facilitators and participants debrief this section of the Pechakucha presentation.

Mentors and life-changing moments

A social justice lens is developed through multiple influences. Compassionate and generous mentorship or acts of kindness from others can be part of the journey. Recognizing those who have guided our vision for a socially just world is the next section of the presentation, which can balance the heavy nature of previous slides and commentary. The slide on mentors is intended to create space for participants to think about who it was in their lives that nurtured and grew their best qualities. For example, in our Pechakucha, one of the facilitators stated,

> *[Mentors]: My sister was my first mentor. She was strong and confident, and always said what she thought. She never backed down when she believed in something. She made me think that maybe one day, I could be like her.*

The next slide, Life-Changing Moments, compels participants to ask a further question: "How are we guiding others?" For example, as one facilitator stated in her Pechakucha,

> *The time that I spent in a convent in Mexico with the radical leftist nuns who wore jeans, drank beer and danced the salsa was my introduction to liberation theology. Their anti-oppression work would forever shift my views on religion, colonization, white privilege and my place in the world.*

These thought-provoking slides require a limited script, as the images of mentors, mentorship, and life-changing moments can reveal poignant aspects of these experiences. Remembering and honoring the life-changing moments that shaped the stories shared by the facilitators and led them on a journey toward social justice is an essential element of the Pechakucha.

Actions

In the subsequent two slides, the facilitators show images in which they have participated in actions toward social justice. This demonstrates to participants that the journey to social justice must move beyond personal reflection. Social justice actions, taken in whatever form, from personal to political, are the culmination of personal introspection and learning, which create the platform for critical thinking and action. An example presented by one of the facilitators was, "I worked with nine women who told stories of their life poverty. They were courageous, so how could I not be? I became politically active, wrote letters, joined feminist groups, and met other people who wanted to see change."

Building community

The work of social justice is difficult, fraught with challenges and conflict. It is therefore critical for social justice workers to develop a community of support. In the slide entitled Building Community, participants are encouraged to envision and share their interpretation of a supportive community. In our Pechakucha, we show an image of ourselves at a large public health care rally, standing alongside a group of people. This photo illustrates for us the importance of building a network of trusted people who help to create a safe place that nurtures one's desire to change the world for the better. While this image was shown on the screen, the accompanying spoken message was as follows: "Social justice work is about intentionally building the world that you believe in—both for yourself and for others."

Now

Summarizing the past and reflecting on the present completes the Pechakucha presentation, capping the discussion in a logical fashion. Participants are asked to share their present point in their social justice journey. An example of this final slide, shared by one of our facilitators, centered on her motherhood role. "[Now]: Motherhood has added an important dimension to my social justice path: I focus on providing my daughter with the grounding of a worldview that does not include bigotry, hate or fear of others who are different from her."

In summary, the Journeys to Social Justice Pechakucha is an engaging presentation that appears to strike a chord with participants. It is a narrative with a logical progression through the human lifespan, outlining key milestones, events, and influences that shape one's views, values, and actions. The difference with Pechakucha over traditional presentations is that it is short, with sharp impact that supports participants to retain, reflect, and interpret what is being presented. Finally, it leaves participants with a sense of connectivity and, it is hoped, an aspiration to chart and share their own personal journeys.

Step 3: Debrief of Facilitator-Led Pechakucha

Following the facilitator-led Pechakucha, participants are asked to debrief and discuss what they have just experienced. The debrief contains two main elements: a discussion of the content and experiences shared through the Pechakucha presentation and a discussion of the Pechakucha as a method for story-telling and group sharing. Process and content sharing are equally important as the core aspects of step 3.

Pechakucha and reflexivity

Facilitators share the intent of the presentation, demonstrating the work they undertook to understand and grow their personal and professional identities as social justice activists. Relayed through stories from different phases of life, from the deeply embedded messages instilled by families of origin, to the recognition of the influence of privilege and oppression, to creating new ways of being that align values and beliefs to action, the facilitators highlight the connections among the various presentation slides. The Pechakucha format, using the life span approach, creates a roadmap that others can follow in order to identify and reflect on their own journeys. The sharing of stories by the facilitators, and the subsequent debriefing session, is intended to create a safe learning environment that encourages and supports participants to create their own narratives. Sharing by the facilitators implicitly gives participants permission to do the same.

Pechakucha as a method

As a teaching method, Pechakucha has been perceived as a new, creative tool that may be used in a variety of social service settings and populations, allowing those who use it full creative license to express themselves in a myriad of ways. A debrief with participants on the use of the Pechakucha as a story-telling method is done to create comfort and respond to any questions that arise regarding this approach. The debrief and discussion set the context for the next step, which is engagement of participants in creating their own social justice narratives using the Pechakucha.

Step 4: Engagement of Participants—Create Their Own Pechakucha

In order to better understand the process and potential of Pechakucha as a sharing method and learning tool, participants are asked to take on the task of creating their own presentations. In groups of three or four, participants are invited to develop their own presentations based on the themes presented in the facilitator-led Pechakucha. Given simple supplies of crayons, colored paper, and markers, each group is given 20 to 30 minutes to create handmade "slides" that will become their own Pechakucha. Even though each individual will develop a set of slides, each work group is encouraged to offer support and suggestions to their peers. For groups that meet on more than one occasion, this approach could be adapted to provide more time for presentation development. Computers and audio-visual equipment could also be used.

Step 5: Presentations and Sharing

Once participants have completed their slides, they are encouraged to share their Pechakucha with others in their small groups. This section of the workshop allows participants to tell their stories, highlighting the parts of their journeys that were most meaningful. The small group format allows participants to share and discuss their experiences without being in front of a large audience and is a catalyst for deepening relationships through compassion and positive reinforcement.

Step 6: Collective Discoveries Through Story-Telling

Story-telling and personal narratives are powerful approaches to building connections among people. Whitmore, Wilson, and Calhoun (2011) asserted that story-telling builds relationships between group members, creating greater empathy and trust, thus "providing a basis for probing for deep levels of understanding and analysis" (p. 159). This creates platforms for reflection through which new learning can emerge (Whitmore et al., 2011).

The story-telling that occurs through the small group Pechakucha presentations is further deepened during the collective discoveries step of this group process. Participants gather once again in a circle with the facilitators to share and harvest the experiences from their small group presentations and discussions. Key questions can be posed by the facilitators, such as, "What did you learn from another person's story in your small group?"; or, "What elements of someone's story resonated with your own?"; and finally, "Has this process changed or deepened your understanding of your own social justice journey?" It is important to allow enough time for this step in the process, as sharing one's personal journey may elicit a broad range of emotions. Facilitators should be mindful of not creating further harm or unwanted vulnerability among participants, who may bring numerous and potentially traumatic life experiences to the discussion table. During this final stage of the process, facilitators may also ask everyone in the room to leave with one new commitment to enhance their social justice journey.

Conclusion

In this article, we explore an adapted Pechakucha process as a liberatory education approach to developing critical consciousness or conscientização. Although the Pechakucha has traditionally been used as a presentation method to a passive audience, we propose that facilitators can engage with participants in a process of interrelational reflexivity to explore, identify, and share individual and collective pathways to developing a social justice lens. In this process, we present six steps, which interweave aspects of story-telling, role-modelling, group discussion, individual reflection, and collective discoveries. The key life-point moments shared in the Pechakucha are the essence of an explored social justice journey. Beginning with childhood and family relationships, the process then includes an articulation of life-changing moments, the influence of mentors, and a reflection on the duality of oppressed and oppressor roles within society. The explored journey "so far" ends with a present-day reflection as well as commitments, through the final phase of the process, of how one's social justice journey can be further advanced. It is our hope that this approach can be used and further adapted for social workers and other participant groups who are interested in developing critical consciousness, enhancing reflexivity in their practice, and centering themselves within a social justice life journey.

References

Baines, D. (2011). *Doing anti-oppressive practice: Social justice social work* (2nd ed). Winnipeg, Manitoba: Fernwood.

Berkowitz, M. W., & Grych, J. H. (1998). Fostering goodness: Teaching parents to facilitate children's moral development. *Journal of Moral Education, 27*(3), 371–391. doi:10.1080 /0305724980270307

Beyer, A., Gaze, C., & Lazicki, J. (2012). Comparing students' evaluations and recall for student Pecha Kucha and PowerPoint presentations. *Journal of Teaching and Learning with Technology, 1*(2), 26–42.

Bishop, A. (2002). *Becoming an ally*. Halifax, NS: Fernwood.

Boal, A. (1979). *Theatre of the oppressed*. New York, NY: Theatre Communications Group.

Brown, J., & Issacs, D. (2005). *Creating hospitable spaces: The world café*. San Francisco, CA: Berrett-Koehler.

Brown, L., & Strega, S. (2005). *Research as resistance: Critical, indigenous and anti-oppressive approaches*. Toronto, Ontario: Canadian Scholars' Press/Women's Press.

Canadian Association of Social Workers. (2005). *Code of ethics*. Retrieved from http://www .caswacts.ca/sites/default/files/attachements/ CASW_Code%20of%20Ethics

Carter, S. M., & Little, M. (2007). Justifying knowledge, justifying method, taking action: Epistemologies, methodologies, and methods in qualitative research. *Qualitative Health_Research, 17*, 1316–1328. doi:10.1177/1049732307306927

Dominelli, L. (2002). *Anti-oppressive social work theory and practice*. Hampshire, England: Palgrave, MacMillan.

Freire, P. (1970). *Pedagogy of the oppressed*. New York, NY: Continuum.

Gilbert, A., & Sliep, Y. (2009). Reflexivity in the practice of social action: From self- to inter-relational reflexivity. *South African Journal of Psychology, 39*(4), 468–479. doi:10.1177 /008124630903900408

Government of Alberta. (2000). *Health professions act: Revised statutes of Alberta 2000*. Retrieved from http://www.qp.alberta.ca/documents/ Acts/h07.pdf

International Federation of Social Workers. (2014). *Definition of social work.* Retrieved from http://ifsw.org/policies/definition-of-social-work

International Federation of Social Workers, Europe. (2010). *Standards of social work practice meeting human rights*. Retrieved from http://cdn. ifsw.org/assets/ifsw_45904-8.pdf

Leonard, P. (2001). The future of critical social work in uncertain conditions.

Critical Social Work, 2(1). Retrieved from http://www1.uwindsor.ca/criticalsocialwork/the-future-of-critical-social-work-in-uncertain-conditions

Lehtonen, M. (2011). Communicating competence through Pechakucha presentations. *Journal of Business Communication, 48*(4), 464–481. doi:1177/00219436114142

Lepp, M., & Zorn, C. (2002). Faculty forum. Life circle: Creating safe space for educational empowerment. *Journal of Nursing Education, 41*(9), 383–385.

Lorde, A. (1984). Age, race, class and sex: Women redefining difference. In A. Lorde (Ed.), *Sister outsider* (pp. 114–123). Trumansburg, NY: Crossing Press.

Lorenzetti, L. (2013). Developing a cohesive emancipatory social work identity: Risking an act of love. *Critical Social Work, 14*(2), 47–59.

McLaughlin, A. M., Rothery, M., Babins-Wagner, R., & Schleifer, B. (2010). Decision making and evidence in direct practice. *Clinical Social Work Journal, 38*, 155–163. doi:10.1007 /s10615-009-0190-8

Mullaly, B. (2002). *Challenging oppression: A critical social work approach.* Don Mills, Ontario: Oxford University Press.

Mullaly, B. (2010). *Challenging oppression and confronting privilege.* Don Mills, Ontario: Oxford University Press.

Pease, B. (2002). Rethinking empowerment: A postmodern reappraisal for emancipatory practice. *British Journal of Social Work, 32*(2), 135–147. doi:10.1093/bjsw/32.2.13

Shaw, I. F. (2007). Is social work research distinctive? *Social Work Education, 26*(7), 659–669. doi:10.1080/02615470601129834

Shields, K. (1994). *In the tiger's mouth: An empowerment guide of social action.* Gabriola Island, British Columbia: New Society Publishers.

Strier, R. (2007). Anti-oppressive research in social work: A preliminary definition. *British Journal of Social Work, 37*(5), 857–871. doi:10.1093/bjsw/bcl062

Sukitkanaporn, T., & Phoocharoensil, S. (2014). English presentation skills of Thai graduate students. *English Language Teaching, 7*(3), 91–102. doi:10.5539/elt.v7n3p91

Whitmore, E., Wilson, M. G., & Calhoun, A. (Eds). (2011). *Activism that works.* Black Point, NS: Fernwood.

Appendix: Our Pechakucha
(Liza Lorenzetti and Joan Farkas)

ROOTS, Facilitator 1: Our people came to Canada like most of your people, if you are not a First Nations. Poverty, struggles of adaptation, and exploitation are family stories, but not my own. In Quebec, you keep your culture close.

ROOTS, Facilitator 2: My mother's family came from England to become homesteaders. Life was hard. But they had community. My dad's story is much more painful. Mom understood community. Dad understood individualism.

FAMILY, Facilitator 1: I was brought up in an intergenerational and multilingual household in Montreal, with three mother-figures and plenty of advice from all over: wanted and unwanted. When I moved to Calgary, people thought that this was strange.

FAMILY, Facilitator 2: We were a traditional family. My mother was a soft place to fall. She was compassionate and kind. My dad, God love him, was authoritarian and very strict.

CHILDHOOD, Facilitator 1: From my mother, I learned compassion and from my father, the courage of taking a stand for what is fair and just. The social well-being and the collective far out-measured the individual. Family loyalty was paramount.

CHILDHOOD, Facilitator 2: I was one of those emotional, anxious children that books are written about. I remember feeling sad and lonely a lot. But still, I always had the vision that one day, I might make things better.

OPPRESSION, Facilitator 1: One in 3 girls will be assaulted prior to age 18. Despite my protection, I joined this statistic.

OPRESSION, Facilitator 2: Depression is anger turned inwards and I was really angry. So I was stalked by the dragon for years. Despite trying to be an ally, I never had the energy to be an activist. I was silent.

OPPRESSSOR, Facilitator 1: I speak out against oppression while benefiting from the spoils of racism, classism and colonization. Children of Italian ancestors get to call themselves Canadians and no one will ask where I am from.

OPPRESSOR, Facilitator 2: My first real job was with Aboriginal women who had been repeatedly victimized. I was angry. But I was young and too scared to rock the boat. Outside of my job, I didn't know how to challenge the racism that was everywhere. I was silent.

MENTORS, Facilitator 1: I have been the grateful recipient of wise teachings from amazing women from many backgrounds. Long ago, I decided to admire women and not compete against them to my own detriment. This decision has made my life abundant.

MENTORS, Facilitator 2: My sister was my first mentor. She was strong and confident and always said what she thought. She never backed down when she believed in something. She made me think that maybe one day, I could be like her

LIFE-CHANGING MOMENT, Facilitator 1: The time that I spent in a convent in Mexico with the radical leftist nuns who wore jeans, drank beer and danced the salsa was my introduction to liberation theology. Their anti-oppression work would forever shift my views on religion, colonization, white privilege and my place in the world.

LIFE-CHANGING MOMENT, Facilitator 2: I turned 40. You should all try it. I decided that I had to be who I was supposed to be. I found my voice through stand-up comedy. Once I found my voice, I could not turn it off. As I got stronger, the depression dragon got smaller. And so did my circle of friends.

ACTIONS, Facilitator 1: When Mandela stepped into freedom, it was my victory too. As committed anti-apartheid activist, I was later invited to meet him when he visited Montreal.

ACTIONS, Facilitator 2: Around this time, I worked with nine women who told stories of their life poverty. They were courageous, so how could I not be? I became politically active, wrote letters, joined feminist groups and met other people who wanted to see change.

NOW, Facilitator 1: Motherhood has added an important dimension to my social justice path: I focus on providing my daughter with the grounding of a worldview that does not include bigotry, hate or fear of others who are different from her.

NOW, Facilitator 2: I am okay. I have a great family, good friends and a wonderful life.

COMMUNITY, Facilitator 2: It took some time, but now I am connected to many wonderful people who care about the same things I do.

COMMUNITY, Facilitator 1: Social justice work is about intentionally building the world that you believe in—both for yourself and for others.

Part 3
Sessional Papers

Developing Facilitator Self-Awareness: Introducing Mindfulness Practices to the Helping Classroom

David Delay & Jennifer Martin

As educators in social work and child and youth care, we prepare students for direct clinical practice with some of the most vulnerable people in society, many of whom struggle with social, emotional, behavioural, and relational problems and are challenged by chronic illness, life crises, violence, and/or complex trauma. Teaching courses that explore sensitive material can be charged with strongly held opinions and intense emotions, as well as the potential for psychologically intimate classroom interactions. As such, we are conscious of our responsibility as educators to manage classroom dynamics effectively as course content is explicated and as stories, experiences, and opinions are shared. During those shared moments, we are assisting students to make connections between theory and practice while at the same time we are role modelling a stance that is analogous to the therapeutic stance taken in professional practice. In those moments, we are demonstrating how to respond to and connect with others with attitudes of openness, nonjudgment, and acceptance; important aspects of mindfulness and self-awareness. Thus, the classroom becomes an andragogical site of engagement. This is in line with the characteristics of the experiential classroom in which students are fully immersed in the experience, not merely doing what they feel is required of them.

We are keenly aware that personal issues will arise with some students, many of whom have had similar critical events occur in their lives as those being discussed in class, and they may find themselves reacting to the course material. This is important given that the American College Health Association's (2013) National College Health Assessment of just over 34,000 post-secondary students indicated that 73% of Canadian participants reported experiencing overwhelming anxiety in the past 12 months, with nearly 90% reporting feelings of being overwhelmed by all they had to do. Ignoring the likely presence

89

of anxiety among our students and its likely manifestation in their classroom engagement may place limits on how the theoretical ideas we introduce in class are understood and, consequently, affect how those ideas are adopted into practice.

There is significant research that suggests mindfulness training can serve as a viable strategy for the promotion of self-care and well-being for practitioners in the helping professions (Bohecker, Wathen, Wells, Salazar, & Vereen, 2014; Newsome, Waldo, & Gruszka, 2012). So it seems that integrating mindfulness into each class would be beneficial for all students as they prepare for direct practice. Practicing mindfulness in the classroom contributes to creating a supportive and inclusive classroom environment and helps students respond rather than react to course materials by helping them to engage in reflective practice and manage their anxiety. We believe in creating a learning climate that engages students in caring about each other and fostering an interest in personal growth; fundamental qualities to practice in social work and child and youth care. At the same time, we believe that adult students are capable and resourceful and able to care about themselves. By introducing mindfulness into our classrooms, we establish a balance between offering caring environments for personal exploration and establishing an expectation that students will take responsibility for their own personal growth by seeking avenues beyond the classroom learning environment to accomplish this.

Mindfulness

Although the present use of mindfulness in the helping professions is rooted in Buddhism, it is a nonsectarian technique. In the vipassana Buddhist meditation tradition, mindfulness meditation is centred on the development of insight and awareness of the reality of all things. In this tradition, a present-moment awareness is achieved through a purposeful attention to the breath. Such a practice assists in the development of present-moment awareness in four areas: body, feeling, mind, and mental qualities and phenomena (Wallis, 2007). Seven factors of awakening are identified within this meditative tradition (present-moment awareness, investigation into qualities, energy, delight, tranquillity, concentration, and equanimity) and these factors are helpfully understood as elements of meditative awakening (Wallis, 2007). Mindfulness-based clinical interventions primarily draw upon the Ānāpānasati Sutta and the Mahāsatipaṭṭhāna Sutta. These teachings on present-moment awareness address its attainment with breathing and its application across the four areas mentioned above. In the mindfulness exercises we have incorporated into our teaching, we try to help students achieve a self-awareness that encompasses the four areas and includes the seven factors.

Mindfulness in the Helping Classroom

The literature discussing the integration of mindfulness practices into the helping classroom primarily contends with the teaching of mindfulness as a separate or supplementary course offering rather than being introduced as a teaching strategy to enhance student self-awareness toward minimizing reactivity (Birnbaum, 2008; Bohecker et al., 2014; Campbell & Christopher, 2012; Napoli & Bonifas, 2011; Newsome et al., 2012; Shapiro, Brown, & Biegel, 2007). Social work and child and youth care are only just beginning to attend to the integration of mindfulness as a component of core course work (Gockel, Burton, James, & Bryer, 2013; Lynn, 2010; Slavik, 2014), with rare mention of mindfulness in teaching practices.

In both social work and child and youth care education, students are asked to develop an awareness of their own biases, power and privilege, and social location. Assisting students with the development of this element of self-awareness can be challenging. Mindfulness practices have been discussed in the professional education literature for both social work and child and youth care within a context of teaching on oppression and diversity, suggesting more of an integrative inclusion of mindfulness practice as a skill used or taught within an andragogical approach. As might be anticipated, when inviting discussion with students on oppression and privilege, disturbances arise for both students and instructors.

Writing in reflection on her experiences teaching about oppression and privilege, Wong (2004) introduced her use of mindfulness as a way to help students to allow discomfort to arise within themselves without reactivity. Encouraging her students to greet with interest any discomfort as it might arise for each in discussions of colonialism and other oppressive realities, Wong invites her students to join her in metaphorically holding space for continuing dialogue. In her class, she advises students to expect the discomfort to arise and encourages them to take note of it and to give it some attention through reflective journal writing. Wong is inviting her students to join her as the instructor in noticing reactivity and making more mindful contributions to classroom discussion.

Mishna and Bogo (2007) have suggested that mindfulness accompanied by a reflective practice may aid the instructor in responding to conflict in the classroom in the teaching of diversity: the focus here is on how the instructor responds. Although the authors suggested mindfulness can be accomplished for the instructor through a practice of meditation, the suggestion is not developed further in their paper; rather, they refer their readers to the work of Kabat-Zinn (1990) and mindfulness-based stress reduction (MBSR). Mishna and Bogo provided some principles for a reflective teaching practice informed by Schön (1987) and, paralleling Wong (2004), they encouraged educators to anticipate conflict arising in the class when topics of diversity and oppression are introduced and discussed.

In their study of 132 incoming graduate students in social work enrolled in multiple sections of a clinical interviewing skills course, Gockel et al. (2013) compared students exposed to brief in-class doses of mindfulness training derived from MBSR exercises (N = 38) with students who had no in-class exposure to mindfulness training (N = 94). The researchers administered several standardized measures of student well-being and two qualitative measures: (a) a qualitative tool developed for the study to measure perceptions of the utility of the training received, and (b) a questionnaire comprised of open-ended questions exploring self-perceptions of skill development. The standardized measures were administered on the first day of class and again on the second to last day of class; the qualitative measures were administered on the second to last day of class and again three months later. Participants in the study "reported that mindfulness training was helpful to their learning in the classroom, assisting them in focusing their attention, managing anxiety, and promoting their ability to be more open to learning" (Gockel et al., 2013, p. 349).

Birnbaum (2005) used mindfulness meditation exercises to encourage students toward a greater connection with the self and essential messages from the self. Similarly, Slavik (2014) incorporated mindfulness into her teaching to aid her child and youth care students to develop a better appreciation of the self in relation with others. Findings from her study indicated that students experienced a positive impact of mindfulness-based activities on their ability to: transition to class, engage with the moment, engage with the learning process, attune/attend, concentrate and process information, decrease stress and anxiety, build capacity for insight and creativity, and be more reflective. (Slavik, 2014, p. 6)

Both Slavik (2014) and Birnbaum (2005) have been using mindfulness practices as integrative teaching strategies. Similarly, Gockel et al. (2013) have examined the integrated use of mindfulness training as a teaching strategy for training social workers studying clinical intervention skills. It is within these frameworks of integration that we discuss our use of mindfulness practices in our respective classrooms toward the enhancement of practitioner self-awareness.

Greeting the Classroom as a Group

Recognizing and attending to group process in the teaching of group work is not new (Schwartz, 1964; Shulman, 1987). As educators, we have developed facilitative approaches to our teaching which have us more tuned in to emerging and evolving group processes within the classroom. Among other courses taught, one of us teaches a group work practice course and the other teaches a course on trauma and trauma-informed practice. Both of us regularly use group work in the classroom to provide students with opportunities to facilitate group discussion and participate in in-class task groups. In doing so, we rely on our group work skills to help our students process their reactions to course content and classroom dynamics. As we set ourselves on this path, we became keenly aware of the presence of anxiety in the classroom and noticed how, at times, its presence was holding back the emergence of new possibility among students who were learning how to be present as practitioners. Students often hesitate to volunteer for the role of discussion facilitator, they may be reluctant to join others in a role-play exercise to demonstrate an intervention skill, or they may not step forward to participate in a "fishbowl" discussion or in a reflecting team; their hesitation limits the possibility of their learning through doing.

Independently, we began incorporating mindfulness exercises into our teaching with the intention to help students to become more mindfully aware of their thoughts and emotions as these were arising in response to the course material, the dynamics of the classroom, their development as practitioners and group facilitators, as well as their performance as group members and group process facilitators within the classroom. Our interest in one another's efforts led to many discussions and eventually to sharing our ideas with other attendees at the 2014 International Association of Social Work With Groups (IASWG) conference in Calgary, Alberta. In the following section, we share some of the mindfulness exercises we have introduced in the classroom and discuss how experiential learning can be connected to an appreciation for practitioner/facilitator self-awareness.

Incorporating Mindfulness

Mindful Breathing

We ask students to arrange the chairs in a circle. While this is the preferred way to organize our classes, it is, at times, dependent upon class size (with numbers ranging from 25 to 65 students) and classroom setup (in some classes seating is stationary). The two-fold intention of sitting in the circle, however, is to have students join in the work of readying the room for our class—building a shared sense of responsibility for the group—and to enhance the possibility for the formation of early connection between students who will face one another without barriers between them. Not surprisingly, this arrangement positions us each as slightly more vulnerable and exposed to one another, but it also creates an environment that highlights the possibilities of interdependence in our learning.

When the room is set up, we take our seats and a welcome is extended; we introduce ourselves, and then the grounding exercise is introduced. We invite students to sit in a comfortable position with their feet firmly touching the floor and advise them that in this exercise the only work they will have to do is breathe. We suggest that students locate a focal point of their own choosing or, for those who are comfortable to do so, close their eyes. Before beginning to guide the breathing exercise (we both join in such exercises in our respective classes), we share some thoughts about the general busyness of our daily routines and the energy we use meeting all the other demands we each have before we take our leave to come to class. We draw parallels to the likely experience of their future group work participants, who will also be leading busy lives before they arrive to participate in group, and suggest that the exercise might be a way in which one can aid group members with the transition into group and into a more purposeful, mindful attention. We reflect on the benefits of stopping to take note of our own arrival at the beginning of each class and to notice that we are here together with others who we will come to know and appreciate just as they will come to know and appreciate us. Finally, we observe that such a grounding exercise, if employed in a group context, is best used separately from any check-in exercise, which has a different intention.

The group is invited to take in a deep breath, and the following words are shared: "Breathing in, I appreciate my own arrival." An invitation to let out their breath is accompanied by these words: "Breathing out, we are here together" Students are invited to continue to breathe and to bring their attention to their breath, and to attend to the feel of their breath as it passes through their nostrils or across their lips. In a gently paced and soft tone, students are reminded that we each find our own way to settle ourselves when in new surroundings and that it is not uncommon to find ourselves unsettled under such circumstances. Students are invited to bring their attention to any feelings of being unsettled and reminded that feeling unsettled is only a part of who we are in any moment and it need not be the only aspect of ourselves that we notice. Students are invited each to take note of their blossoming awareness, "Ah, this is me feeling unsettled." Students are then invited to return their attention to their breath, noticing the inward breath and the outward breath.

Before we end the breathing and grounding exercise, we acknowledge that throughout the course feelings of being unsettled may arise given the material that students are learning. We suggest that in those moments the feeling could be greeted similarly, "Ah, this is me feeling unsettled," and that a few moments of focused silence and an attention to the breath may help them acknowledge the presence of the feeling, to allow the feeling to be experienced and to gradually dissipate in its intensity. Students are reminded that we need not wish away our feelings or thoughts, or blame others or ourselves for their occurrence. Rather, we are better served by greeting each as a part of us and not the sum of us.

When the grounding exercise is complete, we briefly discuss the experience and any similarities or differences in the distractions that arose for each of us. The practice of beginning and ending each class with a similar grounding exercise that attends to the breath is discussed with the students, and they are invited to volunteer to lead the group through such an exercise at any time during the course. In the past, some students have led the class though grounding excises using homemade play dough, mindful eating, humming alongside mindful breathing, and incorporating reflections on the transition into class and the preparation to become fully present. Throughout the term, discussions deepen as students share their reflections on their developing self-awareness and how this helps them to attend to others in group as well as to themselves. These discussions provide opportunities for students to share particular challenges that arise while practicing mindful breathing. The idea of sitting in silence with focused attention to the breath is difficult and unusual for many students, as illustrated in the following quotes from student response journals used with their permission: "I am not used to being silent" (1); "This was the longest five minutes of my life" (2).

For some students it was technology and its ubiquitous presence that proved distracting: "It was difficult for me. I kept looking at my cell phone wondering if my fiancé had texted" (3). Others were able to take their mindful practice from the class and apply it to their personal life: "I usually don't sleep very well, I'm always anxious, always have been. I tried the breathing exercise at home last night. I didn't think it would work but it did. I wanted to share that today. It really helped" (4).

The intention of introducing mindfulness through breathing is to help students develop self-awareness as they ready themselves for working with others. When we are taken up with our own reactivity as practitioners, we are less able to be attentive and present in helping others. For group workers, the work of attending to the other is made complex by the number of others present in group and the need to attend to the group as a whole. When, as group workers, we are unaware of our own reactions within group, we can miss the opportunity to use our own reaction as the jumping off point for inquiry into the reaction of others. We may not notice contrasting or complementary reactions in others, leaving these unacknowledged and robbing us of a richness in our group experience. As groups develop and dynamics (sometimes judged as problematic) emerge and trigger negative emotional reactions, we are aided by our ability to recognize the cues of others in order to intervene in a timely way. For example, when conflict emerges in group and we are disturbed by it, we may hastily end the discussion as a way of avoiding the discomfort that conflict can produce. At these moments many group facilitators call for a time-out: we might call for a break on behalf of others upon whom we have perhaps projected our own discomfort. Whereas if, as the group facilitator, we are more responsive than reactive, we might invite a pause and an attention to the breath, in order to allow space for group members to stay present with the feelings arising alongside the experience of conflict, and, as Wong (2004) has suggested, greet the sudden presence of discomfort with interest and curiosity. In such discussions, students have revealed their surprise at their own initial impulse to flee from rising tension and asserted a commitment to understand themselves better toward becoming more ready to stay present with the moment and available as a helper.

Walking Meditation

We invite students to participate in a walking meditation within class as an early exercise of reflection on patience and the interconnectedness of the group experience. Students are invited to stand in a circle to face one another, to notice one another with a smile as a greeting. The standing group is then asked to turn in a single direction to the right or left and to slowly begin to walk in a circle. The class is invited to take note of the presence of impatience and frustration as it arises. Drawing on the writing of Thich Nhât Hanh (2007), the students are invited to take note of the feet as each foot steps into movement. As we gradually begin to move, in a slow and calm voice, an observation is shared of the many students of group work who have come before us to this place of learning, who have walked the path of a beginning practitioner and whose pathways may have, at first, also seemed unclear and crowded by others. The students are invited into a deeper consideration of slowness and its benefits in the group experience and how slowness can seem, at first, unfamiliar or, perhaps, annoying and unwanted in our busy lives.

As the group's natural rhythm emerges, the class is invited to allow their attention to turn to how the group is working together as we bring our own rhythm into harmony with those sharing our space. Students are again encouraged to allow feelings of frustration and impatience to arise without judgment and an invitation is made to recognize ourselves in our experience of emotion ("Ah, this is me in frustration and impatience"). Students are advised not to worry if distracting thoughts arise ("This is stupid; when will it end?"), and they are invited to consider greeting each judgment or distracting thought with a smile as it arises, to greet it as a welcome part of who we each are, and then to return their attention to their step, noticing their foot touching the floor, landing on and lifting from the floor. We bring the exercise to an end attending to each step and saying, "Breathing in, we have direction; breathing out, we're making progress."

Similar to the grounding exercise, the walking meditation creates an opportunity for the discussion of many aspects of group. The exercise can be used to initiate discussion about the differing needs of those in group and how the pace of group can be allowed at times to emerge organically from within the group and be less subject to the whims or determination of the group worker, while at other times, the group may require more clear guidance in developing a pace for its work. The exercise can be used to discuss how an agenda, when enforced upon a group, can be the cause of frustration and impatience. The exercise allows for some embodied learning related to our interdependence in group and the responsibility we hold for one another for mutual support and growth.

Sitting Meditation

Sitting meditation is introduced early in our courses and developed across each of the courses to come fully into blossom as we discuss silence within group. Following a lecture and discussion of course materials, students are invited to pause and to sit in silence to allow what we have just learned to be present with us. A simple opening meditative phrase is suggested, such as, "I have learned something today; let me acknowledge what I have learned." Later in the course as we begin to discuss the phenomena of silence in group, its meaning, and our reactivity to silence, students will have had some practice with sitting in silence, facing one another, and holding the moment.

What arises for each of us in silence may be different. For some, when in silence, self-doubt and judgment of the self or the other may pay us a visit. Participants in group often experience an intense impulse to share the busyness of their minds when they have been invited into silence. For many, silence is rarely a space of inactivity. When discussing their own use of silence, students often reveal the highly critical self-talk they are made subject to. We discuss the phenomena of negative self-talk as an experience shared by many. As well, we discuss the occasional use of silence by group members toward others or the facilitator as an interpersonal punishment for perceived wrongs within the group experience. Finally, we talk about the assumptions and judgments we make, whether positive, negative, or ambivalent, about silence from the other and its meaning for the self.

The intention for the latter discussion is to enhance students' awareness of the meanings they make of silence and how, when greeted by silence, they may experience rejection and abandonment. Students quickly grasp an appreciation for how, within group, connections are sought and develop a sense that connection comes through the acknowledgement received for one's presence and contribution. To have our contribution greeted by silence can be damaging to our sense of connection. Students are presented with the possibility of learning through action and reflection about the various meanings of silence in group.

Discussion

In this paper, we have discussed some of the ways mindfulness practices have been introduced in the helping classroom as both an intervention-specific training and as an andragogical approach to teaching. Greeting the classroom as a group is central to our teaching philosophy and informs our use of group work practices as teaching strategies. Our integrative use of mindfulness practices in the classroom flows from our teaching philosophy and is strengthened by our use of group work practices in our teaching. We shared three mindfulness practice exercises we use with our students, and we offered insight into how these exercises may provide openings for the discussion of both difficult practice skills and sensitive course content. We offered some reflections on how mindfulness and meditation practice may contribute to the development of practitioner/facilitator self-awareness skills. Integrating mindfulness practices into our teaching has enriched our own capacity for being present and attentive to ourselves and to those we teach.

One of the worries commonly shared by many who begin a

meditative practice is about doing meditation wrong. For many, this worry emerges from a (mis)understanding that mindfulness involves working to clear the mind. For instance, as students are invited to attend to their breathing, they immediately take note of the flood of intrusive thoughts (often before they begin to identify the simultaneous feelings that may be arising) and experience doubt about their ability to engage in the practice of focused attention. The worry that they may be "doing it wrong" can lead to a quick abandonment of the practice.

As instructors, we can also occasionally be burdened by the worry that we are doing it wrong and that another instructor could handle things better. Mishna and Bogo (2007) have suggested that instructors who are handling difficult topics in the classroom should accept that they will, from time to time, mishandle discussions of those topics. One of the assumptions inherent in their suggestion is that the burden for handling such discussions is not usually shared between the instructor and the students. Sharing responsibility with the students for developing more responsive and less reactive contributions to classroom conversations, and incorporating mindfulness practices toward the development of such capacity, may lead to the formation of a classroom principle of acceptance that is adopted more readily by both students and instructors. Instructors and students may have different accountability for the (mis)handling of conflict as it emerges in the classroom, but the responsibility needs to be shared.

The worry of "doing it wrong" or the contrasting imperative of "getting it right" manifests prominently in practice-based classes in both social work and child and youth care education. This worry can become immobilizing for students, inhibiting their willingness to join in group experiential activities. Modeling self-compassion and self-acceptance for students can help them to achieve an understanding that, from time to time, they may not live up to the expectations of others or of themselves. With this in mind, students should be reminded that their future client may experience a similar worry related to achieving desired change. As instructors we value learning through practice, practicing with an openness to feedback and embracing an acceptance of the self in less skilled moments of our practice. Students should be encouraged to adopt a nonjudgmental relationship with themselves in moments of uncertainty and not knowing and to consider how they will remain nonjudgmental in their practice when they are judgmental of themselves in these moments.

In his discussion of the use of group process in the teaching of group work, Shulman (1987) has cautioned educators of the risks of confusing the role of group facilitator/practitioner with the role of instructor of group work skills. He has identified a tension that exists in most training of helping professionals: personal issues inevitably arise among training practitioners (and their instructors) through exposure to course content. Instructors must remember they are not engaged in a clinical relationship with their students. In our role as educators, we each rely on our extensive experience as group work practitioners to enrich our capacity to be responsive to what arises in the classroom. Our practice experience has provided us with the opportunity to establish and maintain good interpersonal and professional boundaries. Additionally, our work with children, youth, adults, and families who have experienced various traumatic events, mental health difficulties, and others' oppressive realities has prepared us in the development of a trauma-informed approach to teaching.

Given the results of the Canadian data for the National College Health Assessment (American College Health Association, 2013), a trauma-informed approach to teaching appears to be well-advised. Among the most concerning statistics presented in the results of the survey were that students reported a current diagnosis of depression (16%), experiences that were either traumatic or very difficult involving their academic life (56%), family problems (30%), issues with intimate relationships (31.9%), health problems of family members (21.5%), personal health issues (21.9%), and sleep difficulties (31.9%; American College Health Association, 2013). Although as educators we understand that we are not in a clinical relationship with our students, it is important to remain aware that some students in our classrooms will reflect the populations they will be serving in their future practice.

Initial studies of the integration of mindfulness practices in the helping classroom have offered support for the practice of enhancing students' appreciation for their improved capacity to maintain greater self-awareness in the classroom (Gockel et al., 2013; Slavik, 2014). These results are encouraging. Further study is required along with the further development of strategies for the integration of mindfulness practices across other courses in both the social work and child and youth care curriculum.

References

American College Health Association. (2013). *National College Health Assessment II: Canadian reference group data report spring 2013.* Hanover, MD: Author.

Birnbaum, L. (2005). Connecting to inner guidance: Mindfulness meditation and transformation of professional self-concept in social work students. *Critical Social Work, 6*(2). Retrieved from http://www1.uwindsor.ca/criticalsocialwork/connecting-to-inner-guidance-mindfulness-meditation-and-transformation-of-professional-self-concept-

Birnbaum, L. (2008). The use of mindfulness training to create an "accompanying place" for social work students. *Journal of Social Work Education, 27*(8), 837–852.

Bohecker, L., Wathen, C., Wells, P., Salazar, B. M., & Vereen, L. G. (2014). Mindfully educating our future: The MESG curriculum for training emergent counselors. *Journal for Specialists in Group Work, 39*(3), 257–273. doi:10.1080/01933922.2014.919046

Campbell, J. C., & Christopher, J. C. (2012). Teaching mindfulness to create effective counsellors. *Journal of Mental Health Counselling, 34*(3), 213–226.

Gockel, A., Burton, D., James, S., & Bryer, E. (2013). Introducing mindfulness as a self-care and clinical training strategy for beginning social work students. *Mindfulness, 4,* 343–353. doi:10.1007/s.12671-012-01234-1

Kabat-Zinn, J. (1990). *Full catastrophe living: Using the wisdom of your body and mind to face stress, pain and illness.* New York, NY: Bantam Dell.

Lynn, R. (2010). Mindfulness in social work education. *Journal of Social Work Education, 29*(3), 289–304.

Mishna, F., & Bogo, M. (2007). Reflective practice in contemporary social work classrooms. *Journal of Social Work Education, 43*(3), 529–541.

Napoli, M., & Bonifas, R. (2011). From theory toward empathic self-care: Creating a mindful classroom for social work students. *Journal of Social Work Education, 30*(6), 635–649.

Newsome, S., Waldo, M., & Gruszka, C. (2012). Mindfulness group work: Preventing stress and increasing self-compassion among helping professionals in training. *The Journal for Specialists in Group Work, 37*(4), 297–311. doi:10.1080/01933922.2012.690832

Nhât Hanh, T. (2007). *Buddha mind, Buddha body: Walking toward enlightenment.* Berkeley, CA: Parallax Press.

Schön, D. (1987). *Educating the reflective practitioner.* San Francisco, CA: Jossey Bass.

Schwartz, W. (1964). The classroom teaching of social work with groups. In Council on Social Work Education (Eds.), *A conceptual framework for the teaching of social group work method in the classroom* (pp. 3–19). New York, NY: Council on Social Work Education.

Shapiro, S. L., Brown, K. W., & Biegel, G. M. (2007). Teaching self-care to caregivers: Effects of mindfulness-based stress reduction on mental health therapists in training. *Training and Education in Professional Psychology, 1*(2), 105–115.

Shulman, L. (1987). The hidden group in the classroom: The use of group process in teaching group work practice. *Journal of Teaching in Social Work, 1*(2), 3–31. doi:10.1300 /J067v01n0202

Slavik, C. (2014). An exploration of the impact of course specific mindfulness based practices in the university classroom. *Relational Child and Youth Care Practice, 27*(1), 6–17.

Wallis, G. (2007). *Basic teachings of the Buddha: A new translation and compilation, with a guide to reading the texts.* New York, NY: Modern Library Paperback Edition.

Wong, Y. R. (2004). Knowing through discomfort: A mindfulness-based critical social work pedagogy. *Critical Social Work, 5*(1). Retrieved from http://www1.uwindsor.ca/ criticalsocialwork/knowing-through-discomfort-a-mindfulness-based-critical-social-work-pedagogy.

The Theory of Trauma-Informed Approaches for Substance Use: Implementing a Seeking Safety Group

Rachael V. Pascoe

Research has demonstrated that addiction or drug dependence is not inevitable for all individuals who use drugs. Methamphetamine, a so-called "hard drug," has been demonstrated to have a low abuse liability (i.e., the likelihood that the drug has addictive pharmacological properties sufficient to result in dependence by the user) among study participants (Comer et al., 2001). Studies have demonstrated that participants who reported daily crack cocaine use chose alternative reinforcements, such as vouchers, instead of a self-administered hit of cocaine under experimental conditions (Higgins, 1997). Therefore, substance use and addiction are not wholly explained by the addictive properties of the drugs alone. Environmental factors may play an important role in explaining addiction.

Researchers studying addictions in Vietnam War veterans with post-traumatic stress disorder (PTSD) have identified a link between isolation, threatening environments, and subsequent drug use behaviours (Herman, 1997). The majority of soldiers who used narcotics during the Vietnam War discontinued their drug use after returning to the United States without requiring treatment methods such as methadone (Robins, Helzer, & Davids, 1975). Fifty percent of the study participants who met the criteria for narcotic addiction in Vietnam ceased using illicit drugs on their return to America, despite the drugs' availability. Although this study did not explain why drug use decreased after their tours of Vietnam, the authors suggested that a stressful social context plays a role in continued drug use (Robins et al., 1975).

The relationship between stressful environment and drug use was further explored in another study of American Vietnam War veterans. McFall, Mackay, and Donovan (1992) determined that there was no difference in drug use between veterans who served in the Vietnam theatre and veterans who did not see combat. However, veterans who were diagnosed with PTSD were more likely to use drugs and alcohol heavily, and be considered drug dependent, than those without PTSD (McFall et al., 1992). Therefore, it appears that a history of trauma may play a role in substance use.

In this paper I examine the complex relationship between trauma and substance use in the addictions literature. I also present a trauma-informed group work model that can be easily implemented in agency settings. Addiction can be a coping mechanism for many individuals who are survivors of trauma, or who have been formerly diagnosed with PTSD. Although it is recognized that trauma and substance use are linked, clinicians and services are often not prepared to provide integrated treatment to address these two issues concurrently. I examine the need for trauma-informed services in a Canadian setting, discuss the barriers to implementing services, and provide suggestions for change.

Trauma: Definition and Symptomology

In the clinical addictions field there has been momentum to integrate a greater understanding of the role of concurrent disorders and the effects of trauma. This move has been spurred by proponents of the trauma-informed approach (Harris & Fallot, 2001b) and increasing advocacy by consumers who are survivors of trauma (Herman, 1997). The Diagnostic and Statistical Manual of Mental Disorders (DSM-5) has defined trauma as "exposure to actual or threatened death, serious injury or sexual violation" (American Psychiatric Association, 2013, p. 271), and this exposure may result from a direct experience of a traumatic event, witnessing an event, vicarious trauma of loved ones, or exposure to aversive details of a traumatic event. Therefore, the term trauma refers to an event that causes significant distress but has also been used to describe the subsequent reaction to that event (Briere & Scott, 2006).

PTSD is a pathology defined in the DSM-5 that involves a response to trauma in which an individual may experience symptoms from four clusters: reexperiencing symptoms, avoidance, numbing, and hyperarousal and hypervigilance, comprising a total of 20 symptoms (American Psychiatric Association, 2013). For the purpose of this paper, the diagnosis of PTSD and self-reported symptoms of trauma are used interchangeably. This is intended to represent a shift away from the biomedical model, to reflect the fact that not all individuals have access to diagnostic services, and to include the narratives of individuals who are suffering from the ongoing effects trauma but who do not meet the criteria for the DSM-5 diagnosis.

The trauma response has been referred to as biphasic, referring to the rapid cycling of trauma survivors between a hyperarousal and a hypoarousal state with a small "window of tolerance" (Siegel, 1999, p. 281). Survivors of trauma often have difficulty in modulating their affect and can be triggered easily to anxiety and anger (Van der Kolk, 1987). Hyperarousal symptoms can include anger as well as panic symptoms such as shortness of breath, choking, nausea, and trembling (Bryant & Panasetis, 2001). Alternatively, a state of hypoarousal will occur for individuals with severe or chronic trauma symptoms, including disengagement, depersonalization, and derealisation, in which individuals are unable to stay present in the moment (Briere, 2006). Over time, the sympathetic nervous system, triggered by environment and traumatic memories, creates greater accessibility to the arousal state and the perpetuation of the trauma response (Van der Kolk, McFarlane, & Weisaeth, 1996). It is imperative that clinicians working with survivors of trauma are able to recognize the symptoms of the trauma response in order to be able to assist their clients in becoming aware of their symptoms and to find strategies to enhance clients' perceived sense of safety.

Unfortunately, exposure to traumatic events is not rare: American community samples found that between 39.1% (Breslau, Davis, Andreski, & Peterson, 1991) and 89.6% (Breslau et al., 1998) of participants had been exposed to trauma. More recent Canadian data revealed that the lifetime prevelence of PTSD diagnosis in a sample of 2991 Canadian adults was 9.2% and exposure to at least one trauma event was reported by 76.1% of survey respondents (Van Ameringen, Mancini, Patterson, & Boyle, 2008). Therefore, clinicians are likely to be working with survivors of trauma across a range of populations. This holds especially true for substance use treatment.

The Prevalence of Trauma and Substance Use

Demographic information on individuals entering treatment for substance use has indicated that there is a high comorbidity of PTSD and substance use (Jacobsen, Southwick, & Kosten, 2001). Early childhood trauma, or the diagnosis of PTSD, is associated with the use of alcohol (Fetzner, McMillan, Sareen, & Asmundson, 2011), heroin (Mills, Lynskey, Teesson, Ross, & Darke, 2005), cocaine (Najavits et al., 2003), and problem gambling (Kessler et al., 2008). Across a number of studies, the prevalence rate for comorbid trauma among samples of individuals in treatment for substance use ranges from 25% to 90% (MacKenzie, Cuff, & Poole, 2014). Early research reviews found that between 30% and 59% of women in treatment have been given a diagnosis of PTSD, and between 55% and 99% of women in treatment for substance use reported having experienced a traumatic event (Najavits, Weiss, & Shaw, 1997).

Alternatively, people diagnosed with PTSD are 4.5 times more likely to have a substance use disorder than individuals without PTSD (Kessler, Sonnega, Bromet, Hughes, & Nelson, 1995). Of individuals diagnosed with PTSD, 46.4% also had a substance use disorder of one or more substances (Pietrzak, Goldstein, Southwick, & Grant, 2011). The concurrent disorder of PTSD and substance use is associated with a number of psychological comorbidities such as depression, sexual dysfunction, suicidality, and self-harm (Briere & Jordan, 2004). Disturbingly, individuals with PTSD in treatment for substance use respond unfavourably to treatment, have earlier attrition than other clients, and are less likely to continue in ongoing care (Brown, Harris, & Fallot, 2013).

Trauma-Informed Care

Trauma Matters, a manual produced by The Jean Tweed Centre (2013) in Toronto, defined trauma-informed care as practices that "take into account an understanding of the prevalence and impact of trauma and integrate that understanding into all components of an organization"

(p. 12). In trauma-informed care, the theory of self-medication posits that the motivation for drug use is to medicate the symptoms of PTSD (Herman, 1997; Khantzian, 1997; Leeies, Pagura, Sareen, & Bolton, 2010; Najavits et al., 1997; Van der Kolk et al., 1996). Individuals with PTSD have reported using alcohol and drugs as a way to improve mood when they are reacting to stressful events (Leeies et al., 2010).

The goal of trauma-informed services is to integrate an understanding of the prevalence of trauma in clients' lives. This differs from trauma-specific services, which directly focus on trauma and trauma recovery (The Jean Tweed Centre, 2013). Trauma-informed services recognize the importance of the client's safety, personal choice, and agency (Poole & Greaves, 2013), and promote collaboration between the client and clinician, facilitate empowerment, and consider cultural competence (Brown et al., 2013). In a trauma-informed context, the service may not be focused on trauma per se, but the care model must take into account the high prevalence of individuals with a history of trauma (The Jean Tweed Centre, 2013; Poole & Greaves, 2013). Trauma-informed services aim to avoid retraumatization. Front-line staff are trained to support clients' coping capacity and successfully manage trauma symptoms so survivors of trauma can benefit from care (Harris & Fallot, 2001a). A number of trauma-informed models exist which can be integrated with substance use treatment.

In order to discuss the use of group work as an effective intervention, a number of theories relevant to social work practice should be considered. Antioppressive practice (AOP) seeks to break down privilege and structural domination in favour of equity for all social groups (Barnoff & Moffatt, 2007). An AOP understanding of trauma considers the multiple ways in which systematic trauma, such as discrimination, can be experienced (Timothy, 2012). This requires practitioners to work from an antiviolence practice in order to reduce retraumatization of clients, as well as to facilitate their empowerment. Feminist theory is also an important foundation for concurrent trauma and addiction work, as it posits that trauma includes gender-based violence (Toner & Akman, 2013) and that women with substance use are coping with additional stressors (Covington, Burke, Keaton, & Norcott, 2008). The feminist perspective requires "gender responsiveness" (Covington et al., 2008, p. 390) in treatment, creating a treatment environment that responds to the strengths, difficulties, and barriers that women face.

Herman's Theory of Trauma Treatment

Herman (1997) stated that traumatic events "overwhelm the ordinary human adaptations to life" (p. 33). Herman described a three-stage theory of trauma recovery in her foundational work, Trauma and Recovery, based on the work of Pierre Janet (1889), a physician who worked with patients experiencing dissociation. These stages are called a consensus model because of how well they are accepted in trauma treatment (Ouimette & Brown, 2013). The first stage of this model is the establishment of safety for trauma survivors in their environment and in their clinical relationships (Herman, 1997). This work often involves aspects of case management that ensure clients are connected to supports in their community (Najavits, 2002). The second stage of Herman's recovery model focuses on remembrance and mourning, which involves telling and processing the story of trauma. The final stage is reconnection, in which the survivor creates a future for him- or herself (Herman, 1997; see Table 1 overleaf). A number of treatment models have been based on Herman's stages of recovery treatment (Briere & Scott, 2006; Najavits, 2002).

Harris and Fallot's Integrated Care Model

Historically, addiction and trauma care were done sequentially, as it was assumed that addiction was of primary concern and therefore should be priority in treatment, and the client should be drug-free before beginning to work on trauma (Harris & Fallot, 2001a). However, these assumptions deny the interrelated nature of trauma and substance use. Furthermore, parallel models that treat both trauma and substance use at the same time but in different programs can be contradictory and send the message that these issues are compartmentalized, when in fact they are complex and interrelated (Harris & Fallot, 2001a). Integrated care models that address both trauma and substance use concurrently are therefore integral for individuals coping with the symptoms of both.

Table 1

Group Work Examples of Herman's Consensus Model

Treatment stages	Goals	Group interventions
Stage 1: Safety	Establish safety from trauma symptoms. Learn self-care strategies. Use psychoeducation to understand trauma and its effects.	Closed groups focused on casework and psychoeducational components teaching self-care skills such as grounding. Example: Seeking Safety (Najavits, 2002).
Stage 2: Remembrance and Mourning	Process the trauma story. Recall suppressed memories. Examine the survivor's affect response to traumatic events (Klein & Schermer, 2000).	Closed trauma-specific groups, focused on creating a trauma narrative for the survivor. Example: Rozynko and Dondershine (1991, as cited in Klein & Schermer, 2000) worked with male veterans with PTSD for three months. Each group member shared their war trauma and processed it with the group.
Stage 3: Reconnection	Create a future. Focus on interpersonal issues (Klein & Schermer, 2000).	Long-term psychotherapy group treatment with heterogeneous membership. Example: Tyson and Goodman (1996, as cited in Klein & Schermer, 2000) described a long-term psychodynamic psychotherapy group with a focus on how interpersonal relationships have been affected by trauma.

Trauma-Informed Care in Diverse Populations

In keeping with AOP, clinicians working from a trauma-informed approach must take issues of diversity into account when working with clients. This means considering the impact that clients' diversity may have not only on their identity, but also on their relationship to their culture. Especially in a Canadian context, it is essential to acknowledge the impact of systemic trauma and its effects on substance use. For instance, according to the Standing Senate Committee on Social Affairs, Science and Technology report, roughly one third of Canada's Aboriginal population, or 330,000 people, have been affected by residential schools directly or indirectly though family members (as cited in Menzies, 2013). Therefore, the effects of past trauma, ongoing systematic oppression of Aboriginal communities, cultural competency, and an understanding of how treatment provision has the potential to retraumatize must be acknowledged by practitioners. Menzies (2012) has recommended therapists assess the level of trauma and assimilation in order to be able to impart how policies have had an impact on a client's identity. During the therapeutic process, clinicians must explore the client's identity and personal histories in the context of public policy in order to shift the client's understanding of his or her behaviours from an internalized perspective to a wider societal context (Menzies, 2012).

Another Canadian group whose diverse backgrounds must be considered are refugees, who may have experienced "traumatic events and difficult situations, such as violence, persecution, multiple loses, social disruption and economic hardship" (Agic, 2012, p. 122). Agic has recommended clinicians develop an awareness of the trauma experienced by refugees before migration as well as the additional stressors they face after migration, including medical problems, housing and income issues, and access to services. Treatment should focus on safety, trust, resiliency, and rebuilding control (Agic, 2012).

Other groups identified in the trauma literature include individuals in diverse and intersectional groups such as those with developmental disabilities, women, men, youth, members of the LGBTQ population, and people with fetal alcohol syndrome (Poole & Greaves, 2013). Not all members of these groups may ascribe to the same issues and not all members of the group may have histories of trauma; however, trauma-informed care must be available to those who need it. Therefore, developing an awareness of trauma along with cultural competency is integral to providing antioppressive practices.

The Applicability of Group Work to Trauma and Addiction Treatment

Group work is well suited to trauma treatment. For survivors of systemic or interpersonal trauma, there is often a pervasive sense of shame or rejection, resulting in social isolation. Therefore, the use of a group to provide a corrective emotional experience of social care and comfort can be an important healing tool for survivors (Weinberg, Nuttman-Schwartz, & Gilmore, 2005). Furthermore, the creation of a trauma narrative with a group of others with similar traumatic histories can provide feedback and empathetic validation (Klein & Schermer, 2000). Group therapy is also beneficial for individuals seeking support for addiction. Group therapy has been shown to bond clients to treatment, provide peer support, and decrease isolation (Center for Substance Abuse Treatment, 2005). Similar to trauma groups, addiction groups can offer a corrective family experience, offer clients a place to learn and practice psychoeducational tools, and make treatment more widely available to more clients. Therefore, group work is an appropriate and helpful treatment modality for clients struggling with both trauma and substance use. Trauma-informed addiction treatment requires group facilitators to integrate the focus of trauma groups (to relieve the symptoms of trauma) with the goal of addiction groups (to decrease substance use or addictive behaviours). To do this effectively, it is important to have an understanding of the phases of trauma treatment and the use of addictive substances or behaviours as a coping mechanism. For clients who are early in seeking treatment, a first stage integrated trauma and addiction group, such as Seeking Safety (Najavits, 2002), is a best practice.

Trauma Informed Group Work: Seeking Safety

Seeking Safety is a manualized, first stage integrated treatment that is present-focused and can be delivered in a group format. It is based on the first stage of Herman's (1997) consensus model and focuses on the clients' need for safety. Seeking Safety has four areas of content: cognitive, behavioural, interpersonal, and case management. The treatment's primary goal is establishing safety from trauma and addiction symptoms (Najavits, 2002). Randomized control trials have found that Seeking Safety groups decrease drug use and the trauma symptoms related to sexual concerns (Najavits, Gallop, & Weiss, 2006). Larger randomized control trials have had mixed results. Seeking Safety was shown to be more effective than community addiction care but was not significantly better than such care at preventing relapse of PTSD and substance use (Boden et al., 2012). Seeking Safety is recommended for clients with complex substance use and avoidance (Ouimette & Brown, 2013). Najavits (as cited in Ouimette & Brown, 2013) has developed a second stage treatment model that is past-focused and serves as a continuation of Seeking Safety called Creating Change, based on clinical experience, pilot research, and literature.

Seeking Safety content

Seeking Safety is a highly flexible program. It has been delivered in residential, prison, and outpatient settings. The program may be offered in an open format with rolling recruitment or on a closed group basis. The length of treatment can vary; from 3 weeks to 25 weeks. Sessions are a minimum of one hour but can be longer. The manual contains 25 topics; however, each topic is independent, and the group leaders can chose which topics best meet the needs of their specific group.

Each session begins with a grounding exercise, which aims to connect the client to the present moment and establish a sense of safety. The grounding exercise is designed to reestablish the perceived autonomy and control of the client. Examples of grounding exercises range from sensory exercises with stones (massaging stones or objects) to directing the group's attention to parts of the room (such as noticing the colours or textures of the walls, floors, or objects in paintings). A number of these grounding exercises are provided in the Seeking Safety manual. This practice establishes the therapeutic relationship with the facilitators as safe and reconnects clients to the group when they are experiencing anxiety or dissociation. Grounding exercises are done at the beginning of the group but can also be provided at any time throughout the duration of the group if clients report feeling anxious or "out of it" (dissociated).

After the grounding exercise, there is a group check-in where members provide an overview of any major events since the last session and any unsafe behaviours they may have engaged in (such as drug taking, avoidance, or isolating behaviours). Clients may also be asked to share examples of their safe coping strategies, such as creating structure for their day or developing alternative strategies to manage their triggers. Check-in also involves following up on any community resources group members may have connected to over the week. Members are also asked whether they were able to follow-up on any commitments that they may have made to the group in the previous session. After the check-in, group handouts may be provided. The handouts provided in the Seeking Safety manual begin with a quote that group members may volunteer to read out loud and interpret or process. After the quote, Seeking Safety material is read or taught and discussed.

Topics covered in Seeking Safety range from information on PTSD (what it is and how it is diagnosed) to an overview of substance use, how to ask for help, constructive anger, and self-care. Other topics include Integrating the Split Self, which discusses any personality splitting that may have occurred as a result of trauma, such as noticing different parts of the ego self to more extreme dissociative identity disorder symptoms. The group ends with a check-out, which involves group members choosing a community resource they will connect with (such as their physician, case worker, housing worker, 12-step sponsor, or financial support office). Additionally, group members make a commitment that they will attempt to complete before the next group. Examples of commitments clients might make include going grocery shopping, blocking a dealer's number on their phone, and using sleep hygiene strategies. Check-out is also an opportunity for clients to provide feedback about the group and the facilitators.

Seeking Safety process

There are a number of ground rules in Seeking Safety groups that are particular to first-stage trauma groups. Given that this group is about establishing safety, no details of drug use or trauma histories are disclosed in group. Groups attempt to remain present-focused and clients are requested not to tell their trauma stories in order to prevent triggering themselves and retraumatizing other group members. Group members are also encouraged not to use triggering language (for example, "shoot up") in order to maintain the safety of the group. Seeking Safety strives to be psychoeducational and content-driven in order to provide clients with the perceived security and skills necessary to process their trauma in the future.

Additional ground rules include protecting client boundaries by discouraging contact with group members outside of group. Clients are not permitted to attend group while intoxicated in order to protect the safety of both the member and the group. However, clients are encouraged to come to group regardless of whether they have used between groups (if not presently under the influence of drugs or alcohol). Honesty is encouraged in group to establish safety and relevance, encourage empathetic support and authenticity as well as group cohesiveness. The process emphasises client control and encourages accountability. Anger is addressed by providing validation and containment strategies. Group dynamics that jeopardize safety are generally addressed with the individual in question, rather than in the group setting, by emphasizing client agency. Care must be taken in such cases in order to validate the client's experience and reduce shame.

Countertransference, Secondary Traumatic Stress, and Vicarious Traumatization

Clinician countertransference is an important factor to consider in trauma and addiction work. Working with clients dealing with addiction may elicit judgmental countertransference in the group worker. Conversely, working with trauma survivors may elicit feelings of sympathy and a strong desire to help or cure the client (Najavits, 2002). Therefore, integrated group care can evoke conflicting and complex countertransference issues for group facilitators. Further countertransference may arise from the different psychoeducational modules of any given session discussed in group meetings. Facilitators may have feelings of frustration when clients express how difficult it is for them to ask for help (Najavits, 2002). For each topic covered by the Seeking Safety program, the relevant countertransference issues are acknowledged and briefly discussed in the clinicians' guide.

Clinicians can be vicariously traumatized by the clients' trauma histories, especially during pregroup assessments, when trauma stories and symptoms are probed for and described. Although traumatic stories are not processed during Seeking Safety groups, present-focused struggles with psychosocial issues and PTSD symptoms experienced by members throughout the week are brought to group. These stories may elicit strong reactions from group facilitators, but they are still required to respond in an empathetic, practical, and nonjudgmental manner. This may be emotionally demanding for the clinician and elicit feelings of helplessness, anger, and sadness, which can contribute to clinician burnout (Canfield, 2005). Bearing witness to shocking stories may create secondary traumatic stress in clinicians and can result in acute or long-lasting symptoms similar to PTSD (Canfield, 2005). Clients who are in the early stages of addiction recovery and trauma are seemingly often in crisis. Group workers may feel that they are frequently "putting out fires," which may exasperate countertransference reactions such as burnout.

Along with the expected challenges of witnessing difficult stories and working with clients who may seemingly be in a state of constant crisis, Seeking Safety sessions may also be influenced by the group dynamics specific to trauma groups. Traumatized clients experience a lack of control and feelings of powerlessness that have been imposed by the perpetrator or perpetrating system (Herman, 1997). Group members may act out and attempt to assert power or control over other members or the facilitator (Weinberg et al., 2005). Alternatively, trauma survivors may also be searching for a saviour in each other or the group facilitator, putting lofty expectations on the clinician to help solve their problems (Weinberg et al., 2005). Group facilitators must also be aware of the group dynamics and how members play out and recreate their interpersonal patterns. Although facilitators may be tempted to address and process these interpersonal dynamics, this technique would be better suited to a second- or third-stage trauma group, once members have developed the awareness and the cognitive tools necessary for examining their interpersonal relationships. These dynamics may be better addressed by using containment strategies and focusing the group's attention on the psychoeducational content. Prescreening for the suitability of members is an important aspect of effective facilitation.

The empathetic engagement required in trauma work can have an effect on the countertransference a group facilitator may experience. However, there is also a serious risk of vicarious trauma from bearing witness to traumatic stories, managing negative client transference, and observing traumatic symptoms such as flashbacks or dissociation. Vicarious traumatization is a consequence of trauma work that creates negative changes in the identity, schemas, and psychological processes of the worker (Canfield, 2005). It may have an effect on the facilitator's personal, professional, and clinical life, as the facilitator experiences anxiety, cynicism, despair, and burnout (Canfield, 2005).

Self-care strategies are especially important for clinicians facilitating Seeking Safety groups to manage negative countertransference, secondary traumatic stress, and vicarious traumatization. Receiving individual or group supervision is an important tool for facilitators to debrief, and process their own experience of the client's trauma (Weinberg et al., 2005). Furthermore, attending supportive group or individual therapy specifically for practitioners working in the trauma field can be helpful, as well as developing self-care activities that are both preventative and restorative (Weinberg et al., 2005).

Conclusion

The need for trauma-informed services is clear: the comorbidity of trauma and substance use is high among individuals seeking services for addiction. However, stage two process groups without a trauma lens have the potential to retraumatize and invalidate clients' experiences, leading to group attrition and disengagement. In this paper I identify the principles of trauma-informed care and provide examples of trauma-informed programming. Seeking Safety is a first-stage trauma group that focuses on gaining safety from trauma and addiction behaviours. It is a trauma-informed practice that is very flexible, accessible, and relatively easily to implement. This form of group work embodies the social work values of antioppressive practice and client-centered care.

References

Agic, B. (2012). Trauma-informed care for refugees. In N. Poole & L. Greaves (Eds.), *Becoming trauma informed* (pp. 121–133). Toronto, Ontario: Centre for Addiction and Mental Health.

American Psychiatric Association. (2013). *Diagnostic and statistical manual of mental disorders* (5th ed.). Washington, DC: Author.

Barnoff, L., & Moffatt, K. (2007). Contradictory tensions in anti-oppression practice in feminist social services. *Journal of Women and Social Work,* 22(1), 56–70.

Boden, M. T., Kimerling, R. E., Jacobs-Lentz, J., Bowman, D., Weaver, C. M., Carney, D., & Trafton, J. A. (2012). Seeking safety treatment for male veterans with a substance use disorder and post-traumatic stress disorder symptomatology. *Addiction, 107,* 578–586.

Breslau, N., Davis, G. C., Andreski, P., & Peterson, E. (1991). Traumatic events and posttraumatic stress disorder in an urban population of young adults. *Archives of General Psychiatry, 48,* 216–222.

Breslau, N., Kessler, R. C., Chilcoat, H. D., Schultz, L. R., Davis, G. C., & Andreski, P. (1998). Trauma and posttraumatic stress disorder in the community: The 1996 Detroit area survey of trauma. *Archives of General Psychiatry, 55,* 626–632.

Briere, J. (2006). Dissociative symptoms and trauma exposure: Specificity, affect dysregulation, and posttraumatic stress. *Journal of Nervous and Mental Disease, 194*(2), 78–82.

Briere, J., & Jordan, C. E. (2004). Violence against women: Outcome complexity and implications for treatment. *Journal of Interpersonal Violence, 19,* 1252–1276.

Briere, J., & Scott, C. (2006). *Principles of trauma therapy: A guide to symptoms, evaluation, and treatment.* Thousand Oaks, CA: Sage.

Brown, V. B., Harris, M., & Fallot, R. (2013). Moving toward trauma-informed practice in addiction treatment: A collaborative model of agency assessment. *Journal of Psychoactive Drugs, 45*(5), 386–393.

Bryant, R. A., & Panasetis, P. (2001). Panic symptoms during trauma and acute stress disorder. *Behaviour Research and Therapy, 39,* 961–966.

Canfield, J. (2005). Secondary traumatization, burnout, and vicarious traumatization: A review of the literature as it related to therapists who treat trauma. *Smith College Studies in Social Work, 75*(2), 75–72.

Center for Substance Abuse Treatment. (2005). *Substance abuse treatment: Group therapy.* Retrieved from http://www.ncbi.nlm.nih.gov/books/NBK64223/

Comer, S. D., Hart, C. L., Ward, A. S., Haney, M., Foltin, R. W., & Fischman, M. W. (2001). Effects of repeated oral methamphetamine administration in humans. *Psychopharmacology, 155*(4), 397–404.

Covington, S. S., Burke, C., Keaton, S., & Norcott, C. (2008). Evaluation of a trauma-informed and gender-responsive intervention for women in drug treatment. *Journal of Psychoactive Drugs, 40*(Suppl. 5), 387–398.

Fetzner, M. G., McMillan, K. A., Sareen, J., & Asmundson, G. J. (2011). What is the association between traumatic life events and alcohol abuse/dependence in people with and without PTSD? Findings from a nationally representative sample. *Depression and Anxiety, 28,* 632–638.

Harris, M., & Fallot, R. D. (2001a). Designing trauma-informed addictions services. *New Directions for Mental Health Services,* 57–73.

Harris, M., & Fallot, R. D. (2001b). *Using trauma theory to design service systems: New directions for mental health services.* San Francisco, CA: Jossey-Bass.

Herman, J. (1997). *Trauma and recovery: The aftermath of violence—from domestic abuse to political terror.* New York, NY: Basic Books.

Higgins, S. T. (1997). The influence of alternative reinforcers on cocaine use and abuse: A brief review. *Pharmacological Biochemistry and Behaviors, 57,* 419–427.

Jacobsen, L. K., Southwick, S. M., & Kosten, T. R. (2001). Substance use disorders in patients with posttraumatic stress disorder: A review of the literature. *American Journal of Psychiatry, 158*(8), 1184–1190.

Janet, P. (1889). *La utomatisme psychologique.* Paris, France: Felix Alcan.

The Jean Tweed Centre. (2013). *Trauma matters guidelines for trauma-informed practices in women's substance use services.* Toronto, Ontario: Author. Retrieved from http://www.addictionsandmentalhealthontario. ca/research-and-tools/trauma-matters-guidelines-for-trauma-informed-practices-in-womens-substance-use-services

Kessler, R. C., Hwang, I., Labrie, R., Petukhova, M., Sampson, N. A., Winters, K. C., & Shaffer, H. J. (2008). DSM-IV pathological gambling in the National Comorbidity Survey replication. *Psychological Medicine, 38,* 1–10.

Kessler, R. C., Sonnega, A., Bromet, E., Hughes, M., & Nelson, C. B. (1995). Post-traumatic stress disorder in the National Comorbidity Survey. *Archives of General Psychiatry, 52,* 1048–1060.

Khantzian, E. J. (1997). The self-medication hyptohesis of substance use disorders: A reconsideration and recent applications. *Harvard Review of Psychiatry,* 231–244.

Klein, R. H., & Schermer, V. L. (2000). *Group psychotherapy for psychological trauma.* New York, NY: The Guilford Press.

Leeies, M., Pagura, J., Sareen, J., & Bolton, J. M. (2010). The use of alcohol and drugs to self-medicate symptoms of posttraumatic stress disorder. *Depression and Anxiety, 27,* 731–736.

MacKenzie, T., Cuff, R., & Poole, N. (2014). Working with clients who have histories of trauma. In M. Herie & W. W. Skinner (Eds.), *Fundamentals of addiction: A practical guilde for counsellors* (4th ed., pp. 399–417). Toronto, Ontario: Centre for Addiction and Mental Health.

McFall, M. E., Mackay, P. W., & Donovan, D. M. (1992). Combat-related posttraumatic stress disorder and severity of substance abuse in Vietnam veterans. *Journal of Studies on Alcohol and Drugs, 53*(4), 357.

Menzies, P. (2012). An intergenerational trauma-informed approach to care for Canada's Aboriginal peoples. In N. Poole & L. Greaves (Eds.), *Becoming trauma informed* (pp. 175–187). Toronto, Ontario: Centre for Addiction and Mental Health.

Menzies, P. (2013). Colonization, addiction and aboriginal healing. In M. Herie & W. W. Skinner (Eds.), *Fundamentals of addiction: A practical guide for counsellors* (pp. 611–634). Toronto, Ontario: Centre for Addiction and Mental Health.

Mills, K. L., Lynskey, M., Teesson, M., Ross, J., & Darke, S. (2005). Posttraumatic stress disorder among people with heroin dependence in the Australian treatment outcome study (ATOS): Prevalence and correlates. *Drug & Alcohol Dependence, 77*, 243–249.

Najavits, L. M. (2002). *Seeking safety: A treatment manual for PTSD and substance abuse.* New York, NY: Guilford Press.

Najavits, L. M., Gallop, E. J., & Weiss, R. D. (2006). Seeking safety therapy for adolescent girls with PTSD and substance use disorder: A randomized controlled trial. *The Journal of Behavioral Health Services & Research, 33*, 453–463.

Najavits, L. M., Runkel, R., Neuner, C., Frank, A. F., Thase, M. E., Crits-Christoph, P., & Blaine, J. (2003). Rates and symptoms of PTSD among cocaine-dependent patients. *Journal of Studies on Alcohol and Drugs, 28*, 601–606.

Najavits, L. M., Weiss, R. D., & Shaw, S. R. (1997). The link between substance abuse and posttraumatic stress disorder in women a research review. *The American Journal on Addictions, 6*(4), 273–283.

Ouimette, P., & Brown, P. J. (2013). *Trauma and substance abuse: Causes, consequences, and treatment of comorbid disorders* (2nd ed.). Washington, DC: American Psychological Association.

Pietrzak, R. H., Goldstein, R. B., Southwick, S. M., & Grant, B. F. (2011). Prevalence and axis I comorbididty of full and partial posttraumatic stress disorder in the United States: Results from wave 2 of the National Epidemiologic Survey on alcohol and related conditions. *Journal of Anxiety Disorders, 25*, 456–465.

Poole, N., & Greaves, L. (Eds.). (2013). *Becoming trauma informed.* Toronto, Ontario: Centre for Addiction and Mental Health.

Robins, L., Helzer, J., & Davids, D. (1975). Narcotic use in Southeast Asia and afterward: An interview study of 898 Vietnam returnees. *Archive of General Psychiatry, 32*, 955–961.

Siegel, D. (1999). *The developing mind.* New York, NY: Guilford.

Timothy, R. K. (2012). Anti-oppresion psychotherapy as trauma-informed practice. In N. Poole & L. Greaves (Eds.), *Becoming trauma informed* (pp. 47–56). Toronto, Ontario: Centre for Addiction and Mental Health.

Toner, B., & Akman, D. (2013). Using a feminist- and trauma-informed approach in therapy with women. In N. Poole & L. Greaves (Eds.), *Becoming trauma informed* (pp. 37–46). Toronto, Ontario: Centre for Addiction and Mental Health.

Van Ameringen, M., Mancini, C., Patterson, B., & Boyle, M. H. (2008). Post-traumatic stress disorder in Canada. *CNS Neuroscience & Therapeutics, 14*, 171–181.

Van der Kolk, B. A. (1987). *Psychological trauma.* Washington, DC: American Psychiatric Press.

Van der Kolk, B. A., McFarlane, A. C., & Weisaeth, L. (Eds.). (1996). *Traumatic stress: The effects of overwhelming experience on mind, body, and society.* New York, NY: Guilford.

Weinberg, H., Nuttman-Schwartz, O., & Gilmore, M. (2005). Trauma groups: An overview. *Group Analysis, 38*(2), 187–202.

The Use of Dream Groups for Developing Professional Self-Care and Spiritual Well-Being

Karen Ring

In this paper I outline the use of group work with social work professionals for the explicit purpose of fostering self-care and spiritual well-being through the introduction of dream work concepts and the mutual sharing of dreams. The connection between self-care, spiritual well-being, and dream work establishes a strong and sustainable foundation for reflective practice and collegial support. Reflective group processes also encourage understanding of self, knowing oneself, and the use of self in the context of social work practice (Thompson & Thompson, 2008). Connecting with their inner dream life, valuing their dreams, and questioning their dreams' meanings can inform the participants' personal and professional lives. Hettler (1976) stated that this search for meaning, and in a broader perspective, a search for understanding of how personal values and beliefs are congruent with how one lives them, along with belief in a greater force than oneself, are the essence of spiritual wellness.

I also discuss the group structure and process that was demonstrated through a 90-minute International Association for Social Work With Groups (IASWG) Calgary symposium workshop of 12 social work professionals. The first half of the workshop focused on the presentation of dream concepts, cultural beliefs about dreams, and personal definitions of spiritual wellness. During the latter half, participants were able to share a significant dream with another participant, and then one dream was chosen and discussed in the larger group. Dream work models and techniques were introduced and demonstrated by the facilitator and practiced by the participants. The group discussed the benefits and lessons learned from a dream group or dream circle, how they might be applied to one's professional and spiritual self-care, and how one might facilitate a dream circle (Castleman, 2009). A dream, The Swim, is included as an example of a dream that contains an important lesson that guided a dream group member's professional life and was processed with the assistance of her dream group.

Professional Self-Care and Spiritual Wellness

According to the National Association of Social Workers' (NASW) policy statement, "Professional self-care is an essential underpinning to best practice in the profession of social work [and is] . . . critical to the survival and growth of the profession" (2009, p. 268). Multiple challenges and stressors that social workers consistently face increase the risk of burnout, compassion fatigue, and vicarious traumatization, and can become realities for many workers. These multiple challenges can include large caseloads, long hours, low pay, limited or inadequate resources, and crises within hostile or inflexible environments, to name a few, that can compromise the efforts of even the most resilient and dedicated professionals.

In order to reduce the effects of these adverse conditions through greater attention and awareness to prevention and management, self-care is seen as an "ethical imperative" (Monk, 2011, p. 4) for social workers. Emphasis on use of self as the main professional tool in their work is important to the integrity of the social work profession and in retaining qualified and valued workers. Professional self-care has implications for delivering quality services to clients across diverse settings (Monk, 2011).

The NASW's (2009) policy statement identifies and supports almost a dozen self-care initiatives, such as organizational policies that foster discussion and negotiation of the issues, address stressors and safety in the workplace, allow for group support and a supportive work environment, encourage supervisory and administrative modeling of self-care, and promote the development of individualized professional self-care plans and continuing education programs. These initiatives also encourage "the development of creative and innovation support services for social workers, which may include support groups, professional retreats, Web site resources, online support, and chat groups" (NASW, 2009, p. 270). This last description and initiative emphasizes the use of groups as a method of collegial support and engagement in self-care. In addition, the policy notes the inclusion of the practice of professional self-care in social work education programs and field instruction, along with the necessity of further research and publications in self-care (NASW, 2009).

Monk (2011) stated that self-care is

> the way a person tends to their emotional, psychological, physical and spiritual well-being. . . . [It is] fundamentally about the ways we show up on our own behalf to care for, nourish, and replenish the Self, while also actively working to reduce and heal stress effects. (p. 5)

The debilitating effects of intense or prolonged stress can affect every aspect of who we are and what we do as social workers. Physical symptoms such as headaches, weight gain, or fatigue are some examples, as well as feelings of being overwhelmed or depressed, having poor concentration, or losing one's sense of humor. Lack of spiritual wellness deeply affects social workers both personally and professionally as it can have a profound effect on how we feel about life and our role in it. Some of the symptoms of this lack are "things feeling meaningless, a sense of disconnection, interpersonal problems, conflict in relationships, and worry about the future" (Monk, 2011, p. 5). Some of these symptoms are similar to the symptoms attributed to burnout and compassion fatigue frequently identified in social workers (Figley, 2002).

When we are spiritually well our personal values and beliefs provide a purpose in our lives, we know who we are, and our search for meaning and purpose leads us closer to a state of harmony and satisfaction with ourselves and with others (Hettler, 1976). Research has indicated that in times of difficulty and disaster, people's faith and connection to Spirit is what sustains them (Pargament, 1997). Additionally, social workers are increasingly challenged to honor the spiritual issues of their clients and bridge the gap between spirituality and social work. The relationship between spirituality and social justice and the role of values is important in informing our spiritual lives. The service aspect of acting on our social work values with the oppressed and poor should move us toward social and political justice as an integral part of our spirituality (Canda, 2007). In the same vein, social work's accessibility to spirituality is in its historic roots in the Christian and Jewish charity movements, helping and caring for those in need by attending to their physical, emotional, psychological, and spiritual needs. McKernan (2007) believes that this progressive return to our roots and emphasis on spirituality will come about due to social workers invested in the spiritual perspective. Thus, it would seem important to assist social workers in their own self-discovery and self-awareness of spirituality through professional self-care and group work initiatives. However, the use and effectiveness of spirituality influenced group work with social workers for professional self-care has been limited.

Although there has been an increase in social work literature that addresses the incorporation of spirituality into the profession, further investigation would be needed to determine whether attending to spirituality actually improves client outcomes (Ai, 2002). Coholic's (2007) exploratory study is an example: using a spiritually influenced group of female adult clients with a history of substance abuse, Coholic found that this approach was useful in helping them to strengthen their self-awareness and self-esteem. Coholic found that when space was created for discussion of spirituality through a variety of activities, members willingly shared their viewpoints and beliefs. Spirituality was an important part of the process. Activities such as dream work, meditation, mindfulness practice, reflective writing, relaxation exercises, and visualizations were used. In a 1-year longitudinal study exploring how spiritual practice might help caregivers and volunteers working with dying hospice patients, the study found that spiritually influenced training and support fosters emotional well-being and spiritual growth in caregivers (Scherwitz, Pullman, McHenry, Gao, & Ostaseski, 2006). My paper explores using dream work in a group setting to support social workers in building self-awareness of their spiritual and self-care needs.

Dreams and Dream Work

Much of the basis for today's dream work models and approaches are products of the early theories on dreams by Freud, Adler, and Jung (Buckley, 1997). Jung (1974) purported that dream analysis "is the primary way to gain knowledge of the unconscious mind through images that are symbolic of conscious and unconscious mental processes" (p. 73). He also emphasized their "balancing" or compensation function between the conscious and unconscious minds, their ability to generate creative ideas, and their commentary function not only on our personal life, but also on society as a whole.

According to Pesant and Zadra (2004), "The usefulness of dream analysis is increasingly being considered across helping approaches and its connection with spirituality is evident in the literature" (p. 503). Historically, the use of dream work or the reluctance to use dream work as a therapeutic tool for personal and professional development has been embedded in practitioners' cultural and personal beliefs about dream work. Since many people have not worked with their own dreams or understand the value of dreams, they are hesitant to pursue knowledge or training in dream work. Therefore, they are not equipped or competent in exploring their dreams, and have not recognized their potential value in professional self-care. However, what the dream means to the dreamer is often much more important than any interpretation a therapist can make (Goelitz, 2009). Also, the contribution of the group members to the dream's meaning takes the emphasis away from the experts, since the dreamers are taking more responsibility and ownership in the interpretations of their own dreams and learning the necessary skills and perspectives through workshops, groups, and diverse approaches to dream work.

Goetlitz (2009), a social worker who uses dream work in her practice, has addressed the gap in knowledge on working with dreams by suggesting that training on dream work could be provided as part of higher education course work; for instance, by teaching it as a component of classes on trauma or end of life issues. Also, there could be post degree programs for credentialing, continuing education, or specialty certification credit for this area of study (Goelitz, 2009, p. 166).

In spiritually influenced group work with clients, participants found dream work helpful and were quite able to connect their dreams with their spiritual perspectives. In the practice-based research of Coholic and LeBreton (2007), group participants reported that working with their dreams led to increased self-awareness and helped with making informed choices. The process of learning dream interpretation also provided them with a technique that they could take with them into their lives and continue to use for the purposes of self-discovery and growth. The researchers ascertained that the inclusion of dream work could be an effective and fun way to help people develop their self-awareness. Since both dreams and spirituality are highly personal areas, when they were shared they served to strengthen the therapeutic alliance and group connection with others. Furthermore, the group participants often linked their dreams with their spiritual perspectives, such as beliefs that dreams contained messages from

God or premonitions of things to come, or they provided an avenue to connect with people who had died.

One area that practitioners are faced with dreams is in trauma work where recurring dreams and nightmares are symptoms of post traumatic stress disorder (PTSD) and other trauma-related symptoms (James & Gilliland, 2013; Schiller, 2012). Professionals and group workers are also faced with their own dreams and trauma as they are at high risk for secondary traumatic stress (STS). STS symptoms are strikingly similar and often identical to those of PTSD (Bride, 2007).

Brown (as cited in Salhany, 2014) has exposed

> the wide spread unspoken stigma inherent to Social Service professionals, especially in students or junior workers, who perceive a stereotype as being attached to asking for help. Many have reported feeling fearful of "appearing unprofessional" or "unable to handle their jobs" should they reveal to peers or superiors that they are suffering psychological after shocks in the wake of one or many clients' heavily trauma laden cases. (para. 8)

Thus, the majority of social workers are simply not asking for assistance. Due to this stigma, individual interventions are avoided, as is the possibility of joining a supportive dream group focusing on self-care, because it may be too threatening to their professional self-image to reveal their dreams and admit to another practitioner or group member their need for therapeutic healing.

Although the literature in the area of spirituality and social work has developed and multiplied, the "matter of dream work and the links between dream work and spirituality remain virtually unexplored" (Coholic & LeBreton, 2007, p. 60). There are practitioners and dream workers that offer validation of those links and connections. Schiller (2014), a clinical social worker and group worker who provides dream circles and supervision for professionals, stated on her website, "Dreams offer us an opportunity to have a direct experience with the sacred" (para. 4). Additionally, some see dreams as playing an important role in psychological development such as accessing deep unconscious feelings and belief patterns (Moss, 2011) or helping to foster deep connections or "spirit–spirit connections" (Coholic, 2007, p. 123) between group members.

Workshop Group Structure and Process

The workshop group was comprised of 12 symposium attendees who were social work educators, practitioners, or students. The group began with introductions and sharing their reasons for attending a workshop on self-care and dream work. The facilitator established an agreement on confidential sharing of information within the 90-minute group and encouraged the attendees to volunteer information at a comfortable emotional level since there was no expectation that anyone had to reveal personal information if they chose not to do so. Creating a safe environment for dream sharing was a priority for the facilitator and the group members (Castleman, 2009).

The objectives of the workshop and other factual information were displayed through a PowerPoint presentation interspersed with discussion and questions by participants throughout the workshop. The results of the workshop were the ability of the participants to

1. identify personal, professional, and cultural knowledge and beliefs about dreams;
2. explore and share their own sense of spiritual well-being; understand the basic concepts of dream work and their correlation to self-care;
3. share a dream that has had a strong influence in their life; and
4. apply dream group processes in social group work.

The initial focus of the workshop was on presenting information on how dreams could be therapeutic in relation to self-care and spiritual well-being by exploring some concepts about dreams presented by dream workers who have researched and practiced in this area.

During the introductory phase of the workshop, the understanding that dreams come to help people rather than frighten them established the therapeutic foundation for the dreams' use. The idea that there can be multiple meanings of dreams addressing a variety levels within the dreamer and his or her environment addresses the richness of knowledge that can be taken from dream exploration. Dreams can address a person's behavioral, emotional, physical, interpersonal, cognitive, and spiritual functioning, as well as the functioning of the collective or societal context. They can be diagnostic, revealing information about a person's process—for instance, where they are in their grief process—or they can be mysterious, with no definitive understanding of what the dream might be attempting to reveal (Taylor, 2009). Social work concepts of empowerment and strengths perspective intersect with dream concepts, as many dreams can address how persons use their power and may even assist them in identifying hidden strengths (Neville, 2004; Norman, 2000).

At this point in the workshop, participants were asked to individually reflect on their personal, professional, and cultural awareness about dreams, since everyone in the group brings diverse understanding and experience of their dream life. During this reflective phase of the workshop, each participant was asked to write down a phrase or sentence in response to one or two of the following questions:

1. Knowledge: What do I know about dreams? How do dreams play a part in my life? What dreams have I had that played a positive influence on me or changed me for the better?
2. Beliefs: What are my beliefs about these dreams? About my spiritual life? What do I believe about people who have dreams?
3. Attitudes: How do I feel about dreams and self-care? Positive, negative, ambivalent? What is my attitude toward dreams and the people who have these dreams?
4. Behavior: How do I act or what are my responses to myself, people, and dreams regarding dreams that bring meaning to my life? What do I say and do when others tell me about these dreams?

Individuals then shared their reflective answers with other group members and discussed how their responses regarding their awareness about dreams could possibly affect or contribute to professional self-care with particular focus on their spiritual well-being (Thompson & Thompson, 2008).

Group members were asked to define what spiritual well-being is for them. In this sharing, it became apparent that although there are similar themes of what this might mean for the participants, very personal and diverse beliefs and approaches emerged. A definition from the Wellness Network (2015) website was presented as a possible guide; it includes the idea that spiritual wellness

is a personal matter involving values and beliefs that provide a purpose in our lives. . . . It is generally considered to be the search for meaning and purpose in human existence, leading one to strive for a state of harmony with oneself and others while working to balance inner needs with the rest of the world. (para. 1)

There was a discussion on how a person's definition of spiritual well-being might affect their personal and professional self-care activities.

The psychoeducational component or content phase of the workshop was guided by Taylor's (1992) basic assumptions about dreams. These were presented and discussed in order to further inform the workshop participants about dream work before the group began sharing their dreams with one another. Taylor (1992) outlined 10 basic assumptions:

1. All dreams come in the service of health and wholeness.
2. No dream comes just to tell the dreamer what he or she already knows.
3. Only the dreamer can say with any certainty what meanings his or her dreams may hold.
4. The dreamer's "aha" of recognition is a function of previously unconscious memory and is the only reliable touchstone of dream work.
5. There is no such thing as a dream with only one meaning.
6. All dreams speak a universal language of metaphor and symbol.
7. All dreams reflect inborn creativity and ability to face and solve life's problems.
8. All dreams reflect society as a whole, as well as the dreamer's relationship to it.
9. Working with dreams regularly improves relationships with friends, lovers, partners, children, self and others.
10. Working with dreams in groups builds community, intimacy, and support and begins to impact society as a whole. (p. 11)

During the dream work phase of the workshop, one of the models used for the actual processing of the dream and its interpretation was Johnson's (1986) concept, which included four steps. The first step is to identify and amplify the dream symbols and make associations as to what they mean to the dreamer. The next step is to look at the structure of the dream, whether it is a story with a plot, image fragments, or the context within which the dream takes place. The third step is to look at how the symbols and structure might be related to the dreamer's present life situation. Finally, Johnson directs the dreamer to "ground" (1986, p. 51) the dream in this reality or to include it as a part of his or her everyday life by creating a meaningful ritual that addresses the dream's meaning. The facilitator briefly applied the model to one of her dreams to demonstrate how the model works.

The workshop group members were then asked to pair up and partner with another individual and to share a recent or past dream that they remember well, one that holds a lot of energy in a way that it is difficult to forget because of the vibrant images or colors it contained or due to the strong emotions it evoked in the dreamer. This is an important process in the group since many persons come to a group or workshop with the intent of needing some understanding or clarity about dreams or at least having an opportunity to share a particular dream. Sharing their dream with another person, along with knowledge from the information presented in the workshop, brings more engagement in the group and the dream work process (Moss, 2011).

When the partners return to the group, they are invited to share their experience of dream sharing and are asked if anyone is willing to have their dream worked on in the group. If there is more than one volunteer, the group decides on which dream they would like to work on first. Usually, when members of the group volunteer to share their dreams in the group, this indicates a readiness to lower defenses and to see more of themselves. Due to the time restraints of the workshop and the number of participants, only one dream could be addressed per group session (Castleman, 2009).

In the exploration phase of the workshop and in preparation for the group processing of the selected dream, Ullman's (2006, p. 8) 5-step model of group sharing was presented:

1. The dreamer shares the dream content with the group.
2. The group reflects on the feelings, images, and metaphors they perceive and empathizes with the dream as "if it were my dream."
3. The dreamer is invited to respond to the group members' reflections.
4. Dialogue with the dreamer ensues, along with questions.
5. The dreamer reflects alone.

Ullman (1994) stated, "While theory is important as a guide in psychotherapy, it is never a substitute for data" (p. 4). He encouraged a practical and workable approach to dreams, "one that demystifies dream work and provides the structure needed to help a dreamer uncover the connections between imagery and waking like experience" (Ullman, 1994, p. 4). Ullman (1994) used experiential dream groups in training therapists and saw the importance of practice. Members of the group are helpers to the dreamer, to the extent that the dreamer wants their help. The concept and model of mutual aid, one of the main components of social work practice with groups (Garvin, 1997), is much in play in dream groups. Although the purpose of the group is to assist the dreamer, other members benefit from the mutual contribution of ideas, as they may provoke memories of similar dreams and themes or bring more awareness to a group member's internal process. And as Taylor (2009) stated in his 10 assumptions, "Working with dreams in groups builds community, intimacy, and support and begins to impact society as a whole" (p. 11).

The role of the social worker or facilitator of a dream group becomes that of a teacher, not a therapist in all phases of the group process. The group worker becomes another member of the group, sharing his or her dream at times, providing information about dream work and guiding the group in their assistance to the dreamer (Ullman, 1994). The major tasks of the group worker are to create a structure and environment where the group members feel safe sharing their dreams and to assist the dreamer in making discoveries about the dream that were difficult to make alone within his or her limits of emotional comfort. However, the dreamer has control of the process and can stop it at any point. The group worker also establishes and encourages confidentiality.

The exploration phase, when all group members participate in taking on the dream as their own, sharing parts of themselves in relation to the dream, and considering the dream seriously as a source of self-knowledge for the dreamer, validates the dreamer and the importance of their work. One technique is the use of the phrase "if it were my dream . . ." (Ullman, 2006, p. 8) when assisting or commenting on a group member's dream. There is the possibility in some groups that members fall into advice-giving and directive comments as to what approaches or decisions other group members should take. By using the phrase "if it were my dream," the member takes ownership of the dream for his or her own situation rather than the dreamer's situation. Therefore, the phrase is a way of taking responsibility for one's projections onto another's dream content.

The dream sharing of the members also increases information that the dreamer can use for more associations and meanings for the dream. The skillful use of listening and questioning by the members are paramount in gaining relevant information about the dream. It is also in this phase that most of the nine processes of mutual aid are in play. The sharing of data, participating in the dialectical process, and the sense of being in this together while offering emotional support in the dreamer's self-exploration are foundational in dream work

(Castleman, 2009). Dreams can surface hidden or taboo subjects that the dreamer has avoided, so the group can provide strength and at times mutual demand for facing those areas of embarrassment or shame (Garvin, 1997).

In the final stage of the dream group, the focus shifts from the group involvement and processes to the dreamer's self-reflection. There is no group pressure for data or meaning. The dreamer takes the information and experience from the group and determines what the dream might be revealing to him or her. Any further understanding or revelations about the dream are shared at the next meeting when the dreamer reports on his or her own inner process and how the group contributed to that work (Ullman, 2006). See The Swim in the appendix for an example of the dream work done within a dream circle and how the dream addressed the dreamer's professional self-care and spiritual well-being.

Lessons From the Dream Circle

Recommendations for professional self-care and spiritual wellbeing practices for social workers can be derived from the uses and models of dream groups. One of the major principles that can be learned from them is the importance of reflective practice in a supportive group setting. Thompson and Thompson (2008) discussed the benefits of group reflective space as sources of learning new ideas and insights, useful for confidence building and promoting double-loop learners. Double-loop learners are capable of "reviewing . . . and renegotiating goals, norms and assumptions about their work" (Thompson & Thompson, 2008, p. 71) in contrast to single-loop learners, who adjust their behavior to suit them. Groups "offer a variety of perspectives and the potential for broadening our outlook" (Thompson & Thompson, 2008, p. 71), thus increasing social workers' flexibility and self-confidence in moving away from habitual ways of approaching their work and issues. According to Thompson and Thompson, "Double-loop learners are therefore better suited to dealing with changing professional environments" (2008, p. 71).

Dreams and dream work provide reflective and effective material for learning and discovering oneself; they fuel the group and reflective processes as well. Opening up oneself to dreams and dream work provides another channel of connecting to an internal source of strength, life, or higher power (Moss, 2005). Attending to and valuing this spiritual connection can be the well-spring that nurtures and cares in ways quite different but as necessary as physical or interpersonal care. Including the concept of spiritual wellness in a professional self-care plan using techniques such as meditation, mindfulness, prayer, and involvement in a spiritual or religious community, besides dream work, can be quite beneficial (Monk, 2011).

Additionally, concepts put forth by dream theorists, such as "all dreams come to heal" (Taylor, 2009, p.11) or Jung's (1974) premise that dreams can be compensatory and come to balance a person, can provide dream group members with internal support through a way of viewing and framing their experiences. These concepts can also be reflected in the group process through the group members' assistance, acceptance, and validation of the dreamer's experience. For social workers, dreams can provide diagnoses of what ails us, commentary on a current situation, or insight into how we use our power, to highlight a few of the benefits of gathering greater self-awareness and self-understanding of who we are and how we do our work. They can also provide us with creative ideas, solutions to our problems, and understanding of the status of our relationships with each other and the world, emphasizing both the personal and collective influences that dreams bring to bear (Taylor, 2009).

The world of dreams and dream groups can provide tools and techniques that can be used and applied in other group settings in addition to assisting in professional self-care and spiritual well-being. Besides the use of the phrase "if it were my dream" mentioned earlier, Castleman (2009) emphasized supportive behavior that includes empathic listening without intervention, which she stated is the goal of a dream circle. Johnson's (1986) final step in his 4-step model of dream interpretation provides a grounding technique, by anchoring dream images, themes, and processes into the dreamer's current life reality through some sort of ritual determined by the dreamer. This can range from lighting a symbolic candle to committing to an altruistic service.

Learning and lessons from dream groups can enrich professional self-care and enhance spiritual well-being. Dream groups may also increase the resiliency of social workers in their interactions with difficult to serve client groups and challenging working environments. As more and more social work practitioners and clients take interest in dream work, or perhaps start to explore their dreams with a dream partner, the possibility of forming dream groups for professionals will increase (Goelitz, 2009). Researchers are challenged to develop and test meaningful outcome measures to assess the impact of dream groups on professional self-care.

Future directions in dream work groups necessarily need to explore theory development in the use of dream work to enhance spiritual and self-care awareness in professionals, as both appear to be protective factors for increasing resiliency (Norman, 2000). Additionally, future studies in social group work could use dream groups as a setting for exploring how the mutual aid dynamics impact members' participation in dream work. There are many areas for potential research and development of the benefits and effectiveness of dream groups in a variety of professional settings.

References

Ai, A. (2002). Integrating spirituality into professional education: A challenging but feasible task. *Journal of Teaching Social Work, 22*(1/2), 103–130.

Bride, B. E. (2007, January). Prevalence of secondary traumatic stress among social workers. *Social Work, 5*(1), 63–70.

Buckley, K. (1997). *An introduction to the psychology of dreaming.* Westport, CT: Praeger.

Canda, E. R. (2007). *Spiritually sensitive social work: Key concepts and ideals.* Retrieved from https://www.bemidjistate.edu/academics/publications/social_work_journal/issue01/pdf/canda.pdf

Castleman, T. (2009). *Sacred dream circles: A guide to facilitating Jungian dream groups.* Einsideln, Switzerland: Daimon Verlag.

Coholic, D. (2007). The helpfulness of spiritually influenced group work in developing self-awareness and self-esteem: A preliminary investigation. In J. Coates, J. R. Graham, & B. Swartzentruber, with B. Ouellete, (Eds.), *Spirituality and social work: Selected Canadian readings* (pp. 111–134). Toronto, Ontario: Canadian Scholars' Press.

Coholic, D., & Lebreton, J. (2007). Working with dreams in a holistic arts-based group: Connections between dream interpretation and spirituality. *Social Work With Groups, 30*(3), 47–64.

Figley, C. R. (2002). Compassion fatigue. Psychotherapists' chronic lack of self-care. *Psychotherapy in Practice, 58*(11), 1433–1441.

Garvin, C. (1997). *Contemporary group work* (3rd ed.). New York, NY: Allyn and Bacon.

Goelitz, A. (2009). *The emotional content of dreams: An exploratory study of trauma survivors dreams.* Saarbrücken, Germany: VDM Verlag Dr. Müller.

Hettler, B. (1976). *The six dimensions of wellness model.* Retrieved from the National Wellness Institute website: http://c.ymcdn.com/sites/www.nationalwellness.org/resource/resmgr/ docs/sixdimensionsfactsheet.pdf

James, R. K., & Gilliland, B. E. (2013). *Crisis intervention strategies* (7th ed.). Belmont, CA: Brooks/Cole.

Johnson, R. A. (1986). *Inner work: Using dreams and active imagination for personal growth.* San Francisco, CA: Harper & Row.

Jung, C. G. (1974). *Dreams.* Princeton, NJ: Princeton University Press.

McKernan, M. (2007). Exploring the spiritual dimension of social work. In J. Coates, J. R. Graham, & B. Swartzentruber, with B. Ouellete (Eds.), *Spirituality and social work: Selected Canadian readings* (pp. 111–134). Toronto, Ontario: Canadian Scholars' Press.

Monk, L. (2011). Self-care for social workers: A precious commodity: An ethical imperative. *Perspectives, 33*(1), 4–5, 7.

Moss, R. (2005). *Dreamways of the Iroquois: Honoring secret wishes of the soul.* Rochester, VT: Destiny Books.

Moss, R. (2011). *Active dreaming.* Navato, CA: New World Library.

National Association of Social Workers. (2009). *Social work speaks: National Association of Social Workers policy statements, 2009–2014.* Washington, DC: Author. Retrieved from https://www.socialworkers.org/nasw/memberlink/2009/supportfiles/ProfesionalSelf-Care.pdf

Neville, D. (2004). *Putting empowerment into practice: Turning rhetoric into reality.* London, England: Whiting & Birch.

Norman, E. (2000). *Resiliency enhancement: Putting the strengths perspective into social work practice.* New York, NY: Columbia University Press.

Pargament, K. I. (1997). *The psychology of religion and coping: Theory, research, practice.* New York, NY: Guilford Press.

Pesant, N., & Zadra, A. (2004). Working with dreams in therapy: What do we know and what should we do? *Clinical Psychology Review, 24,* 489–512.

Salhany, M. (2014, March 18). *Mots sociaux, Secondary traumatic stress and its effect on social workers: A self-care mini-series blog.* Retrieved from http://motssociaux.com/tag/social-services/

Scherwitz, L., Pullman, M., McHenry, P., Gao B, & Ostaseski, F. (2006, July-August). A contemplative care approach. *Explore: The Journal of Science and Healing, 2*(4), 304–313.

Schiller, L. Y. (2012, Winter). Getting unstuck: Using dreamwork to transform trauma through the guided active imagination approach* (GAIA*). *DreamTime*, 4–7, 30–31. Retrieved from http://lindayaelschiller.com/wp-content/uploads/GAIA-article.pdf

Schiller, L. Y. (2014, May 20). *Dreaming: A spiritual experience.* Retrieved from http://lindayaelschiller.com/tag/spirituality-and-dreams/

Taylor, J. (1992). *Where people fly and water runs uphill.* New York, NY: Warner Books.

Taylor, J. (2009). *The wisdom of your dreams.* New York, NY: Tarcher.

Thompson, S., & Thompson, N. (2008). *The critically reflective practitioner.* Basingstroke, England: Palgrave Macmillan.

Ullman, M. (1994). The experiential dream group: Its application in training of therapists. *Dreaming, 4*(4). Retrieved from http://www.asdreams.org/journal/articles/4-4_ullman .htm

Ullman, M. (2006). *Appreciating dreams: A group approach.* New York, NY: Cosimo Books.

Wellness Network. (2015). *Spiritual wellness.* Retrieved from http://wellnessnetworkedmonton .com/wellness-dimensions/spiritual/

Appendix: The Swim

The Swim is the dream of a mental health counselor who was participating in a monthly dream group. She had been invited to counsel prison inmates at the local prison. She had no experience counseling this population but had the support of the staff psychologist and felt she could handle the new challenge.

> I am at the top of a narrow canal in my swimsuit accompanied by a man. As I am about ready to jump in the water, I notice the water is becoming increasingly turbulent and looking dangerous to swim in the longer I stand there. I begin to panic and think that this was not a good idea. The man tells me to go to another part of the canal where the water is calmer and shows me a better place to jump in. I feel grateful for the guidance and jump in the water.

The dreamer, with the assistance of other group members, realized from the dream that this dream was about her new position at the prison. She came to the understanding that the job ahead may be more difficult than she had believed it to be. Maybe she didn't have the skills she needed to work with this population. The water, symbolizing the emotional turmoil she would be encountering (both the inmates' and her own), was more than she could handle. However, she did have assistance in the dream. This was reassuring to her because she had hoped that the psychologist's (the accompanying man) guidance would be there. She realized that her approach with these clients would have to change if she was not going to be taken under by the issues she would possibly encounter. She believed she gained insight into her need to take care of herself professionally in this new position by learning more about this population and their needs, along with what approaches and best practices might be of benefit. Her own emotional care also became an important consideration after the dream, and it helped her to let go of her nonchalant attitude about her current level of competence and her need to prepare for the upcoming challenges. Since she believes that her purpose in life is to help others, she felt that the guidance from the dream came to help her along her path.

Culturally Relevant Group Work With Barbadian Adolescent Males in Residential Care

Sadie K. Goddard-Durant & Nicole N. Lynch

Children come into care as a result of experiences which have all been identified in trauma studies as potentially traumatic (Salazar, Keller, Gowen, & Courtney, 2013). Investigations conducted into the background of the youth in the care of the Barbados Child Care Board indicate that their experiences are no different. For example, child abuse reports to the board for the year 2013 reveal that at least 1,000 such cases were reported (Barbados Ministry of Finance and Economic Affairs, Division of Economic Affairs, 2013). A review of the literature suggests trauma-informed cognitive behavioural therapy (CBT) groups with strong, similarly oriented caregiver components as effective intervention with this population (Schmied & Tully, 2009). However, it is well accepted that Western models of trauma group work are grounded in theoretical constructs, interventions, and evaluation strategies which have been influenced by mainstream American values (Bryant & Njenga, 2006). Standard mental health practices which are developed from a Western mind-set, therefore, require some adaptation in order to be accepted and effective in non-Western cultures (Council on Social Work Education, 2012).

In this paper we identify some of the factors to be considered when creating culturally relevant trauma-informed groups for adolescent males of Afro-Caribbean descent as informed by the culture infused counselling model (Collins & Arthur, 2010). First we discuss the existing research on adapting interventions for clients from non-Western populations. We then apply this knowledge to examine the Western approach to mental health interventions in light of the factors identified by the culture infused counselling model. Finally, we offer some implications for the practice of group work with this population, based on their experience with the creation of a culturally relevant psychoeducational group for adolescent males in care in Barbados. The argument is made for adapting evidence-based interventions to create culturally responsive treatment for persons who are not from the Caucasian American middle class. However, little is known about the trauma experiences of English speaking Afro-Caribbean people, and hence there is an absence of what cultural features might be useful to consider in assessing usefulness of components of any evidence based intervention to be adapted.

Intervening With Clients from Non-Western Cultures

Information on the mental health impact of trauma and the relevant interventions, as with other mental health theories and practices, has long been accepted as universal. Yet, it is now well established that the Western model of perception and intervention in mental health issues cannot be implemented wholesale in other cultures (Sumari & Jalal, 2008). Indeed, Sumari and Jalal (2008) made the point that while the role of culture in counselling has been increasingly explored, little research has been conducted on international populations outside of the United States. According to them, counselling theories of mental health and wellness and intervention are ethnocentric to Caucasian American middle class culture. They are also individualistic, while many non-Western cultures are collectivist. They have asserted that experiences of colonial trauma, where features of Western culture were imposed on indigenous people, may mean that counselling and concepts of mental health may in fact be resisted by people of former colonies. Indeed, Gone and Duran (as cited in Stewart, 2009) have suggested that the act of imposing mental health practices of one culture on another can be perceived in and of itself as colonisation. Hence, what perception of mental health and illness and intervention can be used by clinicians in non-Western contexts, particularly clinicians who may have been trained in Western cultures and practice in former colonies? What cultural factors affect these perceptions and resulting interventions?

Most thinkers in multicultural competence have advocated for the creation of culturally responsive interventions via the adaptation of existing evidence-based interventions (Hwang, 2006). Yet none of these frameworks address specifically what this adaptation looks like for a group intervention where the practice of cofacilitation and the existence of multiple clients per session mean that the therapist–client dynamic is a function of several cultural identities in any given session. Furthermore, our review revealed that most if not all of these frameworks are based on the assumption of knowledge of the various cultures involved and are mainly created from the perspective of a clinician from a dominant culture working with a client considered to be from a minority culture as a result of migration to the clinician's country (Hwang, 2006; Sue, Zane, Hall, & Berger, 2009; Walker, Trupin, & Hansen, 2011).

The culture infused counselling model offers a framework for adaptation to create culturally responsive intervention, which may be helpful to practitioners facing this dilemma. The model identifies four levels of personal cultural identity factors (universal, cultural, personal identity, and contextual) which impact people's worldviews and argues that all interactions between client and counsellor are multicultural as a result. The idea of universality, a commonality as humans across cultures and all interactions being multicultural, allows for the relevance of some of the material from Western models. In addition, the inclusion of the counsellor's personal cultural identity allows more room than other models for application to attempt to create culturally responsive interventions by counsellors from non-Caucasian American middle class cultures.

What knowledge exists, then, about non-Western populations, which can be used to understand mental health experiences and tailor interventions to suit? Much information is still unknown for Afro-Caribbean people. What is known, however, can still be useful in determining the personal cultural identities of the clients and clinicians and hence designing the intervention. In the absence of indigenous programming for group interventions with adolescent males in residential care in Barbados and the Caribbean, and limited information about the personal cultural identity factors, which may need to be considered in order to achieve the same, the task was undertaken by two Barbadian clinicians working in Barbados.

Afro-Caribbean Personal Cultural Identity Factors: Implications for Practice

In the absence of indigenous programming, we used the culture infused counselling model (Collins & Arthur, 2010) to guide adaptations of the trauma-informed CBT approach with groups as outlined primarily by Blaustein and Kinniburgh (2010). As suggested by the culture infused counselling model, universal factors, along with the client's personal cultural identity factors and those of the clinician, were considered in creating a culturally sensitive working alliance and group intervention.

Addressing Universal Factors

Universal factors, according to Collins and Arthur (2010), are elements of experience which are common to everyone; hence, they were a major reason we felt this was a useful framework for creating a culturally responsive intervention. One such feature related to the fact that there is also some evidence that responses to trauma such as PTSD are experienced similarly in people of different cultures (Bryant & Njenga, 2006). However, we acknowledge that the nature and treatment for PTSD needs may vary among adolescents from different countries.

Group therapy has been indicated for adolescents who have experienced psychological trauma (Aronson & Khan, 2004), and boys across cultures tend to be socialised to work in groups (Benenson, Apostoleris, & Parness, as cited in Davis, 2012). This is particularly the case for males in the Caribbean where the kinship system is traditionally underscored as a mechanism to foster mutual aid, cooperation, and unity (Sutherland, 2011). As such, we thought the use of a group intervention to be an appropriate modality for intervention with Afro-Caribbean males in care in Barbados.

To ensure that these universal factors were addressed, we designed the content of the group intervention to include themes which are thought to be essential to the development and trauma recovery of males. Specifically, we focused on the themes of hope, self-esteem, self-protection, self-direction, mutuality, and responsibility, which were identified by Fallot, Freeman, Zasanis, and Dende (1998) as central for this population. The curriculum content was also inclusive of discussions on what it means to be a man and the kind of man participants would want to be when they grew up.

Addressing Cultural Factors

With regard to cultural factors, we thought age to be crucial to consider knowing both the clients' and the clinicians' personal cultural identities. In the Western conceptualisation of adolescence, there is an appreciation that the growing up process involves movement toward greater agency. Cognitive development at this stage entails facilitation of executive functioning (Aronson & Khan, 2004; Blaustein & Kinniburgh, 2010). There is also the acceptance of separation and individuation from caregivers as a normal developmental task (Blaustein & Kinniburgh, 2010). This was also the view of the clinicians. However, Dr. S. Alleyne, child and adolescent psychiatrist in Barbados, noted:

> My observation over the years working with Caribbean families is that in comparison to families in the U.S.A, the adolescents' views are given more weight than that of a child. However, their independent thinking is not as easily accepted, and the ability to act on independent views/ beliefs is not as endorsed as in more developed Western countries. (S. Alleyne, personal communication, December 18, 2014)

Nevertheless, once more, the clinicians' attitudes about adolescents' behaviour were more in keeping with the Western model. A psychoeducational component for the caregivers was included as part of the group intervention to address the discrepancy between the Western model of practice, in which we were trained, and the cultural dynamics surrounding adolescence in Barbados.

According to the culture infused counselling model (Collins & Arthur, 2010), gender is another cultural factor which could be considered as a potential influence on the personal cultural identities of the clinician–client dynamic and hence on creating a culturally sensitive working alliance with this population. In the Afro-Caribbean context, masculinity is defined by traits of aggressiveness, power over others, and sexual prowess (Sutherland, 2011). Emotional expression is limited, and punished unless it is aggressive. However, the trauma-informed care approach, which is both our preferred orientation, calls for clients to learn how to identify and self-regulate their emotional experience, and in so doing broaden their range of acknowledged and expressed feelings and interpersonal relationship-building strategies (Blaustein & Kinniburgh, 2010).

To bridge this gap, we facilitated expression of feelings through nonverbal African-derived features of Caribbean societies such as movement, drumming, music, and art (Sutherland, 2011). Movement was incorporated into the group check-in and soft background music, selected by the boys, was played during the group sessions. In addition, provision was made for the spontaneous use of drumming by boys to moderate group discussions.

Another adaptation to help the boys to identify and regulate their emotions despite the cultural tendency to nonexpression of emotionsm was the use of the superhero metaphor. According to Fallot et al. (1998), males' core values, commitments, and hopes are best explored by way of their heroes. The concept of the superhero was central to the curriculum developed. Video clips and references to superheroes were used to engage the boys in traumatic processing, correct problematic behaviour, and teach alternative coping mechanisms. To further engage the boys in the group process, we framed emotional management as a challenge, and meaningful connections were established to real-life situations in which the boys found it difficult to express or regulate their emotion (King & Gurian, 2006). Specifically, the boys were challenged with seeing how they could use the skills learnt during group to avoid being emotionally overwhelmed at home and at school.

Emotional management was modelled and incorporated at all stages of the group to help the boys to learn new ways to manage emotions. We incorporated the boys' suggestions for physical activities, which calmed them and helped them to focus as part of the beginning ritual. We also actively planned for the physical safety of group members and workers by removing potential weapons and encouraging the use of emotional regulation skills during group. This was especially critical during the second stage of the group when the storming could sometimes become physical.

Another cultural factor, which may be relevant for consideration in adapting the Western evidence-based interventions to be culturally responsive to Afro-Caribbean culture, is language. Many Barbadian adolescent teens use the local dialect, Bajan, to communicate in relaxed or informal settings. However, the interventions often use images and vocabulary which are reflective of Western culture. In this case, we were in agreement with Sutherland (2011), who argued that indigenous languages must be incorporated into the work to be truly relevant to Caribbean clients.

To ensure that the indigenous language was incorporated, we welcomed and incorporated the Bajan dialect and popular sayings into the group process (e.g., "They get you real cruel"; "I tell my self and my self say"). Additionally, we responded to the interpersonal dynamics of language among adults and adolescents in the Caribbean by introducing ourselves by our first names but were accepting when the participants chose to refer to us as "m'am," as this is considered a way of showing respect to elders in Barbadian culture. Sensitivity to the language of adolescence was shown by incorporating superhero gaming language in the curriculum and group discussion (e.g., "power up"; "basecamp").

Religious faith and spiritual factors have been found to influence people's mental health (Tan, Bowie, & Orpilla, 2004). Spirituality and religious beliefs are pervading influences and are traditionally regarded as central to life in the Caribbean (Mordecai & Mordecai, as cited in Tan et al., 2004). Spirituality was, therefore, also considered a key cultural factor. In 2009, Caribbean Development Research Services (CADRES) was commissioned by the Ministry of Family, Culture, Sports and Youth, Bureau of Gender Affairs, to investigate domestic violence in Barbados. Its report (CADRES, 2009) indicated that for survivors of interpersonal violence in Barbados, spiritual resources are often the first accessed intervention—where victims turned to when they felt hopeless even if there was no personal relationship with God. Seeking God's guidance through prayer and meditation and reference to biblical teachings are all strategies used by Barbadians of Afro-Caribbean culture in interpersonal and intrapersonal interactions and self-perception. This perception of religious beliefs as a source of coping also shapes our personal cultural identities as clinicians. However, many of the models on trauma-informed care do not speak to spirituality or religious beliefs as a strategy for use in fostering affect modulation or identity development post trauma.

Given the importance of religion in Caribbean society, we sought to include it as a resource in all phases of the group. All group members' spiritual frameworks were assessed in the intake to create a spiritually safe and receptive therapeutic alliance (Leach, Aten, Wade, & Hernandez, 2009, p. 76). This also allowed us to assess potential spiritual concerns as well as spirituality protective factors and resources for coping. In the beginning stages, spiritual resources such as prayer or calling to a higher power for help when dealing with intense emotions were incorporated in the development of skills to cope with difficult emotions when they arose in or out of group. Mastery of use of these resources to cope with traumatic responses was consolidated during the middle and ending stages of the group. We also responded to the importance placed on religion in the Caribbean through Bibilotherapy, using biblical stories with the group's permission. The Story of Joseph was selected as it was thought to be suited to exploring the themes of trauma, loss, and coping.

Addressing Personal Identity Factors

According to the culture infused counselling model, personal identity factors are another component of the clients' and counsellors' personal cultural identity which must be considered in creating a culturally responsive group intervention. Education is one such factor, which must be considered in designing interventions for persons of Afro-Caribbean descent. This is because the literacy rate for boys in the Caribbean, specifically Barbados, is 70% (UNESCO Institute for Statistics, 2013), and many of the boys in care attend academic institutions catering to persons with learning difficulties and low literacy rates. To address this gap in their Western training and the challenge posed by low literacy in the group, we adhered to the assertions of King and Gurian (2006) that boys learn via experiential and kinesthetic opportunities, spatial visual representations, letting them choose topics which appeal to them, and making reading and writing group activities purposeful. Hence, we created indigenous visual materials to reinforce the emotional regulation and coping skills, which were taught during the group sessions. These materials included visuals such as graduation certificates and "I Have the Power" posters. To encourage participation in activities which required writing or reading during group or for homework, "trying" was reframed as courage and private positive reinforcement was provided for those who made an effort.

Socialisation is another personal identity factor which we thought to be relevant for consideration. Family and community are important in Afro-Caribbean culture (Sutherland, 2011). Indeed, the structure of the facilities for children in care reflects this importance, where the staff are referred to as "Auntie" and "Uncle" and staff positions include "house parents." Group therapy, according to Aronson and Khan (2004), is indicated specifically for adolescents affected by psychological trauma because, among other reasons, group creates the "family" or social support network, which research shows fosters resiliency. Thus no discrepancy existed in this case.

However, parenting practices, a main source of socialisation, have been found to be mainly authoritarian in the Caribbean, and specific to boys, found to be more neglectful than with girls (Lipps et al., 2012; Sutherland, 2011). This is manifested in less monitoring and emotional nurturance (Lipps et al., 2012). Given that many of children come into care in Barbados for physical abuse and neglect, this appears to be true here, although the research is not specific to Barbados (Barbados Ministry of Finance and Economic Affairs, Division of Economic Affairs, 2013). Parenting is guided by principles including religious beliefs such as "if you spare the rod, you spoil the child," and the belief that physical punishment contributes to character formation (Sutherland, 2011). Yet the evidence-based models for working with this population, to which we also subscribe, call for caregivers to be attuned to themselves and their charges towards fostering healthy attachments and supporting youth in developing a sense of consistency; safety via use of praise, limits, and ignoring undesirable behaviours; and ultimately affect identification and modulation (Blaustein & Kinniburgh, 2010).

In the Afro-Caribbean setting masculinity is often defined as power over others and aggressiveness; it is culturally accepted that adolescent males will try this independent of a trauma history (Reddock, 2004). This is compounded by a phenomenon where, culturally, adolescent attempts at independence are not accepted to begin with and are met with authoritarian parenting style. Yet the models call for parents and caregivers to understand adolescence as a developmental phase with certain specific related tasks as well as to not take a child's aggressive, disrespectful behaviour personally (Blaustein & Kinniburgh, 2010) and to respond in non-violent ways. Socialisation with regard to parenting practices then posed a huge discrepancy to be considered in group adaptation.

In adapting the group intervention to the specified population, we were sensitive to the impact of socialisation on parenting practices in Barbados. To address the discrepancy between the Western model and these practices, a positive behaviour management intervention was implemented during the group sessions to help the boys to develop self-management and responsibility. Caregivers were trained to implement this positive behaviour management strategy as a means of developing responsibility and encouraging greater compliance. This was paired with ongoing advocacy for the use of positive disciplinary strategies with an emphasis on self-management techniques.

Addressing Contextual Factors

Contextual factors are another component of personal cultural identity which the culture infused counselling model asserts must be considered in creating a culturally sensitive counselling alliance and intervention. Two systems (mental health and child care) were considered crucial social contextual factors in this case.

Several observed features of the child protective system in Barbados can be considered to affect the personal cultural identity of the clients. Our past interactions suggested that direct caregivers may have had different approaches to managing the behaviour of their charges. There also appears to be limited ongoing opportunities for professional development or staff empowerment to facilitate the development and adherence to a common standard to guide parenting practices. Yet Western models call for consistent caregiver responses and for them to be trained in creating a container by building routines and rituals (Blaustein & Kinniburgh, 2010).

The system is also dynamic in nature, where children are in care temporarily or go home to visit families on weekends. This immediately made some residents ineligible or inconsistently accessible. However, the group therapy model calls for an ideal group size of eight and consistent attendance and this is what we would have desired as well.

Advocacy was the main strategy we used to address the observed features of the child care system in Barbados. Specifically, we used the group evaluation as an opportunity to advocate for a caregiver training component to future group work, formal assessments for boys as part of the intake process, longer group timeframes, coleadership, and greater use of strength-based or creative approaches among colleagues. In the absence of being able to work with the entire system of care, we worked with what was available while advocating for more collaborative care.

Group goals were expanded to reflect the inclusion of support sessions for caregivers—to empower and help them to provide more supportive care for children. These sessions addressed self-care and management of self-affect and provided a listening ear for caregivers to discuss stressors in the child care system. Through these sessions we also sought to equip the caregivers with the skills to increase the likelihood of boys generalising prosocial group behaviour outside of group session.

Coleadership is sometimes seen as an additional expense by those who fund group work. However, given the cultural context of the child care system and the complex dynamics experienced in groups with adolescents who have experienced trauma, cofacilitation was nonnegotiable on our part. Successful cofacilitation depends on a commitment to communication to assist with countertransference reactions and burnout and to facilitate the discussion of disagreements (Aronson & Khan, 2004). To stimulate this ongoing communication, we held weekly peer consultations during which we considered our interactions with each other, the group members, and the child care system while facilitating the group.

The temporary nature of the child care system had implications for how we adapted our approach to termination. Within the child care system, moving from one home to the next and transitioning out of care are common. Residential care also serves as a holding place for youth who are awaiting decisions for status offences. These situations meant that group members may leave the group unexpectedly before its end. To address this, we integrated ongoing skill consolidation and preparation for termination in the group design.

Stigma and discrimination surrounding mental illness, especially schizophrenia and drug abuse, or any remote relationship to the mental health system, are common in the English-speaking Caribbean (Youssef et al., 2014). Indeed, Afro-Caribbean people may see persons as spirit possessed, not mentally ill (Sutherland, 2011). Furthermore, on average, less than 5% of the health budget in Caribbean countries is allocated to mental health (Youssef et al., 2014). Other research has shown that there are too few social workers with too many cases and role-related tasks, which contradict and sabotage the policy mandates (Ken, 2007). In Barbados, there is one psychologist assigned to a child protective system of 90–100 children and one social worker to a home of approximately 7–17 children at any given time. There was also an experienced distrust of mental health professionals, who some believe "want to drive you mad." There is also the fear that mental health professionals may betray a person. This made accessing psychological assessment information challenging. Also, the practice lens speaks to

Western conceptualisation of mental illness, where impact of trauma is viewed according to the Diagnostic and Statistical Manual of Mental Disorders (DSM-IV) classification (Aronson & Khan, 2004). Finally, screening and access to social and psychological assessments are key features of the group intervention (Aronson & Khan, 2004) and evidence-based research calls for helping staff in residential facilities to normalise and provide a therapeutic culture of caring, which evidence-based research calls for (Barton, Gonsalez, & Tomilson, 2012)

We instituted several adaptations to attend to the cultural nuances of the understanding of mental health in the Afro-Caribbean context. Bryant and Njenga (2006) recommended that to be culturally relevant, the group intervention must be clearly explained and understood, especially if the intervention is seen as a challenge to the client's belief system. As such, a sensitisation workshop was held with caregivers to provide an orientation to how the group works, and to discuss roles, collaboration, and confidentiality. Their views of the child care system and the roles of the group workers and caregivers were continually addressed throughout the course of the group intervention to build trust and a working alliance. We also addressed concerns about the effectiveness of the group intervention to bring about a positive change in the boys' behaviour.

When concerns or distrust of the group process arose they were acknowledged, validated, and addressed. We used CBT to challenge assumptions and accusations of "the psychologist come to play with our heads" or using "all this psychology to drive you mad." In light of the cultural distrust of counselling, we placed an emphasis on creating a nonthreatening curriculum by focusing on psychoeducation for the boys instead of therapy during the group sessions.

We negotiated boundaries with both caregivers and the group's participants. With regard to the caregivers, time was spent negotiating the boundaries of confidentiality, as the cultural understanding of "it takes a village to raise a child" entailed an expectation on the part of the caregivers that group workers would divulge everything that happened in the session. Boundaries were also negotiated with boys to help clarify their understanding of the boundaries of helping inside and outside the group context.

We believe that part of working responsibly within a multicultural context involves accounting for the personal cultural identities of individuals within a particular culture. We found that it was in fact possible to facilitate for those known differences in personal cultural identities, outside of techniques, which gave members an opportunity to talk about certain aspects of their culture, as posited by Corey, Corey, Callanan, and Russell (2004). In designing the group intervention, then, we sought to cater to these known individual identities in four main ways. First, individual assessment was conducted with the potential group members. Second, the group members not only were provided with opportunities to share their perspectives verbally, as is the norm for group work, but also were given individual in-group and homework activities specifically designed to elicit and address their personal experiences. Third, we made efforts to accommodate the boys' individual differences by providing options for modes of communication and expression in any given activity. Finally, we made a point of using references and examples reflective of known individual experiences or preferences.

Toseland and Rivas (2005) emphasised the importance of practitioners building their cultural sensitivity by identifying their feelings about their own identity and understanding how this identity may affect their interactions with members from other backgrounds. In this case, although we shared a similar racial background, there were key differences in our personal cultural identity factors. We therefore honed our cultural sensitivity by exploring our feelings about the formation of our cultural identity during these peer consultations. In particular we explored how our view of our cultural identity and the experiences that impacted it affected our values, beliefs, and clinical practices.

During these sessions the group workers also explored questions such as

1. How do we manage the complex dynamics of trauma groups situated in the local child care system?
2. How do we work respectfully within the culture to bring about positive change?
3. How do we model professionalism and maintain healthy boundaries?

Conclusion

While it is accepted that mental health practices developed from a Western mindset require some adaptation in order to be acceptable and effective in non-Western cultures, there is little to guide the adaptation of these practices for use with Afro-Caribbean males. What is known, however, can still be useful in determining the personal cultural identity factors of the clients and clinicians and hence in designing the intervention. The culture infused counselling model provides a good framework for the exploration of these factors when adapting the Western framework for use with Afro-Caribbean clients. Through this model, the identities of both client and clinician can be compared and contrasted with the Western model of thought for group work and implications for practice derived. It should be noted, however, that the implications shared in this article are not exhaustive or instructive but rather are offered for consideration by fellow practitioners who work with this particular population as part of their ongoing process of bringing greater awareness, reflection, and action to the process of making group interventions more acceptable and effective for the Afro-Caribbean population. It would also appear that part of the work of adapting the Western model of group interventions involves a greater emphasis on researching the culture of origin of both the clinician and client and the resulting implications for mental health perception and intervention, as most of the current literature is from the perspective of Western clinicians working with non-Western populations in North America (Hwang, 2006; Sue et al., 2009; Walker et al., 2011).

Further research on the features of Caribbean culture and their impact on group practice is also recommended. Specific areas of relevance include the contribution of religion and spirituality to the mental health of adolescents in the Caribbean, particularly with regard to resilience and the transmission of beliefs and behaviours; the therapeutic use of drumming and storytelling with this population; factors which influence the acceptability of group interventions; and the impact of culturally relevant group work on the facilitation of postcolonial healing and recovery. The continued evaluation of the effectiveness of any adapted group interventions is also recommended, as it would serve to build the currently sparse indigenous knowledge base for group work with this population.

References

Aronson, S., & Kahn, G. B. (2004). *Group interventions for treatment of psychological trauma module 3: Group interventions for treatment of trauma in adolescents.* Retrieved from American Group Psychotherapy Association website: http://www.agpa.org/docs/default-source/practice-resources/3-adolescents.pdf?sfvrsn=0

Barbados Ministry of Finance and Economic Affairs, Division of Economic Affairs. (2013). *Barbados economic and social report 2013.* Retrieved from Divison of Economic Affairs website: http://www.economicaffairs.gov.bb/archive.php?cid=10

Barton, S., Gonsalez, R., & Tomilson, P. (2012). *Therapeutic residential care for children and young people: An attachment and trauma informed model for practice.* London, England: Jessica Kingsley.

Blaustein, M. E., & Kinniburgh, K. M. (2010). *Treating traumatic stress in children and adolescents: How to foster resilience through attachment, self-regulation, and competency.* New York, NY: The Guildford Press.

Bryant, R. A., & Njenga, F. G. (2006). Cultural sensitivity: Making trauma assessment and treatment plans culturally relevant. *The Journal of Clinical Psychiatry, 67*(2), 74–79. Retrieved from http://www.ucalgary.ca/psychiatry/files/psychiatry/ J%20Clin%20Monograph%20Supplement%20Feb%2006.pdf#page=76

Caribbean Development Research Services. (2009). *Domestic violence in Barbados.* Unpublished report. Ministry of Family, Culture, Sports and Youth, Bureau of Gender Affairs, Elsie Payne Complex, Constitution Road, St Michael, Barbados.

Collins, S., & Arthur, N. (2010).Culture infused counselling: A model for developing multicultural competence. *Counselling Psychology Quarterly, 23,* 217–233.

Corey, G., Corey, M. S., Callanan, P., & Russell, J. M. (2004). *Group techniques.* Toronto, Ontario: Brooks/Cole-Thomson Learning.

Council on Social Work Education, Task Force on Advanced Social Work Practice in Trauma. (2012). *Report of the CSWE Task Force on advanced social work practice in trauma.* Retrieved from http://www.cswe.org/File.aspx?id=63842

Davis, K. (2012). Talking to the beat of a different drum: Speaking so he can listen and listening so he can speak. In S. Degges-White & S. Colon (Eds.), *Counselling boys and young men* (pp. 29–40). New York, NY: Springer.

Fallot, R., Freeman, D., Zazanis, S., & Dende, J. (1998). Male survivors. In

M. Harris (Ed.), *Trauma recovery and empowerment: A clinician's guide for working with women in groups* (pp. 354–399). New York, NY: The Free Press.

Hwang, W. (2006). The psychotherapy adaptation and modification framework: Application to Asian Americans. *American Psychologist, 61*(7), 702–715. doi:10.1037/0003-066X.61.7 .702

Ken, P. (November, 2007). *Children without parental care in the Caribbean: Systems of protection.* Retrieved from UNICEF Eastern Caribbean website: http://www.unicef.org/ easterncaribbean/cao_resources_children_without_parental_care.pdf

King, K., & Gurian, M. (2006, September). With boys in mind/teaching to the minds of boys. *Teaching to Student Strengths, 64*(1), 56–61. Retrieved from http://www.ascd.org/ publications/educational-leadership/sept06/vol64/num01/Teaching-to-the-Minds-of-Boys.aspx

Leach, M., Aten, J., Wade, N., & Hernandez, B. (2009). Noting the importance of spirituality during the clinical intake. In J. Aten & M. Leach (Eds.), *Spirituality and the therapeutic process: A comprehensive resource from intake to termination* (pp. 75–91). Washington, DC: American Psychological Association.

Lipps, G., Lowe, G. A., Gibson, R. C., Halliday, S., Morris, A., Clarke, N., & Wilson, R. N. (2012). Parenting and depressive symptoms among adolescents in four Caribbean societies. *Child and Adolescent Psychiatry and Mental Health, 6*(31). Retrieved from http://www.capmh.com/content/pdf/1753-2000-6-31.pdf

Reddock, R. E. (Ed.). (2004). *Interrogating Caribbean masculinities: Theoretical and empirical analyses.* Kingston, Jamaica: University of the West Indies Press.

Salazar, A. M., Keller, T. E., Gowen, L. K., & Courtney, M. E. (2013). Trauma exposure and PTSD among older adolescents in foster care. *Social Psychiatry and Psychiatric Epidemiology, 48*(4), 545–551. doi:10.1007/s00127-012-0563-0

Schmied, V., & Tully, L. (2009). *Effective strategies and interventions for adolescents in a child protection context.* Retrieved from http://www.community.nsw.gov.au/docswr/_assets/ main/documents/effective_adolescent_strategies.pdf

Stewart, S. (2009). Family counselling as decolonisation: Exploring an indigenous social-constructivist approach in clinical practice. *First Peoples Child & Family Review, 4*(1), 62–70. Retrieved from http://journals.sfu.ca/fpcfr/index.php/FPCFR/article/view/138/124

Sue, S., Zane, N., Hall, G., & Berger, L. (2009). The case for cultural competency in psychotherapeutic interventions. *Annual Review of*

Psychology, 60, 525–548. Retrieved from http://www.ncbi.nlm.nih.gov/pmc/articles/PMC2793275/

Sumari, M., & Jalal, F. H. (2008). Cultural issues in counseling: An international perspective. *Counselling, Psychotherapy, and Health, 4*(1), *Counseling in the Asia Pacific Rim: A Coming Together of Neighbors Special Issue*, 24–34. Retrieved from http://www .cphjournal.com/archive_journals/Melati_Sumari_and_F_H_Jalal.pdf

Sutherland, M. (2011). Towards a Caribbean psychology: An African centred approach. *Journal of Black Studies, 42*(8), 1175–1193. Retrieved from the Sage Publications database.

Tan, P. P., Bowie, S., & Orpilla, G. (2004). A Caribbean perspective on spirituality in social work practice. *The Caribbean Journal of Social Work, 3*, 74–88.

Toseland, R., & Rivas, R. (2005). *An introduction to group work practice* (5th ed.). Boston, MA: Pearson.

UNESCO Institute for Statistics. (June, 2013). *Adult and youth literacy: National, regional and global trends, 1985–2015*. Montreal, Quebec: Author.

Walker, S. C., Trupin, E., & Hansen, J. (2011). *A toolkit for applying the cultural enhancement model to evidence-based practice*. Retrieved from http://depts.washington.edu/pbhjp/ downloads/projectsD/models_for_changeD/Toolkit%20Cultural%20Enhancement%20Model.pdf

Youssef, F. F., Bachew, R., Bodie, D., Leach, R., Morris, K., & Sherma, G. (2014, February). Knowledge and attitudes towards mental illness among college students: Insights into the wider English-speaking Caribbean population. *International Journal of Social Psychiatry, 60*(1), 47–54. doi:10.1177/0020764012461236

Validating the Borderlands: Group Work with Queer Latinas

Jayleen Galarza

This paper is inspired by my research study focused on exploring the intersections of queer Latina experiences and identities. From the research interview process, there emerged a call for visibility and understanding with implications and valuable insights for group work practitioners. In addition, my experience of sharing my research findings to a group of queer Latinas at an event called La Palabra further cemented the value of group work in providing emotional support as these women explore and navigate the intricate intersections of gender, ethnic, and sexual identities. Given the theme of the International Association of Social Work With Groups (IASWG) XXXVI Symposium, Unity in Diversity, this paper seeks to highlight not only the significance of group work with queer Latinas but also best practices in approaching such work.

The expanding presence of Latina(o) individuals within the United States presents social work practitioners with a distinct challenge in determining best practices within educational and therapeutic services (Comas-Diaz, 2006; Cruz, 2001). As Latina women begin to make a place for themselves within the United States, their sexuality is also impacted by the dominant culture (Comas-Diaz, 2008), and this influence of the dominant culture on evolving identities is especially evident in the lives of queer Latinas. This continual process of cultural influence impacts how these women experience and label their sexuality. They navigate multiple identities as sexual and ethnic minorities within a dominant heterosexual society (Acosta, 2008, 2011; Ascencio, 2009). For queer Latinas, navigating multiple identities is often marked by experiences of (in)visibility (Acosta, 2008) and isolation with limited opportunities to connect with other individuals of similar life experiences. The journeys and stories emerging within these communities also indicate strength and resistance to the challenges being faced within their daily lives.

According to the IASWG (2010) Standards for Social Work Practice With Groups, a core understanding that is essential for group workers practicing under the parameters of developing a "socially just society" (p. 4) is the workers' "appreciation and understanding of such differences as those due to culture, ethnicity, gender, age, physical and mental abilities and sexual orientation among members that may influence practice" (p. 4). Such professional obligations and importance of comprehending as well as valuing diversity among group members' experiences warrants understanding of cultural identities, experiences that are often marginalized within society. Therefore, it is essential for social workers developing groups to fully understand the unique needs and strengths of the queer Latina community. In addition to providing a review of the relevant literature of queer Latina experiences and group work with Latina(o)s, I highlight a subset of data from my larger research study, which provides further rationale for conducting group work with this community. I also reflect on my experience with informally facilitating a community group in discussing some of these findings. And, lastly, I offer recommendations for group work practitioners based on this research and my review of the literature.

Queer Latina Experience

Anzaldua (1999) stated, "Most of us unconsciously believe that if we reveal this unacceptable aspect of the self our mother/culture/race will totally reject us. To avoid rejection, some of us conform to the values of the culture, push the unacceptable parts into the shadows" (p. 42). Anzaldua's words reflect the difficulties of revealing and navigating multiple identities as queer Latinas existing in the borderlands. For these women, the borderlands serve as both physical and symbolic space. According to Anzaldua, "A borderland is a vague and undetermined place created by the emotional residue of an unnatural boundary. It is in a constant state of transition. The prohibited and forbidden are its inhabitants" (1999, p. 25). These inhabitants include Latina(o) sexual minorities, but Anzaldua specifically focused her writing on the experiences of Latina sexual minority women, who encounter a unique challenge in explaining their Latina culture within both the dominant culture of the United States and within lesbian, gay, bisexual, transgender, and queer (LGBTQ) spaces. There is also a parallel process of confronting the sexism and homophobia present in Latina(o) communities. Anzaldua emphasized that despite the experiences of multiple oppressions, borderlands are spaces of resistance, activism, and change. Occupying this borderland space offers an opportunity to embody an identity that empowers the individual to challenge the traditional scripts of culture and society.

Espin's (1997) qualitative study on lesbian identified Cuban women is one of the few studies focused on exploring the intersecting identities of Latina women who have sex with women (WSW); her results highlighted the struggle participants experienced with coming out to their families and communities, which includes the potential loss of connection due to oppressive structures of racism, sexism, and heterosexism. As Anzaldua (1999) emphasized, "For the lesbian of color, the ultimate rebellion she can make against her native culture is through her sexual behavior. She goes against two moral prohibitions: sexuality and homosexuality" (p. 41). Most notable is the act of publicly disclosing this identity, otherwise known as coming out, that confronts family and community expectations and presents an opportunity for family members to condemn, dismiss, or acknowledge women's sexuality (Greene, 1994).

Greene (1994) further explored these ideas and the impact of indirect communication within Latina(o) communities on relationship dynamics. Greene asserted that such methods of navigating identities was used as a means of saving face and retaining respect within the culture. Therefore, as Greene wrote, "To label oneself gay or lesbian implies not only consciously participating in behavior that is condemned but actively confronting others with your choice to do so, thus violating the injunction to be indirect" (1994, p. 244). There is an emphasis on silencing women's expression of both sexuality and sexual minority identity, which is a determined effort by the family and individual woman to maintain good standing within their culture. This is significant as the literature indicates that Latina(o) cultures stress a collectivist identity and heterosexuality is a valued component of this identity (Anzaldua, 1999; Comas-Diaz, 2006; Espin, 1997).

Within research focused on Latina WSW experiences, participants often distinguish silence and invisibility as significant markers of their experience (Acosta, 2011; Alimahomed, 2010; Ascencio, 2009; Espin, 1997). Espin's (1997) study revealed that Latina(o) communities often contend with lesbian family members through "silent tolerance" (p. 101). According to Espin, lesbian women are not always overtly rejected; the lack of acknowledgement of their sexuality is often explained to other family members or acquaintances as "the woman hasn't found the right man" or "she is not interested at this stage of her life," which encourages a double life.

Although there is negativity associated with silence in the family system, Acosta's (2011) research on the language of (in)visibility revealed that participants discovered power in both implicit and explicit disclosures of their sexual identity. Acosta (2011) elaborated on the role of visibility among Latina sexual minorities:

> It is both empowering and disempowering because there are risks that come with being visible. Being visible leaves one susceptible to negativity, rejection, and potential violence. In light of these risks, it becomes important to understand the choices made about when and where to be visible and the relationship between choices and silence. (p. 886)

Leading a double life or nondisclosure of sexual identity may represent a way to manage multiple identities within family and community. Acosta (2011) noted participants found a particular strength in their invisibility as they were in control of the logistics around disclosing their sexual identity, and the silence surrounding their sexual identity aided them in navigating the intricacies of family relationships.

Additionally, Acosta's (2008) research focused on individuals' attempts at visibility while navigating multiple communities. Her study touched on Latina lesbians' feelings of otherness within LGBTQ organizations and social spaces due to their ethnic identification. Ascencio's (2009) study also confirmed sexual minority Latinas' experiences of isolation from LGBT communities. Ascencio's participants found that connecting with the nuances of Latina(o) culture, such as language and religion, was a valuable component of being immersed in primarily Latina(o) spaces and was often absent within LGBTQ social contexts.

Research

Given the cultural nuances of queer Latina experience, I embarked on a research study dedicated to further exploring the multiple meanings and experiences associated with navigating ethnic, gender, and sexual identities. I conducted a qualitative, phenomenological study in which I recruited and interviewed 15 self-identified Latina women, who had previously been involved in or were currently in a relationship with another woman. The participants were recruited within 1.5 hours of the Philadelphia area. A phenomenological approach was used in order to better comprehend the essence of this phenomenon attached to experiences of multiple identities among these women. These semistructured interviews yielded several themes that provided further insight into the experiences of navigating identities as queer Latinas; however, within this paper and in order to emphasize the value of intentionally creating space for queer Latinas to gather, I highlight two specific themes that emerged from the data: navigating multiple communities and finding an authentic self. Within these discussions, participants stressed desires for community and visibility.

Navigating Multiple Communities

Within the theme of navigating multiple communities, participants spoke of both managing their identities as well as the importance of and challenges associated with being visible. In managing identities, individuals reflected on the decisions they made as they encountered different social groups and spaces. Within this subtheme, individuals highlighted several strategies that were used, such as shifting sexual identity labels, being open, reading the space that you're in, and compartmentalizing lives. Many of the participants who discussed shifting sexual identity labels did this in order to facilitate simpler communication with different communities and avoid any misunderstandings or misgivings associated with any particular identity label. As individuals spoke of strategies for maintaining and negotiating relationships within various settings, there also emerged a discussion related to their desires and attempts at visibility within both Latina(o) and LGBTQ spaces. For many of the participants, there was recognition that visibility was an issue for their involvement in these settings. In addition, individuals articulated desires to "claim a space" in which all of their identities could be validated.

Furthermore, all of the participants talked of attempts at and struggles with finding and expressing their true selves. Throughout their discussions of navigating family, multiple communities, religion, and politics, there was a common thread of finding authenticity. Participants elaborated on this theme in different ways. For some individuals, there was a need and desire to be read as Latina, which was often associated with feelings of not being quite enough Latina and complicated by histories of assimilation. In an email discussion about the findings that emerged from this study, Renee wanted to emphasize, "The way in which the legitimacy of one's Latina(o) identity can be questioned, especially within queer communities." For other participants, finding authenticity had less to do with being read as Latina but more related to their search for validation of their Latinidad within queer spaces and desires to connect with others experiencing similar journeys.

Group Work With Latina(o)s

The voices of these participants, as well as the existing research on queer Latina experiences, indicated usefulness in finding a place, both emotional and physical, for queer Latinas to gather and share their stories in order to gain support and understanding. However, the group work research focused on this specific population is scarce. Although the literature concentrated on organizing, developing, or leading groups with Latina(o)s is limited (Comas-Diaz, 1981; Torres-Rivera, Wilbur, Roberts-Wilbur, & Phan, 1999), especially with queer Latina(o)s (Torres, 2014), overall there is indication of an increased interest in exploring best practices in facilitating groups with women of color (Short & Williams, 2014).

Short and Williams (2014) focused on the effectiveness of group work in addressing the intersections of identities and life experiences of women of color, specifically the value of group work in assisting women of color to process internalized messages related to gender, race, and ethnic identities. The authors explored two specific group models: the SisterCircle approach and the group relations model. The SisterCircle approach is described as focusing on the internalization of "unhealthy" (Short & Williams, 2014, p. 77) identity formation and the impact of external sociocultural discourses on this process. One of the key aspects of this practice model is the development of mindfulness in order for participants to gain further understanding of themselves while applying this knowledge to improving their relationships. In implementing the SisterCircle approach, Short and

Williams elaborated that this model operates from an "integrative theoretical framework" (2014, p. 77), which includes tenets from liberation psychology and systems theory. These theories emphasize the interconnectedness of identity development and social, political, and economic influences. Ultimately, the SisterCircle model emphasizes the goal of assisting participants in internalizing healthier visions of themselves while also strengthening interpersonal relationships. Integral to implementing this approach is the group worker's use of self within the group process, which centers on her or his ability to openly discuss systems of oppression, especially emphasizing the intersections of these experiences and creating space for group members to also engage in this dialogue. Furthermore, Short and Williams stated, "The use of homework assignments and experiential exercises, which encourage members to give voice to their conceptualization of identity, can facilitate this process" (2014, p. 83).

The group relations model attends to the group process, especially dynamics among participants and the development of group. An essential part of applying this group model is assessing, exploring, and addressing dynamics that may potentially obstruct the group's "optimal functioning" (Short & Williams, 2014, p. 84). According to Short and Williams (2014), "The Group Relations Model creates a context in which the group worker can assist members to identify and challenge projections by owning, disowning and or correcting them, which can illuminate unconscious basic assumption functioning and enhance group movement, developmentally" (p. 86). The authors have proposed that the roles enacted by various group members could be linked to conceptions of self that have been adopted as a result of different encounters with oppression, discrimination, and assimilation. Defense mechanisms that may be displayed within group interactions, such as projection or splitting, are rooted in these experiences. Therefore, in applying this model, it is the group workers' primary function to recognize, interpret, and work through these dynamics. Short and Williams proposed the integration of the SisterCircle approach and group relations model to focus on both the internal aspects of identity as well as the external group processes, which emphasize the usefulness of group work in helping women of color confront and tackle the internalized messages about identities they have come to believe and accept.

In reviewing the limited research on conducting groups specifically with Latinas, there were clear links between group practice and the value of cultural attunement in successful treatment outcomes (Comas-

Diaz, 1981; Torres-Rivera et al., 1999). Comas-Diaz (1981) found that cognitive behavioral groups were successful in reducing depression among Puerto Rican women. Such results may be attributed to cultural values that are reflected within the group process, such as the concept of extended families and contextual culture. Additionally, in Comas-Diaz's (1987) work on feminist therapy with Puerto Rican women, she further highlighted the importance within the therapeutic process in recognizing the influence of sociocultural factors on the lives of Puerto Rican women. Feminist therapy emphasizes the importance of gender consciousness-raising, especially within group contexts. However, developing any clinical relationship (individual, family, and group) warrants cultural considerations. As Comas-Diaz (1987) stated, "As an interactive process, feminist therapy allows for the accommodation of the ethno-sociocultural world and inner reality, and their consequent impact on the etiology, presentation, expectations, and approach to the treatment of ethnic minority group members" (p. 469).

Torres-Rivera et al. (1999) have presented a psychoeducational model for group work with Latinas. They maintained the importance of acknowledging the possible effects of Latinas' experiences of dual culture and how acculturation within the United States often produces dissonance. As Torres-Rivera et al. stated, "Latinos not only experience dissonance among their beliefs and behaviors but they also question who they are and how and why they do things and behave in ways that are contrary to their own cultural values and beliefs" (1999, pp. 392–393). By facilitating a psychoeducational group for Latinas, participants are able to make sense of their beliefs and experiences in order to organize any "dissonant beliefs into a more congruent belief system" (Torres-Rivera et al., 1999, p. 393). Given the findings on queer Latina identities and experiences previously discussed, there is evidence that queer Latinas may resonate with such dissonance as they navigate borderland experiences. Existing within borderland space often means having to negotiate the norms and expectations of two or more cultures; as one participant described it, "the push–pull."

Although not always discussed within academia, research, or practice, there is a history of queer Latinas organizing and creating group space (Acosta, 2010; Tijerina-Revilla, 2009; Torres, 2014). Torres (2014) focused specifically on two influential groups organized by lesbian Latinas within the Midwest, Latina Lesbians en Nuestra Ambiente (LLENA) and Amigas Latinas. In undertaking this project, Torres hoped to contribute to the visibility of queer Latinas in the histories of LGBTQ movements as well as focus on Latina lesbians as "agents of change" (2014, p. 42). This work acknowledged the efforts of queer Latinas in providing spaces where the unique needs and culture of Latina lesbians could emerge and be seen. As Tijerina-Revilla (2009) discovered in her work exploring the experiences of sexual identity among members of a queer Latina student organization, "Raza Womyn not only engaged in activism and consciousness-raising about multiple, interlocking identities, but it also pushed members to reconstruct their sense of self and identity" (p. 59). Such a distinction is powerful, as rarely are queer Latinas afforded meaningful opportunities to gather and connect either in predominantly LGBTQ or Latina(o) communities (Tijerina-Revilla, 2009).

La Palabra:
Example of Latina Group Work Experience

With the emerging interest in exploring group work with women of color and an existing gap within the literature on group work with queer Latinas, it is imperative for group workers to understand the implications for practice as well as the impact of such work. In order to illustrate the value of intentional group space for queer Latinas to meet and relate, I share my experience leading and facilitating a discussion with other queer Latinas at an event called La Palabra (The Word), which was hosted by the Gay and Lesbian Latina(o) AIDS Education Initiative (GALAEI) in Philadelphia, PA. La Palabra was designed to create intentional space for queer Latina(o)s to gather, connect, and share stories. GALAEI advertised within various communities in Philadelphia but paid particular attention to geographical areas most populated and concentrated by Latina(o)s in order to provide access to an experience not so readily available in these sections of the city. The event itself occurred in one of these locations of North Philadelphia. With the exception of directions posted on the front door, indicating where the event was taking place, the building did not contain many identifiable markers, which is important in maintaining safety for those individuals who did not wish to outwardly express their identities.

The meeting space evoked a comfortable, living room quality with sofas and worn chairs arranged in a circle. GALAEI provided refreshments, and as individuals from the community gathered, they were welcomed and asked to join the group. Approximately 20 people were in attendance. Once the community had gathered, I was introduced by the executive director of GALAEI, herself a queer Latina, and asked to initiate the conversation. This experience was not a typical research presentation; rather, it was a community discussion. I discussed the purpose of my work as well as the results of the study; however, most important, I shared the words and stories of the participants. This is what generated the most reaction and conversation. One after another, individuals in this circle revealed personal accounts that related with the themes generated by the study. There were no restrictions placed on this exchange, and participants were encouraged to freely express their thoughts and feelings. From this space, personal narratives emerged. For many, there were calls for action—to create more spaces where these intersections of identities could thrive. Most important, what surfaced from these conversations were not only indications of some participants' experiences of isolation and invisibility but also stories of strength and resistance.

Implications for Group Work

What I gained from my experience of interviewing other queer Latinas, as well as facilitating the informal group at La Palabra, was the profound impact not only in validating my own experiences but also in acquiring a better understanding of the needs of this community. One of the most significant concerns that was expressed within the interviews was a desire for "home space." Group work professionals can help individuals find home space by deliberately creating opportunities for individuals to be visible and united. Such spaces can help provide validation and support to group members, as well as opportunities to discuss any divisive experiences of identities they may be experiencing. The significance of applying a mutual aid model to this work is in ensuring the safety of participants as they express their individual stories while connecting with others, resulting in the development of universality (Steinberg, 2014). However, in forming group space for queer Latinas, there are various recommendations that must be integrated into the group development process. Some of the most significant considerations in developing and facilitating group with queer Latinas primarily concern the pregroup phase (IASWG, 2010), specifically planning, recruitment, and group facilitator demographics.

Planning and Recruitment

Pregroup planning is one of the most crucial aspects of developing a mutual aid group (Steinberg, 2014). In order to establish a strong foundation for successful group work, systemic factors such as location and setting must be considered (Steinberg, 2014). As such, essential to group planning with this population is understanding that the process must be community driven. As Torres-Rivera et al. (1999) stated in their implications for group workers, "Socio-process groups for Latinos in need of such groups should be made available to members of the Latino community through their own community organizations and meeting places" (p. 390). Therefore, when exploring locations to host these gatherings, group workers should explore spaces that are readily accessible by the community. Group workers also must be vigilant of the various community dynamics at play, such as any hostile incidents that may have occurred within that particular area. Although not necessarily inherent in the planning process of La Palabra, the group space provided anonymity to participants but was also centrally located in the heart of the Philadelphia Latina(o) community. By establishing such anonymity via the group's location, individuals were able to relax into a more open dialogue about identities and experiences without the restrictions and limitations at times felt in either primarily White, LGBTQ, or Latina(o) spaces.

Group Facilitator Demographics

Additionally, facilitator identity and demographics, including level of and capacity for appropriate cultural attunement, are important to consider in the development of group. They may impact potential group dynamics as well as the success of the group experience for participants. As several authors have noted, the group worker's use of self is essential to the process of conducting groups with women of color (Comas-Diaz, 1981; Short & Williams, 2014). Many of the participants who participated in my own research study expressed how validating it was to speak with me, as I also identified as a queer Latina. The success of La Palabra hinged on the fact that it was hosted and led by community members, individuals who could relate with this cultural experience. As Comas-Diaz (1981) indicated, group therapeutic results may be improved if the group practitioner is of the same ethnic and/ or cultural background.

In working with women of color, it is important to be mindful of power dynamics that may affect relationships between participants and the group worker (Gutierrez, 1990). For example, Gutierrez (1990) discussed the significance of teaching skills in the process of empowering women of color, which is a potential aspect of a group experience, and stated, "When teaching these skills the worker should adopt the role of a consultant or facilitator rather than an instructor, so as not to replicate the power relationships that the worker and client are attempting to overcome" (p. 152). For the Latina(o) community, there is a significant history of colonization and marginalization that impacts experiences within and outside of the community (Anzaldua, 1999). For many Latina(o)s, emphasis is placed on trusting and relying on the cultural community for support. As such, it is imperative that group workers acknowledge this history and the potential impact on the experiences of group members.

Describing the best practices for implementing a SisterCircle model of group practice with women of color, Short and Williams (2014) stated,

> Best practices would include the group worker making the implicit explicit through open discussion about systems of race/ethnicity and gender and underscores the significance of the group worker's knowledge, awareness, and skills to effectively implement identity work in groups with women of color. The group worker's interventions can raise members' consciousness by: (a) Establishing his/her trustworthiness for the work, (b) Providing models of integrative articulation of identity concepts, and, (c) Providing a platform by which members may begin to own their identity experiences within the group. (p. 81)

In order to achieve this work, the group would benefit from having a facilitator who is either personally connected with this community and culture or is knowledgeable of cultural nuances. As such, the worker must guide the group discussion toward acknowledging these challenges, including experiences of oppression and discrimination, as well as resilience.

Conclusion

In this paper I aimed to provide group work professionals with insight into the distinct experiences of queer Latinas navigating ethnic, sexual, and gender identities, as well as explore implications for practice. With the developing discourse on intersectionality and the impact on social identities, there is also need for spaces where individuals can exchange life stories and receive support. For group work practitioners, this process entails being mindful of cultural nuances and acknowledging experiences of oppression and resiliency within this community. As individuals access these groups or "home spaces," individuals can shape new meanings, and these narratives can emerge and be validated.

References

Acosta, K. L. (2008). Lesbianas in the borderlands: Shifting identities and imagined communities. *Gender & Society, 22*, 639–659. doi:10.1177/0891243208321169

Acosta, K. L. (2010). Boundaries, identities and layers of belonging in one Latina lesbian social group. *Conference Papers—American Sociological Association, 231.* Retrieved from SocINDEX database.

Acosta, K. L. (2011). The language of (in)visibility: Using in-between spaces as a vehicle for empowerment in the family. *Journal of Homosexuality, 58*(6/7), 883–900. doi:10.1080 /00918369.2011.581932

Alimahomed, S. (2010). Thinking outside the rainbow: Women of color redefining queer politics and identity. *Social Identities, 16*(2), 151–168. doi:10.1080/13504631003688849

Anzaldua, G. (1999). *Borderlands: La frontera, the new mestiza.* San Francisco, CA: Aunt Lute Books.

Ascencio, M. (2009). Migrant Puerto Rican lesbians negotiating gender, sexuality, and ethnonationality. *NWSA Journal, 21*(3), 1–23. Retrieved from Ebscohost database.

Comas-Diaz, L. (1981). Effects of cognitive and behavioral group treatment on the depressive symptomatology of Puerto Rican women. *Journal of Consulting and Clinical Psychology, 49*(5), 627–632.

Comas-Diaz, L. (1987). Feminist therapy with mainland Puerto Rican women.

Psychology of Women Quarterly, 11, 461–474.

Comas-Diaz, L. (2006). Latino healing: The integration of ethnic psychology into psychotherapy. *Psycotherapy: Theory, Research, Practice, Training, 43*(4), 436–453. doi:10.1037/0033-3204.43.4.436

Comas-Diaz, L. (2008). Our inner Black Madonna: Reclaiming sexuality, embodying sacredness. *Women & Therapy, 3*(1), 5–20. doi:10.1080/02703140802145094

Cruz, C. (2001). Toward an epistemology of a brown body. *Qualitative Studies in Education, 14*(5), 657–669. doi:10.1080/09518390110059874

Espin, O. M. (1997). *Latina realities: Essays on healing, migration, and sexuality.* Boulder, CO: Westview Press.

Greene, B. (1994). Ethnic-minority lesbians and gay men: Mental health and treatment issues. *Journal of Consulting and Clinical Psychology, 62*(2), 243–251.

Gutierrez, L. (1990). Working with women of color: An empowerment perspective. *Social Work, 35*(2), 149–153.

International Association of Social Work With Groups. (2010). *Standards for social work practice with groups.* Retrieved from http://iaswg.org/docs / AASWG_Standards_for_Social_Work_Practice_with_Groups2010.pdf

Short, E. L., & Williams, W. S. (2014). From the inside out: Group work with women of color. *The Journal for Specialists in Group Work, 39*(1), 71–91. doi:10.1080/01933922.2013 .859191

Steinberg, D. (2014). *A mutual-aid model for social work with groups* (3rd ed.). New York, NY: Routledge Press.

Tijerina-Revilla, A. (2009). Are all Raza womyn queer? An exploration of sexual identity in a Chicana/Latina student organization. *NWSA Journal, 21*(3), 46–62. Retrieved from Ebscohost database.

Torres, L. (2014). Companeras in the middle: Toward a history of Latina lesbian organizing in Chicago. *GLQ: A Journal of Lesbian and Gay Studies, 20*(1-2), 41–74. doi:10.1215 /10642684-2370360

Torres-Rivera, E., Wilbur, M. P., Roberts-Wilbur, J., & Phan, L. (1999). Group work with Latino clients: A psychoeducational model. *The Journal for Specialists in Group Work, 24*(4), 383–404. doi:10.1080/01933929908411445.

La supervision combinée comme soutien à l'apprentissage du travail social de groupe d'étudiants à la maîtrise en travail social

Ginette Berteau, Sylvie Cameron, et Étienne Guay

Cette communication décrit une expérience de supervision combinée auprès de huit étudiantes de maîtrise en travail social de l'Université du Québec à Montréal (UQÀM) dont le stage avait comme objet le travail de groupe. Dans un premier temps, les aspects théoriques de la supervision combinée seront explorés. Puis, l'expérience de supervision sera décrite. Une analyse critique de celle-ci suivra. L'article se termine par des recommandations.

À l'École de travail social de l'UQÀM, tout comme ailleurs, la supervision individuelle ou dyadique auprès de stagiaires ou d'intervenants sociaux demeure, de façon générale, la modalité privilégiée en travail social. Kadushin et Harkness (2002) expliquent ce phénomène par le fait que la supervision dyadique ou individuelle se rapproche le plus du travail d'intervention habituel, notamment chez les travailleurs sociaux. Nous définissons la supervision individuelle ou dyadique comme étant une forme de supervision qui se réalise en dyade pendant laquelle un superviseur offre, sur une base individuelle, l'encadrement pédagogique d'un étudiant. Ce mode de supervision comporte sans aucun doute ses bienfaits. À cet effet, il permet au supervisé de bénéficier d'une attention individualisée aux difficultés qu'il rencontre en intervention. Toutefois, pour la formation des stagiaires au travail social de groupe, d'autres modalités de supervision sont à considérer, notamment la supervision de groupe. De l'avis des formateurs en travail social de groupe, cette modalité de supervision est essentielle pour l'apprentissage chez les stagiaires en travail social de groupe. Elle permet aux stagiaires d'apprendre par l'expérience, de vivre à la fois le processus d'intervention en travail social de groupe et le processus de groupe. Cette modalité de supervision doit intégrer, dans sa mise en œuvre, les principes d'intervention du travail social de groupe.

C'est en ce sens qu'une première expérimentation de supervision combinée auprès de huit étudiantes de maîtrise ayant choisi d'orienter leur stage en travail social de groupe a été mise en place en 2012. Dès le départ, les initiateurs du projet avaient pour intention de créer un contexte d'apprentissage visant le transfert de notions théoriques du travail social de groupe et l'expérimentation d'un processus de groupe. À la fin de cette expérimentation, un bilan oral et écrit ont été réalisés avec les étudiantes, les superviseurs et les directeurs du stage/essai. Ce bilan a permis de dégager certains constats quant aux possibilités d'apprentissage et à leur transfert dans les projets d'intervention de groupe réalisés en stage. Par conséquent, cet article décrit les différentes étapes de la réalisation de cette expérience, fait état de l'appréciation des principaux acteurs y ayant joué un rôle, identifie les retombées observées sur le plan professionnel chez les stagiaires et se termine par des recommandations.

Recension des écrits

D'entrée de jeu, précisons que la supervision combinée est l'utilisation simultanée de la supervision individuelle et de groupe. Cette association de deux modes de supervision permet de profiter des forces réciproques et de partager la responsabilité de l'encadrement des étudiants (Walter & Young, 1999). Malheureusement, la supervision combinée est jusqu'à maintenant peu traitée dans la littérature. Par conséquent, pour pouvoir identifier les forces et les limites de cette modalité de supervision, il faut s'attarder aux particularités, avantages et inconvénients de chacune de ses composantes : la supervision individuelle et la supervision de groupe.

L'une des grandes forces de la supervision individuelle ou dyadique auprès de stagiaires est la possibilité pour l'étudiant d'avoir des moments personnalisés avec son superviseur et de développer avec ce dernier, une relation privilégiée (Boutin & Camaraire, 2001; Gagnier & Bigras, 2000). La confiance ainsi établie favorise une rétroaction régulière, consistante (Ray & Altekruse, 2000) et prédispose l'étudiant à exposer plus facilement ses forces, limites et vulnérabilités (Sussman, Bogo, & Globerman, 2007). Ceci permet d'ajuster de façon continuelle les objectifs d'apprentissage en lien avec le rythme de l'étudiant et le contexte d'intervention. Il est donc possible d'avoir un meilleur contrôle du processus d'apprentissage (Walter & Young, 1999) facilitant ainsi le parcours de l'étudiant. La supervision individuelle est aussi reconnue pour favoriser le développement d'habiletés cliniques. Par contre, deux désavantages sont souvent mentionnés dans la littérature : un risque de rendre l'étudiant dépendant du superviseur et une exposition limitée à une variété d'idées, d'opinions, de cultures et de façons de voir et d'être.

Pour sa part, la supervision de groupe est définie comme:

> Un processus continu d'échanges qui se réalisent à travers l'analyse des pratiques professionnelles. Les objectifs, les expériences, les ressources des supervisés et du superviseur ainsi que le processus de groupe sont mis à contribution dans le but d'offrir des services de qualité et de répondre aux besoins de développement des compétences de cette communauté apprenante. (Berteau & Villeneuve, 2005, p. 2)

Longtemps, cette modalité de supervision a été perçue comme un complément ou une variante à la supervision dyadique (Bernard & Goodyear, 1992; Glickauf-Hughes & Campbell, 1991). La supervision de groupe reste encore une modalité plutôt méconnue, peu exploitée, souvent utilisée de façon improvisée sans référence à des appuis théoriques (Bogo, Globerman, & Sussman, 2004; Glickauf-Hughes & Campbell, 1991; Holloway & Johnston, 1985; Prieto, 1996).

Paradoxalement, la pertinence de la supervision de groupe est largement reconnue (Arvidsson, Lofgren, & Fridund, 2001; Gagnier & Bigras, 2000; T. Lindsay, 2005; Sussman et al., 2007). À titre d'exemple, une recension des écrits sur l'utilisation de la supervision dans la formation des infirmières, arrive à la conclusion que la supervision de groupe est aussi efficace que la supervision individuelle (Kangasniemi, Ahonen, Liikanen, & Utriainen, 2011).

La plupart des auteurs s'entendent pour dire qu'un groupe de supervision s'apparente à un milieu naturel d'apprentissage par les pairs. Ainsi, par l'intermédiaire du groupe, ce cadre de supervision permet au stagiaire de développer ses compétences, de réfléchir sur ses actions, d'améliorer sa conscience de soi, sa sécurité personnelle et son fonctionnement interpersonnel. Participer à un groupe de supervision aide à consolider l'identité professionnelle, à augmenter le sentiment de solidarité professionnelle puis à donner de meilleurs services à la clientèle. Confronter sa vision à celle de ses pairs permet aux membres de développer des visions communes et d'implanter des nouvelles façons de faire. La supervision de groupe permet aussi d'atténuer le risque de dépendance au superviseur.

Les avantages sont multiples sur le plan de l'apprentissage du travail de groupe. En vivant le groupe, l'étudiant intègre divers aspects de la dynamique d'un groupe, développant ainsi son sens du groupe et par conséquent l'amène à mieux saisir les valeurs et les habiletés de la pratique de groupe. D'ailleurs, vivre une expérience de groupe comme membre serait un élément incontournable pour la formation au travail de groupe (Dennison, 2005). Du côté du travail social de groupe, la participation d'un stagiaire à la supervision de groupe peut aider à la consolidation de ses apprentissages académiques en l'amenant à vivre, comme membre, toutes les étapes d'une intervention de groupe.

L'ensemble des bénéfices précédents contribue souvent à pallier au manque fréquent de formation en travail social de groupe chez les étudiants (Grossman-Leeman, 2013; Lindsay, Roy, Turcotte, et Labarre, 2010). D'ailleurs, cette lacune sur le plan de la formation au travail social de groupe est également présente chez les superviseurs de stage. On observe donc des difficultés à accompagner adéquatement les stagiaires dans l'expérimentation du travail social de groupe (Knight, 2000).

La réussite d'une supervision de groupe comporte un certain nombre d'exigences. La littérature note entre autres que la supervision de groupe avec des étudiants nécessite une homogénéité des besoins sur le plan de l'apprentissage. De plus, les étudiants peuvent facilement se sentir incompétents dans une supervision de groupe amenant plusieurs auteurs à dire que la supervision de groupe, par le haut degré d'exposition de soi, peut exacerber l'anxiété.

Sur le plan des désavantages, cette modalité n'est pas à l'abri d'une dynamique de groupe malsaine, de la présence de la rivalité et de la compétition entre les membres et de la critique à outrance. Certaines difficultés sont repérées sur le plan de la facilitation de la supervision de groupe. Ainsi, il est parfois difficile d'équilibrer les besoins émergeants versus l'agenda prévu, et les besoins personnels versus ceux du groupe. Enfin, on note que trop souvent les supervisions de groupe sont consacrées aux fonctions administratives et éducatives de la supervision au détriment de la fonction de soutien.

Quelques caractéristiques de la supervision combinée

Plusieurs recherches notent la nécessité d'offrir de la supervision individuelle. Spontanément, les étudiants préfèrent la supervision individuelle (Ray & Altekruse, 2000) puisque celle-ci leur permet un accompagnement où ils pourront traiter plus en profondeur de leurs besoins d'apprentissage et de leurs enjeux professionnels. S'ils ne participent qu'à une supervision de groupe, ils se montrent insatisfaits (Walter & Young, 1999). La supervision combinée permet à la fois de satisfaire leurs besoins personnels et de profiter de la richesse d'un apprentissage fait en groupe. Par contre, la combinaison des deux modalités s'avère complexe, surtout du côté de la mise en application. Pour faire de l'expérience, un succès, cela nécessite de bonnes connaissances en supervision individuelle et de groupe (Sussman et al., 2007). Par ailleurs, ces mêmes auteurs notent la difficulté pour les étudiants de traiter des malaises vécus dans l'un ou l'autre des modes de supervision lors de l'utilisation de la supervision combinée.

Contexte à l'origine du projet de supervision combinée

Précisons que la structure du programme de maîtrise en travail social à l'École de travail social de l'UQÀM ne permet pas toujours aux étudiants de suivre le cours en travail social de groupe. Or, depuis quelques années, on observe chez les étudiantes de ce programme de formation, un intérêt marqué pour le travail social de groupe. Au cours de l'année 2012–2013, 50% des projets d'intervention développés par les étudiantes de ce programme étaient orientés en ce sens. Pour ces deux raisons, la professeure en travail social de groupe et la responsable de la formation pratique ont initié une expérience de supervision combinée avec un groupe de huit étudiantes ayant choisi l'option stage dans le cadre du programme de maîtrise en travail social.

Pour ce groupe de stagiaires, la supervision combinée représentait un contexte d'apprentissage incontournable : d'une part pour ses effets bénéfiques sur les apprentissages (tels que présentés dans la littérature qui y est consacrée); d'autre part, parce que ces étudiantes n'avaient pu suivre de cours sur le travail social de groupe. Certaines d'entre elles, avaient cependant un peu d'expérience pratique en intervention de groupe alors que d'autres n'en avaient aucune.

Structure du projet de supervision combinée

L'expérience s'est donc déroulée comme suit : 27 heures ont été consacrées à la supervision de groupe (neuf séances de trois heures de supervision de groupe) en alternance avec 40 heures de supervision individuelle (20 séances de deux heures). Chaque étudiante bénéficiait d'une supervision individuelle orientée vers le développement de besoins d'apprentissage spécifiques, pour chaque projet d'intervention de groupe implanté dans le milieu de stage.

Les huit étudiantes ayant participé au projet de supervision combinée ont été intégrées à deux groupes formés de quatre étudiantes et de deux superviseurs maitrisant le travail social de groupe. Le mandat initial des superviseurs de groupe était de transmettre des notions théoriques, de faire vivre une expérience d'aide mutuelle et de favoriser l'apprentissage du groupe par le groupe.

Précisons que quatre des huit étudiantes étaient encadrées individuellement par les superviseures responsables de la supervision de groupe alors qu'un second superviseur a été attitré aux autres étudiantes pour l'encadrement individuel. Ces dernières ont donc travaillé avec des superviseures différentes : une superviseure dans le cadre de l'encadrement individuel (durée de 40 heures) et les deux co-facilitateurs de la supervision de groupe (durée de 27 heures).

Application du processus d'intervention de groupe dans le cadre de la supervision combinée

L'objectif de ce projet visait à offrir un contexte d'apprentissage alliant à la fois le transfert de notions théoriques et une expérience pratique basée sur les principes d'intervention du travail social de groupe. Les initiateurs ont respecté les différentes étapes du processus d'intervention. Plusieurs moyens ont été déployés pour s'assurer du bon fonctionnement de ce projet. La section qui suit présentera les démarches réalisées à chacune des phases du processus d'intervention de groupe, mais adaptées à un contexte de supervision combinée.

Phase pré-groupe

Il est largement reconnu en travail social de groupe que la phase pré-groupe constitue une étape essentielle pour le succès du groupe. En ce sens, voici les démarches réalisées lors de cette phase auprès des acteurs ayant eu un rôle à jouer dans ce projet de supervision combinée.

Auprès des superviseurs. La première tâche a été d'identifier des superviseurs selon les critères suivants : posséder une formation en travail social (maîtrise ou baccalauréat avec dix années d'expérience en intervention), une expérience en supervision, être en mesure de faire des liens théorie-pratique et avoir une solide expérience en travail social de groupe, en particulier pour les facilitateurs de la supervision de groupe. Nous avons communiqué avec chaque superviseur potentiel afin de vérifier leur ouverture et intérêt à vivre cette expérience pilote. Pour s'assurer de la cohérence entre la supervision individuelle et la supervision de groupe, une rencontre a été proposée à tous les superviseurs afin de (a) clarifier les raisons à l'origine de ce projet de supervision; (b) préciser les objectifs pédagogiques; (c) traiter de la répartition des rôles, des responsabilités et des tâches entre la supervision individuelle et la supervision de groupe; et (d) vérifier la perception des superviseurs face au projet proposé. Ces démarches semblaient essentielles auprès de l'ensemble des superviseurs et davantage, auprès des quatre superviseurs qui devaient partager leur rôle avec les co-facilitateurs assumant la supervision de groupe.

Auprès des directrices du stage/essai. Les professeurs ayant un rôle de direction d'études auprès des stagiaires ont été interpelés. Le rôle du directeur est d'accompagner l'étudiant dans la rédaction de son projet de stage, de s'assurer du bon déroulement du stage et d'évaluer les apprentissages. Or, ces rencontres s'effectuent en présence du stagiaire et de son superviseur de stage assumant la supervision individuelle. Nous devions donc informer les directeurs d'études du projet de supervision combinée pour qu'ils puissent comprendre le bien-fondé de cet encadrement privilégié dans un contexte où les stagiaires avaient peu ou pas de notions théoriques sur le travail social de groupe alors que leur projet de stage visait à maîtriser cette intervention. Les directeurs ont, au point de départ, appuyé de façon informelle l'idée de mettre en place un contexte de supervision combinée. Pour formaliser la démarche, ils ont été invités à la rencontre avec les superviseurs, mais malheureusement, ils n'ont pu être présents.

Auprès des instances universitaires. La direction du programme de maîtrise a été sollicitée afin d'obtenir sa collaboration et son appui, ce qui a permis de poursuivre les démarches auprès des instances administratives de l'université. Depuis de nombreuses années, les Écoles de travail social au Québec consacrent une enveloppe budgétaire pour défrayer les coûts associés de la supervision associés au stage. Or, ce budget est versé, soit au milieu qui accueille la stagiaire lorsque la supervision est assumée par ce dernier, soit au superviseur engagé au privé si aucun intervenant du milieu ne peut assumer la supervision. Précisons également que l'encadrement, comme il a été mentionné dans la section précédente, est centré sur la supervision individuelle puisqu'en tout temps, ce cadre de supervision est celui privilégié dans la discipline du travail social. Or, la supervision combinée venait modifier ce paramètre. Nous avons donc rédigé un texte présentant les bénéfices, sur le plan pédagogique, de la supervision combinée auprès des instances universitaires afin d'utiliser de manière différente le budget, bien que les coûts demeuraient les mêmes.

Malgré les espaces restreints à l'UQÀM, les deux groupes de stagiaires et leurs co-facilitateurs ont eu accès à des locaux à l'École de travail social afin que se déroule la supervision de groupe. Par ailleurs, les coûts de photocopie ont été assumés également par l'École de travail social dont un budget est alloué à la formation pratique.

Auprès des étudiantes : Identification des besoins. Les besoins d'apprentissage ont été identifiés tant pour la supervision individuelle que la supervision de groupe. Soulignons que les stagiaires doivent élaborer un projet d'intervention avant le début de leur stage. De celui-ci découlera des besoins d'apprentissage. Ceux-ci serviront de balises pour le contrat d'apprentissage en supervision individuelle.

Pour la supervision de groupe, une identification des besoins d'apprentissage a été effectuée en groupe réunissant les co-facilitateurs et leur groupe de stagiaires. Voici un résumé des besoins identifiés : (a) comprendre le rôle de l'intervenant; (b) apprendre certains rudiments théoriques du travail social de groupe; et (c) développer des habiletés spécifiques en intervention de groupe, notamment celles reliées à l'émergence de l'aide mutuelle et aux possibilités d'extériorité.

Enfin, les étudiantes ont manifesté le souhait que la supervision de groupe soit un lieu d'échanges sur les différentes expériences vécues dans le cadre de leur stage. Sur le plan expérientiel, elles ont exprimé la volonté de vivre le groupe comme groupe.

Phase début

Cette section est consacrée en grande partie à la réalisation de la supervision de groupe. Cette phase se caractérise par la mise en commun des besoins, des objectifs d'intervention ainsi que des normes de fonctionnement. Le rôle de l'intervenant y est également discuté. Lors de la phase début de la supervision de groupe, l'élaboration d'un contrat d'apprentissage commun entre les étudiantes a été la première démarche réalisée par les superviseurs de groupe. D'une part, les besoins d'apprentissage identifiés préalablement (rencontre pré-groupe) ont été intégrés à ce contrat. D'autre part, les objectifs à atteindre à la fin de la démarche, les normes de fonctionnement du groupe de même que le rôle des facilitateurs ont été abordés. Plusieurs besoins d'apprentissage issus de la rencontre pré-groupe ont été repris lors de la formulation du contrat. Ce dernier a été rediscuté à la mi-parcours pour valider la pertinence des objectifs ciblés.

Durant la phase de travail, phase consacrée à la réalisation des objectifs et à l'émergence du système d'aide mutuelle, l'engagement des étudiantes est à souligner. Pour favoriser les apprentissages, les co-facilitateurs ont misé sur les occasions d'utiliser l'expérientiel, par exemple, rendre les étudiantes responsables de la réalisation de la syntonisation. Le groupe a été aussi appelé à réfléchir sur son processus. Tous les événements propices au développement du système d'aide mutuelle ont été exploités et portés à la connaissance du groupe. Tout comme il est souhaitable, lors de la phase de travail, les deux groupes de supervision se sont distingués par une forte cohésion et par la présence d'un système d'aide mutuelle significatif. Tout en se souciant de développer le groupe comme groupe, les facilitateurs ont su maintenir l'équilibre entre les besoins individuels et ceux du groupe et ont favorisé le transfert des apprentissages faits en supervision de groupe vers l'expérimentation en stage.

Parallèlement à la supervision de groupe, la supervision individuelle a mis l'accent sur l'accompagnement des projets de stage particuliers à chacune. Les étudiantes ont pu à ce moment aborder en profondeur l'opérationnalisation de leur projet, tels que l'implantation d'un projet dans un milieu de pratique, le recrutement des membres et les aspects organisationnels. C'était aussi le lieu pour viser une cohérence entre les objectifs d'intervention, le processus à l'œuvre dans chacun des groupes et les habiletés de la stagiaire en fonction de ses objectifs d'apprentissage.

Phase évaluation

À la fin du projet de supervision combinée, plusieurs démarches ont été effectuées pour connaitre l'appréciation des différents acteurs au sujet de cette expérience. Dans un premier temps, à la fin des rencontres de supervision, lors de la phase terminaison, les facilitateurs ont réalisé les tâches requises par cette phase. Une évaluation de satisfaction auprès des deux groupes fut l'occasion de faire un bilan des apprentissages et d'exprimer son point de vue sur l'appréciation générale de l'expérience de supervision en groupe. À cet effet, il faut souligner que l'évaluation de satisfaction des étudiantes s'est fait à la fin de la dernière rencontre sous forme d'un échange informel. Environ six mois après l'expérience, chaque groupe d'acteurs a été invité à faire part de sa perception des forces et des limites de cette expérience. Selon les situations, certains l'ont partagé par courriel et d'autres oralement.

Les opinions recueillies permettent d'avancer que les objectifs d'apprentissage, notamment pour la supervision de groupe ont été atteints à l'unanimité, les stagiaires reconnaissant que la supervision de groupe a favorisé l'apprentissage expérientiel. En tant que membre d'un groupe, elles ont été en mesure de développer leur empathie envers le rôle de participant dans un groupe. Elles ont ainsi pris conscience du processus de groupe et ont pu mieux comprendre le développement du système d'aide mutuelle. À l'instar de Denison (2005), force est de constater que la participation comme membre d'un groupe est incontournable dans la formation. L'observation du travail de co-facilitation leur a permis de cerner des habiletés en travail social de groupe. Notons ici l'apport particulier de la supervision de groupe en ce qui concerne l'apprentissage de comprendre et transférer la notion d'extériorité dans leur projet d'intervention personnel. Expérience faite, plusieurs des groupes menés par les stagiaires sont manifestement parvenus à l'extériorité, soit en se développant comme groupe d'action sociale, soit en permettant aux membres de leur groupe à entreprendre des actions de sensibilisation.

Les co-facilitateurs des supervisions de groupe confirment les propos des stagiaires. Selon leurs dires, l'expérience fut riche à la fois sur le plan du développement des connaissances en travail social de groupe et d'une prise de conscience des phénomènes d'aide mutuelle de même que du processus de groupe. Ce fut aussi l'occasion, pour les étudiantes, de partager leurs croyances et leurs connaissances à l'égard du travail social de groupe. Les co-facilitateurs ajoutent avoir apprécié l'expérience de supervision combinée. Tous sont d'avis que le double rôle (supervision individuelle et de groupe) ne leur a posé aucune contrainte. Au contraire, ils estiment que les deux modes se complétaient.

C'est aussi l'opinion de la plupart des superviseurs qui assumaient une supervision individuelle. L'expérience s'est avérée des plus positives, la supervision individuelle et de groupe couvrant des aspects différents du stage. Pour eux, la supervision combinée est un mode de supervision plus complet pour des stagiaires en travail social de groupe.

Par contre, quelques limites ont été soulignées lors de ces évaluations. Ainsi, il a été mentionné que quelques étudiantes ont dû composer avec des rétroactions qui leur apparaissaient contradictoires entre la supervision individuelle et de groupe. Pour ces superviseurs, la supervision combinée comporte donc des risques de créer de la confusion chez les étudiantes.

Ces risques de confusion ont été aussi relevés de la part de certains directeurs d'études. Par ailleurs, ces derniers ont déploré les nombreux acteurs entourant l'étudiante plus particulièrement chez celles ayant deux superviseurs. Ils ont aussi partagé leurs doléances en ce qui a trait au manque de communication lors de l'implantation du projet.

Retombées chez les étudiantes

es retombées de cette expérience sont positives pour le développement du travail social de groupe. Nous observons que plusieurs des étudiantes ayant participé à cette supervision combinée s'investissent en travail social de groupe. Cela se manifeste de diverses manières : reprise de l'intervention de groupe mise sur pied en stage dans leur pratique professionnelle, participation à une communauté de pratique sur le travail social de groupe (cinq sur huit) et enseignement du travail social de groupe.

Analyse

Les commentaires des divers acteurs mettent en évidence la pertinence de l'utilisation des forces réciproques de la supervision individuelle et de groupe (supervision combinée) pour l'apprentissage du travail social de groupe (Walter & Young, 1999).

Plusieurs raisons peuvent expliquer ce degré élevé de satisfaction. D'abord, les différentes démarches entreprises et l'adhésion des étudiantes, des superviseurs et des milieux de stage avant le début de l'expérience, ont mis en place un cadre assez clair pour permettre aux étudiantes de cheminer dans l'expérience de façon sécuritaire (Berteau & Villeneuve, 2005). De plus, le défi commun qui les unissait (réaliser un projet d'intervention de groupe dans le cadre d'un stage de maîtrise sans avoir eu de formation théorique) a été un levier important du succès obtenu. A cela s'ajoute le fait que les stagiaires se connaissaient préalablement. Ceci a probablement contribué au développement d'un climat de confiance, d'une cohésion et d'un engagement du groupe face aux objectifs poursuivis. Ces trois derniers aspects constituent des conditions de succès pour une supervision de groupe (Bogo et al., 2004).

Puis, le fait que chaque étudiante pouvait traiter de son projet d'intervention, à la fois en supervision individuelle et de groupe a été nettement favorable à l'apprentissage : la supervision individuelle permettant d'approfondir l'intervention de groupe menée par chacune ; la supervision de groupe permettant de puiser de nouvelles perspectives et d'apprendre l'intervention de groupe à partir du processus présent dans le groupe de supervision. Comme l'affirment Walter et Young (1999), les avantages de la supervision combinée sont manifestes dans ce projet puisqu'une part, les besoins particuliers ont été répondus et d'autre part, un apprentissage de qualité a été soutiré de l'expérience de groupe.

Sur le plan de la facilitation des supervisions de groupe, nous avons été à même de compter sur des personnes possédant une formation ainsi qu'une solide expérience en travail social de groupe ainsi qu'en supervision individuelle. Par ailleurs, la complémentarité des co-facilitateurs a été un atout dans la réalisation des supervisions de groupe. L'un mettait l'accent sur les dimensions pratiques alors que l'autre s'appuyait davantage sur les notions théoriques. Enfin, ces dernières furent intégrées à partir de l'ici et maintenant.

Tout comme l'indique Sussman et al. (2007), la mise en application de la supervision combinée a été plus complexe que prévu. La multiplicité des acteurs présente un défi d'importance puisque plusieurs contextes sont engagés auprès des étudiantes : le milieu de stage, le contexte universitaire, la supervision de groupe et la supervision individuelle. Ceci entraine des difficultés sur les plans de la communication et de la concertation entre les acteurs.

Conclusion

En somme, la supervision combinée a été une option de choix pour répondre aux besoins d'apprentissage de ces étudiantes qui possédaient peu de connaissances théoriques et pratiques en intervention de groupe. Les deux modalités étaient nécessaires pour optimiser les apprentissages en travail social de groupe. Lors de la supervision de groupe, les étudiantes ont été en mesure d'apprendre de l'expérience des pairs, de vivre comme membre le processus de groupe et de bénéficier d'un contexte favorable à l'apprentissage expérientiel. Alors que la supervision individuelle a permis d'aborder les besoins spécifiques d'apprentissage liés à leur propre expérience de stage. Essentiellement, les résultats viennent confirmer la nécessité de combiner ces deux modalités de supervision. Les retombées positives de cette expérience militent en faveur de l'utilisation de ce mode de supervision pour l'apprentissage du travail social de groupe.

Par contre, si l'on veut maximiser les bénéfices de ce mode de supervision, certaines conditions doivent être respectées. D'abord, cela exige une préparation rigoureuse où chaque acteur engagé dans l'apprentissage des étudiants est consulté et donne explicitement son accord. Il faut aussi que les rôles et les responsabilités de chacun des acteurs soient clarifiés. Idéalement, le superviseur à l'individuel et de groupe devrait être le même. Sinon, il faut mettre en place un mécanisme de communication qui permettrait des allers retours entre les deux superviseurs. Par ailleurs, il semble de première importance d'encourager les étudiants à partager les contenus entre les supervisions individuelle et de groupe et surtout les inciter à exprimer leurs malaises par rapport à des messages qui peuvent leur sembler contradictoires.

Afin de mieux intégrer la supervision de groupe au processus d'apprentissage il semble important de développer des outils permettant d'évaluer au fur et à mesure le déroulement de celle-ci tant sur le plan du processus que sur celui de la progression des objectifs. À cet égard, il serait souhaitable que les superviseurs de groupe tiennent une transcription écrite portant sur l'évolution du groupe en ce qui concerne les interactions, l'étape d'évolution et l'évaluation générale de chaque rencontre. Ceci permettrait de donner un portrait plus exact de l'évolution de chaque stagiaire. En adoptant une telle stratégie, il sera plus facile de déterminer clairement les éléments d'évaluation des apprentissages des étudiants qui sont communs entre les deux modes de supervision et spécifiques à chacun.

Références

Arvidsson, B., Lofgren, H., & Fridund, B. (2001). Psychiatric nurses' conceptions of how a group supervision program in nursing care influences their professional competence: A 4-year follow-up study. *Journal of Nursing Management, 3,* 161–171.

Bernard, J., & Goodyear, R. (1992). *Fundamentals of clinical supervision.* Boston, MA: Allyn & Bacon.

Berteau, G., & Villeneuve, L. (2005). *Du travail social des groupes à la supervision collective de groupe...Réalités ou fictions.* Bordeaux, France : Journée d'études. « La supervision des actions collectives : Comparaison : Belgique-France-Québec, document inédit.»

Bogo, M., Globerman, J., & Sussman, T. (2004). The field instructor as group worker: Managing trust and competition in group supervision. *Journal of Social Work Education, 40*(1), 13–26.

Boutin, G., & Camaraire, L. (2001). *Accueillir et encadrer un stagiaire.* Montréal, Québec: Éditions Nouvelles.

Dennison, S. (2005). Enhancing the integration of group theory with practice: A five-part teaching strategy. *Journal of Baccalaureate Social Work, 10*(2), 53–65.

Gagnier, J.-P., & Bigras, M. (2000). La supervision de groupe dans les équipes autonomes. Dans D. Boisvert (Dir.), *L'autonomie des équipes d'intervention communautaire modèles et pratiques* (pp. 69–85). Sainte-Foy, Québec: Presses de l'Université du Québec.

Glickauf-Hughes, C., & Campbell, L. (1991). Experiential supervision: Applied techniques for a case presentation approach. *Psychotherapy, 28*(4), 662–634.

Grossman-Leeman, D. (2013). In the boat with only one oar: The creation and adventures of an MSW consultation group. *Journal of Teaching in Social Work, 33*(3), 266–279.

Holloway, E., & Johnston, R. (1985, June). Group supervision: Widely praticed but poorly understood. *Counselor Education and Supervision,* 332–340.

Kadushin, A., & Harkness, D. (2002). *Supervision in social work* (4th ed.) New York, NY: Columbia University Press.

Kangasniemi, M., Ahonen, S.-M., Liikanen, E., & Utriainen, K. (2011). Health science students' conceptions of group supervision. *Nurse Education Today, 31*(2), 179–183.

Knight, C. (2000). Critical content on group work for the undergraduate social work curriculum. *Journal of Baccalaureate Social Work, 5,* 93–112.

Lindsay, J., Roy, V., Turcotte D., & Labarre, M. (2010). Tendances actuelles au sujet de la formation en service social des groupes. *Intervention, 132,* 15–24.

Lindsay, T. (2005). Group learning on social work placements. *Groupwork, 15*(1), 61–90.

Prieto, L. R. (1996). Group supervision: Still widely practised but poorly understood. *Counselor Education and Supervision, 35,* 295–307.

Ray, D., & Altekruse, M. (2000). Effectiveness of group supervision versus combined and individual supervision. *Counselor Education and Supervision, 40,* 19–30.

Sussman, T., Bogo, M., & Globerman, J. (2007). Field instructor perceptions in group supervision: Establishing trust through managing group dynamics. *Clinical Supervisor, 26*(1-2), 61–80.

Walter, C. A., & Young, T. M. (1999). Combining individual and group work supervision in educating for the social work profession. *The Clinical Supervisor, 18*(2), 73–89.

"Without Them, I Probably Wouldn't Be on This Planet": Benefits and Challenges of Groups for Parents of Children with Disabilities

Alice Home

Parenting a child with special needs means dealing with difference on a daily basis, both at home and in the community. In a society geared to typical families, those whose children cannot meet societal expectations are offered few accommodations and little understanding (Green, 2007). Parents face heavy demands, high costs, social exclusion, and inequality in most life domains, particularly when their children have invisible disabilities that can affect emotional or social behaviour (Dowling & Dolan, 2001). Many of these parents feel isolated, overwhelmed, and unsure of how to avoid burnout or where to turn for help. Group workers know that connecting to others in similar situations can be an important strategy for finding acceptance, practical help, and comradeship. Although the literature sets out potential benefits of various kinds of groups, few studies have examined how different groups benefit parents living with child disability. Similarly, there is limited research exploring challenges facing parent-led and professionally led groups and how they play out in different family or disability situations. This makes it difficult for parent organizations and professionals to know how to structure groups so they can be most helpful to parents.

In this paper I present findings from two of my unpublished qualitative studies that shed some light on these questions. The first explored groups as a resource for parents of children with hidden disabilities, through the eyes of professional and peer facilitators in Canada and New Zealand (Home & McNicoll, 2008). The second focused generally on which formal supports were seen as most helpful in raising adopted children with disabilities by Canadian parents, associations, and social workers (Home, 2010). After a short summary of background literature and research methods, I present findings on benefits and challenges for each study, with most data drawn from the first. Findings are then discussed together and connected with theory. The paper ends with some implications for group work practice with these "different" parents.

Background: Parenting Children With Disabilities and How Groups May Help

Many parents raising children with disabilities face inequalities in work, leisure, finances, and quality of family life, yet receive limited societal support. Invisible disabilities can bring greater misunderstanding and exclusion, as they manifest suddenly in the form of social and behavioural problems in children whose difference is not always readily apparent (Dore & Romans, 2001). Parents of children with disabilities such as attention deficit hyperactivity disorder (ADHD), autism spectrum disorder (ASD), and fetal alcohol spectrum disorder (FASD) have difficulty accessing early diagnosis or services, regularly need to educate people who attribute child problems to poor parenting, and must constantly advocate to ensure their child's rights are met. Exhausted and overwhelmed by their struggle and unsupported by the community, many of these parents feel powerless and isolated. Research has indicated that adoptive parents are more likely to be raising children with invisible emotional or behavioural disabilities, often combined with environmental special needs from prior abuse, neglect, or multiple placements (Wind, Brooks, & Barth, 2007). Many feel unprepared for special needs that emerge or change after placement, yet little post-adoption support is available to help these parents cope with their difficult situation (Reilly & Platz, 2004).

The challenges facing parents of children with certain invisible disabilities have been well documented, but research on benefits and difficulties of parent groups is more limited. Most work has focused on professionally led psychoeducational groups which provide training in parenting skills or communication, along with information on child development and specific disabilities (Knoke, 2008). A meta-analysis found these groups can reduce distress in parents of children with developmental disabilities, especially if focused on improving parents' well-being as well as on changing children's behaviour (Singer,

Ethridge, & Aldana, 2007). One study found increased confidence and reduced anxiety in group members raising children with ASD (Todd et al., 2010); another reported that lower stress found in parents raising children with ADHD had diminished a year after the group ended (Ferrin et al., 2014). In contrast to mutual aid groups, few parent education groups address members' feelings or mobilize peer helping (Home & Biggs, 2005), though one group for parents of children with emotional or behavioural disorders developed content from member concerns and built in time for sharing and support (McClendron, Pollio, North, Reid, & Jonson-Reid, 2007).

A small number of studies have focused on support groups led by parents of children with disabilities. Main benefits reported were emotional support, information exchange, a sense of belonging, and opportunities to develop coping or advocacy skills (Law, King, Stewart, & King, 2001). Peer-led groups helped parents of children with ADHD increase knowledge, self-efficacy, sense of parenting competence, and ability to seek and use resources (Singh et al., 1997). However, a study of group longevity found benefits depend on participation level, while difficulties arise from a dearth of committed leaders and new members, insufficient community contacts, and low adaptation to evolving needs (King, Stewart, King, & Law, 2000). Online groups are an alternative for parents with accessibility issues due to distance, timing, cost or lack of competent child care, and need for anonymity. One study suggested parents of children with autism derived support, empowerment and advocacy strategies from group participation but had difficulty with overwhelming, confusing, or unreliable information (Carter, 2009). Another found inconclusive evidence these groups had any stress-buffering impact, though members appreciated sharing experiences and information (Clifford, 2013).

There is virtually no research on groups for adoptive parents of children with special needs, but a few studies of post-adoption support programs have suggested parent-led groups are important. Participants in a peer mentoring program attended group meetings for emotional support and information (Bryan, Flaherty, & Saunders, 2010), whereas parents in an adoption preservation program found groups to be the most helpful component. This program was unusual, however, in that parent group facilitators were trained and hired to do this work and had access to a professional adoption specialist (Atkinson & Gonet, 2007). Another study reported that adoption professionals saw parent support group development as a major way of overcoming barriers to accessing post-placement services (Ryan, Nelson, & Siebert, 2009). As these groups may allow members to put their struggles in perspective while learning about community resources, several adoption associations are helping parents set them up (Stevens, 2012).

Methods: Two Canadian Studies on Parenting Children With Disabilities

I drew findings from two of my unpublished exploratory studies, which had different goals but used similar methods, described in this paragraph. Specific goals and method adaptations for each study are presented in separate paragraphs. As both studies sought to understand and compare perceptions based on lived experiences of different "insiders" whose voices are rarely heard, a qualitative design was deemed most useful (Padgett, 1998). After receiving ethics approval, recruitment was carried out in both English and French. To reduce the influence of regional factors, data collection took place in the two culturally and geographically distinct Canadian provinces of Ontario and British Columbia. [1] A purposive, maximum variation sampling strategy was selected in order to identify shared patterns while mapping diversity on important factors (Patton, 2002). Semistructured interview guides included similar questions to explore common themes, as well as some questions adapted for each respondent group. This was done to balance structure and flexibility, allow triangulation of sources, and facilitate comparison of perspectives (Patton, 2002). After transcribed interviews had been checked by participants, data were subjected to thematic content analysis using a qualitative–interpretive approach.

Despite these methodological similarities, the studies differed in several ways. The first explored groups specifically as a formal support for parents of children with any of three invisible disabilities (FASD, ASD, ADHD), through the eyes of both professional and peer facilitators (Home & McNicoll, 2008). The goals of the research were to learn facilitators' perspectives on how their groups attempted to meet parent needs, along with the main benefits and challenges observed, in order to identify some similarities and differences across culture, language, and type of group and disability. The interview guide focused on agency and community context, member and group characteristics, benefits observed, challenges encountered, and resource and access issues. In keeping with a contrast strategy, recruitment involved approaching relevant groups from lists in each region, with a view to balancing peer and professional leadership, as well as specific disability focus. A special effort was made to reach out to cultural and linguistic minorities, including French language groups in Ontario. The contrast strategy was successful in recruiting a diverse sample, including 16 groups in Canada (10 in Ontario, 6 in British Columbia) along with 6 in different regions of New Zealand. Ten groups were facilitated by paid professionals with varying types of credentials, whereas the 12 peer facilitators were volunteers whose expertise was rooted in their experience parenting a child with a disability. Roughly equal numbers of groups addressed each disability type and six targeted parents of minority cultural or linguistic backgrounds (Chinese, Indigenous, and Franco-Ontarian). The researchers conducted interviews in English or French as needed and coded the transcriptions using the Ethnograph.

The second study focused only on parents of adopted children with disabilities, asking participants to identify the most helpful supports including but not limited to groups (Home, 2010).[2] Existing adoption research is based largely on either parent or professional perspectives, so this study sought to learn and compare the views of three types of stakeholders: adoptive parents, social workers, and parent associations. As lack of distinction between special need types has been a limit of many adoption studies, this study focused on raising adopted children diagnosed with bio-behavioral needs stemming from disabilities, disorders, medical conditions, or prenatal substance exposure, though these may not have been fully known at placement (Wind et al., 2007). Parents of children whose difficulties came from trauma, abuse, neglect, or multiple placements were included only if one of the above diagnoses was present. To reduce the impact of prior environment, transitional, and developmental factors, children had to be aged 2 to 12 at the time of the study and living with the adoptive family from 1 to 4 years. This study asked all participants to describe the main challenges of this parenting, most useful supports, and main action priorities. The sample, evenly divided between Ontario and British Columbia, included 16 families, five workers from different types of adoption agencies, and three associations. Participating parents, five of whom had adopted internationally, were raising children aged 2 to 12 with a range of disabilities. FASD, ADHD, and mental health disorders predominated, and some children also had a history of abuse, neglect, or multiple placements. Children ranged in age, race, and culture, and families varied in size, socioeconomic situation, and composition, with five from minority ethnocultural backgrounds (Home, in press).

The following section presents findings on benefits and challenges of groups. For clarity, findings supported by quotes are presented on each study separately. Sources of quotes are identified both by research participant number (1, 2, etc.) and type. For the parent group study, SH indicates parent facilitator and PR indicates professional, whereas type of stakeholder (Par for parent, Ag for agency, and Assoc for association) distinguishes between participants in the adoptive parenting study.

Findings on Benefits of Groups for Parents of Children With Hidden Disabilities

Facilitators noted five advantages these groups provided to members: a safe place, an opportunity for mutual helping and learning, an anchor in difficult times, empowerment, and camaraderie. The first three were mentioned most often. Having a safe place to share their experiences and be believed by others who had "been there" was critical, as few parents had anyone that really understood how different their family life was. Many had learned to put on a brave face and keep silent, rather than risk dismissal or criticism from parents of typical children and some professionals. Being able to vent their feelings without fear of judgment or blame was an essential first step toward breaking through their isolation. Parents reported feeling less alone in their struggle, as "it was like someone held up a mirror to my life" (SH 6, Home & McNicoll, 2010, p. 2). The unspoken understanding of those "who recognize they are really trying very hard under difficult circumstances" (PR 7, Home & McNicoll, 2008) made this group one place they could relax and "have a good laugh" (PR 3, Home & McNicoll, 2008).

A second important benefit was the opportunity for mutual learning and helping. By the time some parents get to the group, they are stuck, in distress, or at their wits' end after years of struggling with a difficult child: "I don't know what to do anymore, I'm tearing my hair out" (PR 2 [translated], Home & McNicoll, 2008). Others are overwhelmed by a new diagnosis:

> They've got nowhere to go, no one to turn to, don't know what to do, what they're entitled to .... They don't want professionals; they want to

talk to families about the nitty-gritty of what happens and learn some survival skills. (SH 12, Home & McNicoll, 2008)

The group can help parents learn to negotiate the maze of services, manage their child's behaviour at home, and deal productively with unhelpful reactions of teachers and others. This information can be a first step to getting unstuck: "By giving them the resources, they're better able to advocate for their child" (PR 6, Home & McNicoll, 2008). Other members' experiences can be an important source of learning, especially to those who are new to the group or who are losing hope. The facilitator of a FASD group described how the mother of a younger child saw what was possible: "So he can work? I need to hear that" (Home & McNicoll, 2009, p. 10). Members can find renewed energy to keep going at times when slow progress and frequent setbacks make goals seem unattainable.

For many, mutual helping was the key to finding creative new solutions in this marathon struggle: "Some parents have had success in one way and are struggling in another way and they help each other" (PR 7, Home & McNicoll, 2008). In a peer-led group, "One person was really, really stuck and this woman said, 'Oh wait, now there's one thing that worked for me'" (SH 6, Home & McNicoll, 2008). This process builds both cohesion and ownership: "It's really a group that belongs to the members .... There is a certain solidarity that comes from all of them sharing something in common'" (SH 5 [translated], Home & McNicoll, 2008).

Although these two benefits have been reported in other populations, the three others stand out when members are raising children with unpredictable behaviour that can cause crises at any time. Groups were described as "an anchor in a stormy family life [and] . . . a way to stay connected when things go wrong" (PR 5, Home & McNicoll, 2008). This is one reason some think "these parents need more than a six-week group .... What they need is a long-term commitment" (SH 8, Home & McNicoll, 2010, p. 3). As these lifelong disabilities present different challenges at various developmental stages, parents face both continuity and change. They have to feel free to come and go: "People come when they're in need, stick around for a while, then everything's fine .... A few years later they come back in a crisis" (SH 6, Home & McNicoll, 2008). As one grandmother put it: "He's getting older so his moods are changing, his behaviour, his way of being .... I remember your videos, I remember the sheets you gave me, but now I have to come back" (SH 2; Home & McNicoll, 2010, p. 3).

Although cited less often, the fourth and fifth benefits, empowerment and camaraderie, are of special interest because of the marginalized situation of these families. Parents have to resist community blame and misunderstanding while advocating to ensure their children's rights are respected. Facilitators of some groups noticed empowerment developing over time. Parents begin to validate their resilience, strengths or strategies: "The external brain—that's what I've been doing all along. I thought it wasn't the right thing" or else find their voice: "Now I can talk to teachers, police" (Home & McNicoll, 2009, p. 3). Some begin to demonstrate empowerment as a group, even if the latter is facilitated by a professional: "When we did FASD day, they were all there. It was all their idea. I just organized it" (PR 3, Home & McNicoll, 2008). The peer facilitator of a long-standing group observed a ripple effect, as members began to speak on behalf of the group, educate professionals and the community, or start new services.

Camaraderie was the last benefit mentioned by most facilitators. Connections with others who share similar experiences can blossom into friendships for these isolated parents, replacing others lost during their intense parenting. Some groups are structured to facilitate this, such as one for carers of Aboriginal children that starts with an informal time and family supper. Groups like this one that also provide child care during formal meeting time give children a rare opportunity to build social connections: "They can come and recognize that there are other children with FASD, and they're not alone" (PR 7, Home & McNicoll, 2008). These groups become "a way for the ones affected to expand their friendships and still feel safe and secure" (PR 3, Home & McNicoll, 2008), which is crucial as "friendship is very hard to come by for ASD kids" (SH 7, Home & McNicoll, 2008).

Findings on Challenges Encountered by Groups for Parents of Children With Hidden Disabilities

These groups were not without their challenges, which fall into three main categories: lack of resources, recruitment or participation issues, and dealing with member differences. Resource issues were mentioned most often by the widest variety of groups. Funding was elusive in professionally led groups, as support came mainly from short-term grants. Facilitators had to devote considerable energy to securing stable funding, taking scarce professional time but also causing uncertainty, which limited options for outreach, offering needed services such as child care, and evaluating outcomes with a view to strengthening benefits. These professionals felt frustrated at not being able to respond fully to member and group needs and worried about continuity. The situation was worse, however, for peer-led groups, which run on a shoestring with only targeted support for some necessities like venues. One facilitator noted, "We really have no resources except ourselves" (SH 5 [translated], Home & McNicoll, 2008); another explained, "Whenever there's a new video I'll buy it . . . photocopying, phone, long distance sometimesbut I don't worry about it, I just do it." She is aware that this is not be a workable solution for most people and worries "a group could fold because of that" (SH3, Home & McNicoll, 2008). Lack of material support makes these groups especially vulnerable to the precariousness that besets most groups for parents with hidden disabilities. Peer-led groups are vulnerable for another reason. Although they sometimes get professional guidance and/or financial help with set-up, their long-term survival depends on the energy, resilience, and deep commitment of a limited pool of parent volunteers. Living with the same issues as other members, they too are at risk of sudden family crises and personal burnout. In one group, "Mrs. B. found it very difficult to continue, and it just fell to us. We have a lot of burn-outs; it's not unusual .... The stress kind of got to her" (SH 1, Home & McNicoll, 2008). For other facilitators, it is one burden too many in an overcommitted life, juggling this parenting with employment. Professionally led groups struggle with staff turnover from stress of working in this field, but peer-led groups can be unable to continue due to lack of renewal:

> The biggest challenge is lack of new blood on the board. As it's basically the same people, there's always a worry that if they stop, our group will fall apart .... We can't do it unless people volunteer. So there are times it's on and times it's off. (SH 6 [translated], Home & McNicoll, 2008)

This precariousness of human resources helps explain why parents cannot count on these groups to be there when they need them.

The other two challenges are familiar to many group workers: recruitment and dealing with differences. Getting people to join any type of parenting group has become more challenging with families busier and with more activities competing for their time. Adding to these practical obstacles is concern that attending means admitting parental incompetence. Facilitators found these practical and psychological issues more of an obstacle when children have hidden disabilities. A chaotic and unpredictable family life makes any commitment difficult, while finding affordable, competent child care is nearly impossible if behaviour and safety issues are present. Some parents are too exhausted from their daily struggle to invest in a group, whereas others are not ready to face tough family issues in the presence of others. A few groups offer a list-serve format to circumvent these difficulties while avoiding chat rooms due to safety concerns. More complex issues face minority linguistic or cultural groups, who are dealing with double difference. Some parents had to "choose" between the right group in English and a less appropriate group in their own language (PR 1, Home & McNicoll, 2008); others risked rejection of relatives for admitting a child's disability, especially outside the family circle (SH 5 [translated], Home & McNicoll, 2008). One Aboriginal group dealt with stigma around FASD by offering families cultural activities while encouraging discussion of disability issues that were brought up by members (PR 3, Home & McNicoll, 2008).

The last challenge, dealing with member differences, was particularly difficult. As these hidden disabilities can have a strong genetic component, parent groups often included "members who are on the [ASD] spectrum themselves" (SH 4, Home & McNicoll, 2008) or whose ADHD impulsivity led them to blurt out socially provocative comments which could upset others (PR 1 [translated] , Home & McNicoll, 2008). The extra time and attention required by needier members sometimes brought impatience from their peers (Home & McNicoll, 2009). Age differences of affected children posed a challenge in some groups because intensive parenting continued into the teens and beyond. Some groups ended up either dividing in two or separating members for part of each meeting. As explained by the facilitators: "A mom with a 4-year-old with ADHD has no clue what a 13- [to] 14-year-old is going through" (SH 12) and "[parents of older children] have a lot of baggage .... I don't want that negativity to affect those parenting the younger ones" (PR 6; Home & McNicoll, 2010, p. 2).

Finally, FASD groups faced a particular dilemma, as this disability is due to maternal drinking during pregnancy. Many children are raised by adoptive or foster parents, who are the main clientele in FASD parent groups. One facilitator worried about inclusion of birth parents: "Sometimes people do get quite upset and . . . speak out bluntly about somebody doing the drinking. So it might be kind of hard sometimes for a birth mother to be there" (SH 3, Home & McNicoll, 2008). Another had discussed this with members: "The group as a whole feels that they would welcome biological families .... If we get a biological parent interested, some parents have agreed to mentor the parent in" (PR 5, Home & McNicoll, 2008).

Findings on Groups for Adoptive Parents of Children With Special Needs

The adoptive parent study asked three types of stakeholders which supports they saw as being most helpful (Home, 2010). A striking finding is that despite their different roles, all stakeholders agreed that connection with other parents in similar situations was critical. Less than half the families did not mention groups and for several, this was only because they were unable to access one. Connecting with peers was a major unmet need for these families facing unusual challenges. As explained by a mother whose black child had complex disabilities,

> Anything with other adoptive parents—any kind of group where you could just share your experiences and go, "Oh, they're doing this; what can I do?" Anything that is outside of society's ways of dealing with normal children. "No I'm not a bad parent, this is the way it is." (Par 13, Home, 2010)

Benefits similar to those found in the first study were also subtly different. Having a safe place to vent was vital to these parents, who worried that approaching the adoption agency could be interpreted as their not being up to the job or result in a refused subsequent adoption. Asking agency help was "filled with anxiety, so we put it off until really, we needed help so badly that there was just no other option" (Par 2, Home, 2010). Mutual helping and learning were other reasons adoptive parents' support groups stood out as the best support. Members provided inside information such as the best doctor, and the parent facilitator was available to give immediate, practical advice in a school crisis. Some parents had no doubt about the critical role played by that group: "I'm sure the adoption could have ended up breaking down if we hadn't had that [support] .... You don't think you're going to need it, then bang! You need it!" (Par 2, Home, 2010). Another parent had a similar experience with an adoptive parent association when facing a crisis: "We had meetings. We had on-line chats .... Families all visit each other and we share war stories . . . but we know we will be confidential" (Home, 2013, p. 8.). A single mother of several high needs children noted, "If weren't in that organization, I probably wouldn't be on this planet" (Par 14, Home, 2010). However, not everyone knew these resources existed as some workers did not share this vital information. To avoid parents having to struggle alone, one participant suggested giving a fridge magnet listing the support group contact to new adoptive parents the day the child arrives.

For some of these very different families, it was the camaraderie and socializing that was most important, as "other parents don't want their kids with our kind of kids" (Par 14, Home, 2010). For example:

> Once I got into the adoption circle . . . I felt like our family just blossomed .... We have our supports in place and not only for ourselves. Our children know they're not the only adoptive family with special needs and of different races. (Par 15, Home, 2013, p. 8)

Parents without access to an adoptive parent group or association in their community developed informal networks at family fun days or picnics organized by adoption agencies. This sometimes led to stronger bonds: "And out of that networking comes a lot of peer support . . . they're working together, two moms that have some similar issues or are at similar stages" (Assoc 2, Home, 2010). Other adoptive parents participated in peer-led groups for any parents of children with a specific disability such as FASD. These groups provided information and helped some people realize their child's condition was "mild compared to what some other parents are dealing with" (Par 7, Home, 2010). Others, however, found these groups offered little interaction and were of limited use if children were young.

Participants in this study also pointed to challenges. As in the previous study, "support groups kind of come and go" (Assoc 1, Home, 2010), as they depend on the availability of competent, committed leaders. Taking this on can be daunting for adoptive parents dealing with multiple differences at the same time. In addition to coping with their child's special needs from disability and/or past history, many have children of a different racial or ethnic background, some of whom are still in contact with their birth family and community. When children have multiple, complex needs, it may be that no one group fits. For example, cultural groups for adopted children are often not developmentally appropriate for those with special needs, and disability groups may be "not a welcoming place for us [adoptive parents]" (Par 1, Home, 2010). Parents such as these have few options. Some start their own very specific group, such as one for parents of gay and lesbian children, which fill an important gap but rarely last. For adoptive parents in remote communities and those reluctant to "just show up at a support group with a group of strangers and start venting or sharing personal information" (Assoc 2, Home, 2010), online and Facebook groups can be a solution: "They connect most of the year through Internet, on-line, telephone, webcam, whatever they need to do, then have two to three major get-togethers per year" (Assoc 2, Home, 2010). This study participant concluded: "There's no one model for support groups .... You have to find out what works for you" (Assoc 2, Home, 2010).

Discussion and Implications

These findings reveal that groups can bring benefits to these families raising children who are so different from most others. Several benefits are similar to those offered by mutual aid groups, including reducing isolation, providing a place to feel safe and less "abnormal," learning new strategies, and getting mutual support (Shulman, 2005). Similarly, peer-led parent groups allowed sharing and venting, as well as a chance to help and be helped both on an emotional and practical level (Kurtz, 2004). A few peer-led groups helped empower members to advocate on behalf of their children and work for change on a societal level, supporting King et al.'s (2000) findings with a similar population.

For these families who struggle constantly to deal with their child's hidden differences and others' reactions to them, certain benefits less reported in the literature take on particular importance. Parents of children with unpredictable lifelong disabilities need to be able to count on a long-term group, which can act as an anchor when things get rough. Secondly, camaraderie is vital to both children and parents, who find friendship elusive due to their difference and to community rejection. This is one place where they know they belong, as they are accepted in their difference. For adoptive families facing double and triple difference, being connected to like others is of survival value, according to parents, agencies, and associations. Having a safe place to share is unusually important to these parents because of their reluctance to seek help from the adoption agency except as a last resort (Home, 2013).

The challenges that emerged from these studies are food for thought for group workers. The number one concern of facilitators was the constant uncertainty around whether these groups could keep going. Lack of stable funding plagued professionally and peer-led groups, but the latter's survival was under constant threat because of leadership renewal issues, as noted by King et al. (2000). This raises the question as to whether it is realistic to expect overburdened families to carry alone the full load of setting up, facilitating, and managing this vital resource. Although professional presence at meetings may not be required or even recommended in all peer-led groups, they can fall apart if members have no access to professional consultation. Group workers could provide help not only during set up but also at times of transition or crisis, if requested by the group. They could help groups deal with common challenges such as those related to recruitment and member differences. As suggested by one study participant, they could offer workshops on facilitating these groups, perhaps with an experienced peer group leader.

However, the low status of group work in agencies, coupled with increasingly heavy workloads, make freeing up priority time for such preventive work daunting. Only by working in close partnership with parent disability and adoption associations can such an approach be successful. Drawing on their specialized knowledge of parents' needs and relevant resources, these associations can help both parents and group workers learn about creative solutions, such as online alternatives to face-to-face meetings. Working collaboratively with university-based scholars, group workers and parent associations could use evaluative research to monitor outcomes of various group approaches and make results widely known. Mobilizing different partners' expertise could be a way forward toward a more solid footing for these vital but precarious resources.

Notes

1   Six of the 22 groups were located in New Zealand. Paule McNicoll was not involved with the New Zealand sector of the parenting groups study.
2   Further information on findings of this study can be found in Stakeholder Study [Video 2], which can be downloaded free of charge from the Adoption Council of Canada website: http://www.adoption.ca/special-needs-parenting. The other videos in this series may also be of interest to readers.

References

Atkinson, A., & Gonet, P. (2007). Strengthening adoptive practice, listening to adoptive families. *Child Welfare, 86*(2), 87–104.

Bryan, V., Flaherty, C., & Saunders, C. (2010). Supporting adoptive families: Participant perceptions of a statewide peer mentoring and support program. *Journal of Public Child Welfare, 4*, 91–112.

Carter, I. (2009). Positive and negative experiences of parents involved in online self-help groups for autism. *Journal on Developmental Disabilities, 15*(1), 44–52.

Clifford, T. (2013). Logging on: Evaluating an on-line support group for parents of children with autism spectrum disorders. *Journal of Autism and Developmental Disability, 43*, 1662–1675.

Dore, G., & Romans, S. (2001). Impact of bipolar affective disorder on family and partners. *Journal of Affective Disorders, 76*, 147–158.

Dowling, M., & Dolan, L. (2001). Families and children with disabilities: Inequalities and the social model. *Disability and Society, 16*(1), 21–35.

Ferrin, M., Moreno-Granados, J., Salcedo-Marin, M., Ruiz-Veguilla, M., Perez-Ayala, V., & Taylor, E. (2014). Evaluation of a psychoeducation programme for parents of children and adolescents with ADHD: Immediate and long-term effects using a blind randomized trial. *European Child and Adolescent Psychiatry, 23*, 637–647.

Green, S. (2007). "We're tired, not sad": Benefits and burdens of mothering a child with a disability. Social Science and Medicine, 64(1), 150–163.

Home, A. (in press). Working with special needs adoptive parents: Insiders' perspectives on what professionals need to know. *Professional*

Development: The International Journal of Continuing Social Work Education, 15(1).

Home, A. (2010). [Special needs adoptive parenting: Stakeholders' views on parents' experiences and support needs]. Unpublished raw data.

Home, A. (2013). *What's going on? Disentangling children's disabilities and getting the right support.* Monograph 1 in the series Special Needs Parenting: Working Together for success. Retreived from http://www.adoption.ca/uploads/Image/Monograph1-Alice-FINAL.pdf

Home, A., & Biggs, T. (2005). Evidence-based practice in the real world: A group for mothers of children with invisible disabilities. *Groupwork, 15*(2), 39–60.

Home, A., & McNicoll, P. (2008). [Parenting children with diverse invisible disabilities: Role of group and cultural factors]. Unpublished raw data.

Home, A., & McNicoll, P. (2009, March). *Groups for parents of children with FASD and other hidden disabilities: A study of facilitators' views.* Research poster presented at the Third International FASD Conference: Integrating Research, Policy and Promising Practice, Victoria, British Columbia, Canada.

Home, A., & McNicoll, P. (2010, April). *Evolving needs: Parenting adolescents and young adults with hidden disabilities.* Research poster presented at the Fourth National Conference on Adolescents and Adults with Fetal Alcohol Spectrum Disorder, Vancouver, British Columbia, Canada.

King, G., Stewart, D., King, S., & Law, M. (2000). Organizational characteristics and issues affecting the longevity of self-help groups for parents of children with special needs. *Qualitative Health Research, 10*(2), 225–241. doi:10.1177/104973200129118381

Knoke, D. (2008). *Parent training programmes* (Centre for Excellence in Child Welfare Information Sheet 68E). Retrieved from the Canadian Child Welfare Research Portal website: http://cwrp.ca/sites/default/files/publications/en/parenttraining68E.pdf

Kurtz, L. (2004). Support and self-help groups. In C. Garvin, L. Gutiérrez, & M. Galinsky (Eds.), *Handbook of social work with groups* (pp. 139–159). New York, NY: Guilford.

Law, M., King, S., Stewart, D., & King, G. (2001). The perceived effects of parent-led support groups for parents of children with disabilities. *Physical & Occupational Therapy in Pediatrics, 21*(2/3), 29–48.

McClendron, J., Pollio, D., North, C., Reid, D., & Jonson-Reid, M. (2007). School-based groups for parents of children with emotional and behavioral disorders: Pilot results. *Families in Society: The Journal of Contemporary Social Services, 124–129.*

Padgett, D. (1998). *Qualitative methods in social work research: Challenges and rewards*. Thousand Oaks CA: Sage

Patton, M. (2002). *Qualitative evaluation and research methods*. Newbury Park, CA: Sage.

Reilly, T., & Platz, L. (2004). Post-adoption service needs of families with special needs children: Use, helpfulness and unmet needs. *Journal of Social Service Research, 30*(4), 51–67.

Ryan, S., Nelson, N., & Siebert, C. (2009). Examining the facilitators and barriers faced by adoptive professionals delivering post-placement services. *Children and Youth Services Review, 31*, 584–593.

Shulman, L. (2005). *The skills of helping individuals, families and groups* (5th ed.). Itasca, IL: Peacock.

Singer, G., Ethridge, B., & Aldana, S. (2007). Primary and secondary effects of parenting and stress management interventions for parents of children with developmental disabilities: A meta-analysis. *Mental Retardation and Developmental Disabilities Research Reviews, 13*, 357–369.

Singh, N., Curtis, W., Ellis, C., Wechsler, H., Best, A., & Cohen, R. (1997). Empowerment status of families whose children have serious emotional disturbance and attention deficit hyperactivity disorder. *Journal of Emotional and Behavioral Disorders, 5*(4), 223–229.

Stevens, K. (2012, Spring). Families benefit from parent-led post-adoption services. *Adoptalk*, 8–9.

Todd, S., Bromley, T., Ioannou, K., Harrison, J., Mellor, C., Taylor, E., & Crabtree, E. (2010). Using group-based parent training interventions with parents of children with disabilities: A description of process, content and outcomes in clinical practice. *Child and Adolescent Mental Health, 15*(3), 171–175.

Wind, L., Brooks, R., & Barth, D. (2007). Adoption preparation: Differences between adoptive families with and without special needs. *Adoption Quarterly, 8*(4), 45–74.

An Inventory for Enhancing Cross-Cultural Group Work

Tomasz Michal Rapacki & Dawn Lorraine McBride

The purpose of this article is to introduce "101 Strategies for More Culturally Responsive Mental Health Services—Group Facilitator Version," an inventory and practical learning tool meant to help group-based counselors, social workers, and psychologists address the growing need for culturally responsive mental health services. This tool is based on a review of over 160 peer-reviewed publications and contains an inventory of 101 concrete strategies focused on how to adapt services to take advantage of the scientifically demonstrated benefits of cultural customization. Each strategy is presented along with endnote references in order to facilitate self-directed learning. This article contains an overview of the development process of this tool, whereas the inventory itself is located within the appendix. Our hope is that this tool will encourage helping professionals to connect their abstract ethnocultural knowledge to concrete therapeutic practices that may improve the mental health outcomes of diverse clients.

Rationale

The provision of culturally informed mental health services to diverse clients is a central challenge for today's helping professionals, many of whom live in increasingly multicultural societies (Collins & Arthur, 2010). The high ethical value of cultural competence has been communicated through cultural competency guidelines published by numerous professional bodies, including the American Psychological Association (2002), the National Association of Social Workers (2001), and the Canadian Psychological Association (2001).

Although there is some evidence that ordinary mental health interventions may be adequate for ethnic minorities (Miranda et al., 2005), there is also evidence that these services may not be an ideal fit for culturally diverse peoples. In the United States and Canada, people from racial and cultural minority groups are consistently less likely to seek mental health services and more likely to drop out of counseling or receive less therapeutic benefit than their European–American counterparts (Kirmayer, du Fort, Young, Weinfeld, & Lasry, 1996; Melfi, Croghan, Hanna, & Robinson, 2000; Mok, Lao, Lin, Wong, & Ganesan, 2003; Snowden & Yamada, 2005; Stewart, 2008; U.S. Department of Health and Human Services, 2001; Wang et al., 2005).

Although many mental health professionals may be surprised to learn that cultural modifications contribute significantly to client outcomes, there is in fact a good deal of evidence that culturally tailored interventions are superior to unmodified protocols (Benish, Quinana, & Wampold, 2011; Griner & Smith, 2006; Smith, Domenech Rodríguez, & Bernal, 2011). Cultural customization results in such benefits as increased session smoothness, depth, and satisfaction, as well as improved perceptions of practitioner credibility, higher service usage rates, and decreased no-show and dropout rates (Griner & Smith, 2006; Lefley & Bestman, 1991; Leong, 2007; Zane et al., 2005). These benefits have been demonstrated in a variety of interventions from one-on-one psychological services to group-level social work programing.

The effect size of culturally customized treatment over treatment-as-usual has been consistently estimated at $r = .22–.24$ (Griner & Smith, 2006; Huey & Polo, 2008; Smith et al., 2011). This compares favorably to factors such as the working alliance, at approximately .25 (Safran & Muran, 2006), and theoretical orientation, at up to .20 (Wampold et al., 1997), which are currently given a central weight in research and training. In fact, with less-acculturated clients, clinical samples, or when treatment was customized to a single ethnic group, effects were found to approach or exceed .25 (Griner & Smith, 2006; Smith et al., 2011). In more concrete terms, this indicates that clients who receive mental health services customized for their ethnic group achieve better outcomes than 69% of those who receive ordinary treatment. Furthermore, these clients report satisfaction levels greater than 82% of clients who received nonadapted services. Therefore, culturally tailoring services can have a substantial positive impact on mental health professionals' collaboration with diverse clients. This article and the included inventory were created in order to promote the incorporation of cultural adaptations into mental health practice.

Procedure

The present article is part of a collection of materials developed from a single literature review (see Rapacki & McBride, 2013, 2014a) aimed at collecting information to help mental health professionals practice cross-culturally. The focus of this review was primarily on multicultural competency frameworks, therapeutic adaptation models, and outcome-focused research related to the delivery of counseling across cultures. An extensive search was undertaken to locate relevant academic journals through online databases including PsycINFO, ERIC, Medline, and Google Scholar, as well as all 51 databases available through EBSCOHost. Searches concentrated chiefly on studies that had been published since the year 2000 and included, but were not limited to, various combinations of keywords such as counseling, therapy, psychotherapy, psychology, meta-analysis, intercultural, cross-cultural, multicultural, cultural competence, assessment, outcomes, matching, adaptation, and modification.

We also consulted the databases for lists of publications by leading authors in the field: Professors Derald Wing Sue, Wei-Chin Hwang, Sandra Collins, and Nancy Arthur, and browsed abstracts since the year 2000 in the Journal of Cross-Cultural Psychology and Journal of Counseling Psychology for studies of clinical significance. Finally, we also reviewed the books Counseling the Culturally Diverse: Theory and Practice (Sue & Sue, 2008), Culture-Infused Counselling: A Model for Developing Multicultural Competence (Collins & Arthur, 2010), and Culture & Psychology (Matsumoto & Juang, 2008). In addition, we also contacted Professors Timothy Smith and Wei-Chin Hwang, who directed us to several recent publications on cultural adaptation.

Ultimately, we selected over 160 publications for review, with the final number having been chosen when we judged that the point of theoretical saturation had been reached. The studies were selected based on our judgment of their relevance to the topic of applied multicultural counseling after examining their abstracts. Selection criteria included having (a) a clear focus on applied cultural competence, (b) a topic that was clearly psychological or sociological in nature, and (c) a publication date after the year 2000 and/or evidence of frequent citation that demonstrated the publication as influential in the field of multicultural competence.

Information from this review was then selected for inclusion in cultural competency training materials according to our appraisal of its practical relevance and educational value. During this phase, approximately 30 additional sources were selected based on their potential to enhance the interactivity and effectiveness of training materials. This information was used to create an online workshop for counsellors-in-training (Rapacki & McBride, 2013, 2014a), a website (Rapacki, 2014), an academic presentation delivered to the International Association of Social Work With Groups (Rapacki & McBride, 2014b), and the present paper. The 101 strategies for more culturally responsive mental health services—group facilitator version inventory was developed as a direct summary of the strategies introduced in the cultural adaptation workshop.

Results

In recognition of the time pressures faced by many practitioners, the strategies from the literature review and workshop were presented in the inventory primarily as single sentences organized into six application-focused domains adapted from the psychotherapy adaptation and modification framework (PAMF; Hwang, 2006). These domains include (a) dynamic issues and cultural complexities, (b) orientation to group work, (c) cultural beliefs, (d) relationships, (e) cultural differences in expression and communication, and (f) cultural issues of salience.

In order to take advantage of the self-reference effect (Rogers, Kuiper, & Kirker, 1977), which has been shown to enhance recall, the inventory was structured as a self-evaluation form. We adopted an endnote referencing format in order to manage the length and complexity of the inventory. Using an endnote system allowed us to create a less cluttered inventory that still provided the potential for readers to engage in self-directed learning (Loyens, Magda, & Rikers, 2008) by following up on the original sources of strategies.[1] In addition, we adopted a nearly identical content order to the cultural adaptation workshop, providing further opportunities for practitioners to investigate the strategies of their choice.

Discussion

It is important for counselors, facilitators, and social workers to be aware of the strengths and limitations of the training tools they use, as this allows them to ensure that they are suitable for their needs. In this spirit, we discuss the strengths and weaknesses of this tool below. Subsequently, we offer a few thoughts on the possible directions of future developments in culturally adapted mental health treatments.

Strengths

One considerable strength of this inventory is the extensive, balanced, and diverse literature review upon which it is based, which has allowed for common themes to emerge from expert recommendations and program outcome studies. Over 190 publications were cited, including both methodologically rigorous research and the experiential writings of veteran clinicians. Consequently, the resulting review may be considered broadly representative of a large segment of professionals in the field.

More quantitative than qualitative studies were used in order to address the criticism that culturally competence literature relies too heavily on theory and qualitative research (Hays, 2009; La Roche & Christopher, 2008). This strong foundation in quantitative research has helped to ensure that many of the strategies presented in the inventory have been validated as part of broad collections of effective, diversity-friendly modifications. However, the inclusion of recommendations sourced from the experiential writings of senior clinicians is valuable as well, as this has lent considerable face validity to many of the strategies described, potentially benefitting concrete-minded learners. The fact that the content of the inventory closely follows the PAMF (Hwang, 2006), one of the most current frameworks for cultural adaptation presently concluding clinical trials (Hwang, 2012), is also a positive indicator of the validity of its content. Despite a more predominant quantitative research base, we believe the inventory is broadly reflective of expert consensus between practitioners and researchers in a number of areas.

In regards to the inventory itself, considerable effort was taken to create a concise, accessible, and practitioner-friendly learning tool. The information is organized according to several empirically supported learning principles: it is concrete; organized by logical, application-focused goals; offers opportunities for self-directed learning; and encourages practitioners to relate strategies to themselves. Finally, this tool is part of a full range of free, publicly available materials including an extensive literature review, website, and downloadable online workshop. Therefore, there are a number of closely related learning materials which are easily accessible to complement this inventory at no cost to practitioners.

Limitations

Despite having considerable strengths, this inventory also has several notable limitations worth highlighting to potential learners. These limitations come in three broad categories: those relating to scope, depth, and methodology of the underlying literature review; the brief, textual format of the inventory; and the need for testing and consultation to further refine this tool. In terms of methodology, despite the extensive literature review that was undertaken, it is possible that the information selected by the principal author may reflect researcher bias. Although every effort was made to select studies according to their applied relevance, we may have inadvertently expressed personal biases in the information that we attended to and selected.

In terms of scope and depth, the literature review was not limited solely to quantitative and methodologically rigorous studies. Even though some examples and suggestions shared in the inventory were based on randomized controlled trials (RCTs) and rigorous, empirical research, a significant part of the review and resulting strategies was theory-driven. Therefore, at times, specific strategies were extended from broader quantitative findings or generated based on theoretical principles or clinical expertise shared in peer-reviewed articles. Consequently, although many of the strategies have been empirically validated as a group through cultural adaptation outcome research, the individual strategies have not yet been validated as discrete elements.

In terms of the brief, textual format of this tool, a deliberate trade-off was made between brevity and depth in order to ensure the form was short enough to possess clinical utility. Thus, the scope of the tool was intentionally limited to cultural diversity only, which is merely a single dimension of human diversity. Practitioners are strongly encouraged to consider how they will incorporate other important aspects of diversity such as religion, language, gender, sexual orientation, and socioeconomic status.

Additionally, learners should be aware that the included inventory is based on broad generalizations stemming from research with a number of disparate groups from a variety of different countries, ethnic backgrounds, immigration statuses, and acculturation levels. Therefore, it will be important for practitioners to treat the strategies provided as tentative and pursue additional, group-specific research on their own initiative. Additionally, given that the inventory is designed to use self-directed learning, its effectiveness as a teaching tool is dependent on the motivation of the learner and his or her comfort with individual learning.

Perhaps the most important limitation to bring to the attention of readers is that the included learning tool still requires further testing and refinement. It has not yet been tested empirically nor formally evaluated by cultural competency experts. Furthermore, it could likely benefit from further refinement based on the feedback of potential users. Thus, it will be important to continue improving this tool based on practitioner feedback.

In summary, strengths of the 101 strategies for more culturally responsive mental health services—group facilitator version include a broad and diverse literature review, strong face validity, and careful attention to clinical and educational utility. Weaknesses may include a lack of empirical, expert, and user review; a scope limited to cultural diversity only; and broad generalizations that may not necessarily apply equally well to all cultural groups. Prospective users are encouraged to consider these strengths and weaknesses to determine whether this professional development tool is suitable for their individual needs.

Future Developments

The 101 strategies for more culturally responsive mental health services—group facilitator version inventory was created to help address a central challenge in the field of cultural competence, which is the lack of integration of the cultural competency movement and evidence-based practice research (Hays, 2009; La Roche & Christopher, 2008). To date, there is only limited evidence available on the effectiveness of completely novel, culture-specific therapies (Griner & Smith, 2006; Huey & Polo, 2008), yet the effectiveness of unadapted evidence-based treatments for diverse clients has also not been firmly established (La Roche & Christopher, 2008; Miranda et al., 2005). The included inventory was developed to help practitioners pursue a sensible, middle ground approach (see Hwang, 2006) by adapting existing evidence-based protocols rather than using generic interventions as-is or developing completely new, culture-specific treatments.

Recent research trends suggest that this middle-ground approach is set to blossom. With the creation of the ecological validity model (EVM; Bernal, Bonilla, & Bellido, 1995) and the PAMF (Hwang, 2006), there are now two frameworks actively being tested for adapting psychosocial interventions (Walker, Trupin, & Hansen, 2011). Two RCTs of the EVM have been completed (Rossello & Bernal, 1999; Rossello, Bernal, & Rivera-Medina, 2008), and Hwang (2012) has reported that one using the PAMF is being prepared for publication. Therefore, it is likely that information available on the effectiveness of cultural adaptation is set to increase.

Another current development is the adoption of bottom-up therapeutic adaptation frameworks emphasizing customization of services based on collaboration with communities and stakeholders. This is evidenced by the creation of the formative method for adapting psychotherapy (Hwang, 2009) to enhance the PAMF, and the cultural adaptation process model (Domenech Rodríguez & Weiling, 2004) to complement the EVM. It appears that therapeutic adaptation research is increasingly integrating theory, practice, and community.

Another encouraging development is the steady establishment of novel culture-based treatments in parallel to the culturally adapted interventions movement, such as cuento therapy (Costantino, Malgady, & Rogler, 1986), strengthening of intergenerational/intercultural ties in immigrant Chinese American families (SITICAF; Ying, 1999), and Chinese Taoist cognitive psychotherapy (Zhang et al., 2002). As cultural diversity in Western countries increases, these innovative new therapies are likely to gather additional interest and support.

A meta-analysis of culturally adapted therapies by Griner and Smith (2006) indicated that interventions targeted to specific cultural groups were four times more effective than interventions for heterogeneous groups, and interventions conducted in a client's native language were twice as effective as interventions in English. Therefore, an increased convergence between culture-specific and culturally adapted therapies may occur, as emphasis shifts to progressively more targeted interventions rather than on broad racial or ethnic groups such as "Asian" or "African."

Finally, as we have highlighted the need for refinement of the 101 strategies for more culturally responsive mental health services with further testing and consultation, this process is also an expected future development. The present publication is part of the current effort to refine this tool through academic collaboration and peer review. It is our hope that this inventory will constitute one small step forward towards helping psychotherapy, counseling, and social work to continue to stay relevant and effective within a rapidly changing world.

References

American Psychological Association. (2002). *Guidelines on multicultural education, training, research, practice, and organizational change for psychologists.* Washington, DC: Author.

Benish, S. G., Quintana, S., & Wampold, B. E. (2011). Culturally adapted psychotherapy and the legitimacy of myth: A direct-comparison meta-analysis. *Journal of Counseling Psychology, 58,* 279–289. doi:10.1037/a0023626

Bernal, G., Bonilla, J., & Bellido, C. (1995). Ecological validity and cultural sensitivity for outcome research: Issues for cultural adaptation and development of psychosocial treatments with Hispanics. *Journal of Abnormal Child Psychology, 23,* 67–82.

Canadian Psychological Association. (2001). *Guidelines for non-discriminatory practice.* Retrieved from www.cpa.ca/cpasite/userfiles/Documents/publications/ NonDiscPractrev%20cpa.pdf

Collins, S., & Arthur, N. (2010). Culture-infused counselling: A model for developing multicultural competence. *Counselling Psychology Quarterly, 23,* 217–233. doi:10.1080/09515071003798212

Costantino, G., Malgady, R. G., & Rogler, L. H. (1986). Cuento therapy: A culturally sensitive modality for Puerto Rican children. *Journal of Consulting and Clinical Psychology, 54,* 639–645.

Domenech Rodríguez, M. M., & Weiling, E. (2004). Developing culturally appropriate, evidence-based treatments for interventions with ethnic minority populations. In M. Rastogin & E. Weiling (Eds.), *Voices of color: First person accounts of ethnic minority therapists* (pp. 313–333). Thousand Oaks, CA: Sage.

Griner, D., & Smith, T. B. (2006). Culturally adapted mental health intervention: A meta-analytic review. *Psychotherapy: Theory, Research, Practice, Training, 43*, 531–548. doi:10.1037/0033-3204.43.4.531

Hays, P. A. (2009). Integrating evidence-based practice, cognitive–behavior therapy, and multicultural therapy: Ten steps for culturally competent practice. *Professional Psychology: Research and Practice, 40*, 354–360. doi:10.1037/a0016250

Huey, S. J., & Polo, A. J. (2008). Evidence-based psychosocial treatments for ethnic minority youth. *Journal of Clinical Child and Adolescent Psychology, 37*, 262–301. doi:10.1080/15374410701820174

Hwang, W. (2006). The psychotherapy adaptation and modification framework: Application to Asian Americans. *American Psychologist, 61*, 702–715. doi:10.1037/0003-066X.61.7 .702

Hwang, W. (2009). The formative method for adapting psychotherapy (FMAP): A community-based developmental approach to culturally adapting therapy. *Professional Psychology: Research and Practice, 40*, 369–377. doi:10.1037/a0016240

Hwang, W. (2012). Integrating top-down and bottom-up approaches to culturally adapting psychotherapy: Application to Chinese Americans. In G. Bernal & M. M. Domenech Rodríguez (Eds.), *Cultural adaptations: Tools for evidence-based practice with diverse populations* (pp. 179–199). Washington, DC: American Psychological Association Press.

Kirmayer, L. J., du Fort, G. G., Young, A., Weinfeld, M., & Lasry, J. C. (1996). *Pathways and barriers to mental health care in an urban multicultural milieu: An epidemiological and ethnographic study.* Montreal, Quebec: McGill University, Culture and Mental Health Research Unit. Retrieved from https://www.mcgill.ca/files/tcpsych/Report6.pdf

La Roche, M., & Christopher, M. S. (2008). Culture and empirically supported treatments: On the road to a collision? *Culture & Psychology, 14*, 333–356. doi:10.1177/1354067X08092637

Lefley, H., & Bestman, E. (1991). Public–academic linkages for culturally sensitive community mental health. *Community Mental Health Journal, 27*, 473–491.

Leong, F. T. L. (2007). Cultural accommodation as method and metaphor. *American Psychologist, 62*, 916–927. doi:10.1037/0003-066X.62.8.916

Loyens, S. M., Magda, J., & Rikers, R. M. (2008). Self-directed learning in problem-based learning and its relationships with self-regulated learning. *Educational Psychology Review, 20*(4), 411–427. doi:10.1007/s10648-008-9082-7

Matsumoto, D., & Juang, L. (2008). *Culture & psychology* (4th ed.). Belmont, CA: Wadsworth.

Melfi, C. A., Croghan, T. W., Hanna, M. P., & Robinson, R. L. (2000). Racial variation in antidepressant treatment in a Medicaid population. *Journal of Clinical Psychiatry, 61*, 16–21. doi:10.4088/JCP.v61n0105

Miranda, J., Bernal, G., Lau, A., Kohn, L., Hwang, W., & LaFromboise, T. (2005). State of the science on psychosocial interventions for ethnic minorities. *Annual Review of Clinical Psychology, 1*, 113–142. doi:10.1146/annurev. clinpsy.1.102803.143822

Mok, H., Lao, D. W. L., Lin, D., Wong, M. P., & Ganesan, S. (2003). Chinese Canadians in a cross-cultural psychiatry outpatient clinic: Some exploratory findings. *BC Medical Journal, 45*, 78–81. Retrieved from http://www.bcmj. org/article/chinese-canadians-cross-cultural-psychiatry-outpatient-clinic-some-exploratory-findings

National Association of Social Workers. (2001). *NASW standards for cultural competence in the practice of social work.* Washington, DC: NASW Press.

Rapacki, T. M. (2014). *Cultured psychology*. Retrieved from http://www. culturedpsychology .com

Rapacki, T. M., & McBride, D. L. (2013). *From awareness to practice: An online workshop on bringing culture into the counselling room.* (Master's project, University of Lethbridge, Lethbridge, Canada). Retrieved from: https://www. uleth.ca/dspace

Rapacki, T. M., & McBride, D. L. (2014a). *From awareness to practice: An online workshop on bringing culture into the counselling room.* Retrieved from ERIC database. (ED545469)

Rapacki, T. M., & McBride, D. L. (2014b, June). *From awareness to practice: Bringing culture into the counselling room.* Paper presented at the XXXVI Annual Symposium of the International Association for Social Work With Groups, Calgary, Alberta, Canada.

Rogers, T. B., Kuiper, N. A., & Kirker, W. S. (1977). Self-reference and the encoding of personal information. *Journal of Personality and Social Psychology, 35*(9), 677.

Rossello, J., & Bernal, G. (1999). The efficacy of cognitive-behavioral and interpersonal treatments for depression in Puerto Rican adolescents. *Journal of Consulting and Clinical Psychology, 67*, 734–745.

Rossello, J., Bernal, G., & Rivera-Medina, C. (2008). Individual and group CBT and IPT for Puerto Rican adolescents with depressive symptoms. *Cultural Diversity & Ethnic Minority Psychology, 14*, 234–245. doi:10.1037/1099-9809.14.3.234

Safran, J. D., & Muran, J. C. (2006). Has the concept of the therapeutic alliance outlived its usefulness? *Psychotherapy: Theory, Research, Practice, Training,*

43, 286–291. doi:10.1037/0033-3204.43.3.286

Smith, T. B., Domenech Rodríguez, M. M., & Bernal, G. (2011). Culture. *Journal of Clinical Psychology, 67*, 166–175. doi:10.1002/jclp.20757

Snowden, L., & Yamada, A. M. (2005). Cultural differences in access to care. *Annual Review of Clinical Psychology, 1*, 143–166. doi:10.1146/annurev. clinpsy.1.102803.143846

Stewart, S. L. (2008). Promoting Indigenous mental health: Cultural perspectives on healing from Native counsellors in Canada. *International Journal of Health Promotion and Education, 46*, 49–56. doi:10.1080/14635240.2008 .10708129

Sue, D. W., & Sue, D. (2008). *Counseling the culturally diverse: Theory and practice.* Hoboken, NJ: John Wiley & Sons.

U.S. Department of Health and Human Services. (2001). *Mental health: Culture, race, and ethnicity—A supplement to mental health: A report of the surgeon general.* Rockville, MD: Author. Retrieved from http://www.ncbi.nlm.nih. gov/books/NBK44243/pdf/TOC .pdf

Walker, S. C., Trupin, E., & Hansen, J. (2011). *A toolkit for applying the cultural enhancement model to evidence-based practice.* Retrieved from http:// depts.washington.edu/pbhjp/ downloads/projectsD/models_for_changeD/ Toolkit%20Cultural%20Enhancement%20Model.pdf

Wampold, B. E., Mondin, G. W., Moody, M., Stich, F., Benson, K., & Ahn, H-N. (1997). A meta-analysis of outcome studies comparing bona fide psychotherapies: Empirically, "all must have prizes." *Psychological Bulletin, 122*, 203–215.

Wang, P. S., Lane, M., Olfson, M., Pincus, H. A., Wells, K. B., & Kessler, R. C. (2005). Twelve-month use of mental health service in the United States. *Archives of General Psychiatry, 62*, 629–640.

Ying, Y. W. (1999). Strengthening intergenerational/intercultural ties in migrant families: A new intervention for parents. *Journal of Community Psychology, 27*, 89–96.

Zane, N., Sue, S., Chang, J., Huang, L., Lowe, S., Srinivasan, S., . . . Lee, E. (2005). Beyond ethnic match: Effects of client–therapist cognitive match in problem perception, coping orientation, and therapy goals on treatment outcomes. *Journal of Community Psychology, 33*, 569–585. doi:10.1002/jcop.20067

Zhang, Y., Young, D., Lee, S., Zhang, H., Xiao, Z., Hao, W., . . . Chang, D. F. (2002). Chinese Taoist cognitive psychotherapy in the treatment of generalized anxiety disorder in contemporary China. *Transcultural Psychiatry, 39*, 115–129. doi:10.1002/(SICI)1520-6629(199901)27:1<89::AID-JCOP6>3.0.CO;2-O

Appendix:
101 Strategies for More Culturally Responsive Mental Health Services—Group Facilitator Version

The purpose of this inventory is to help group-based mental health practitioners to explore and evaluate strategies to enhance their work with diverse clients. This document is adapted from the workshop entitled "From Awareness to Practice" and is grounded in the psychotherapy adaptation and modification framework. Complementary materials are publicly available on the ERIC database (reference number ED545469). The endnotes are available from the first author's website: www.culturedpsychology.com/. Facilitators are advised to employ these recommendations only in combination with their best clinical judgment and consideration of a client's individual characteristics and preferences, as well as with in-depth knowledge of the client's specific cultural group.

Please rate the following cultural competency strategies from 1 to 5 based on how well they fit with your personal helping style, with 1 being not at all and 5 meaning very well.

Domain 1: Dynamic Issues & Cultural Complexities					
Section 1: Self-Esteem	1	2	3	4	5
1. Include interdependent traits[3] in self-esteem building	☐	☐	☐	☐	☐
2. Inquire about group membership when assessing self-esteem	☐	☐	☐	☐	☐
3. Ask the question "what would your mother (friend, etc.) say are your personal strengths?"[4]	☐	☐	☐	☐	☐
Section 2: Acculturation and Personal Values	1	2	3	4	5
4. Use clients' level and strategy of acculturation to inform how to "size"[5,6] cultural interventions	☐	☐	☐	☐	☐
5. Personalize statements recognizing clients' cultural values without stereotyping[6]	☐	☐	☐	☐	☐
6. But, discuss common cultural experiences if doing so normalizes stigmatized experiences or emphasize the customization of a counseling program[7]	☐	☐	☐	☐	☐
7. Assess acculturation formally; e.g., through the GEQ[8], VIA[9], AVS[10], etc.[11,12]	☐	☐	☐	☐	☐
8. Assist a client with finding and employing a comfortable acculturation[13] strategy	☐	☐	☐	☐	☐
9. Ask clients about the role of culture and context in their lives when unsure of how to dynamically size interventions	☐	☐	☐	☐	☐
Section 3: Minority Identity Development	1	2	3	4	5
10. Utilize a model of minority identity development[14] to set developmental goals when appropriate	☐	☐	☐	☐	☐
Section 4: Personality in Context	1	2	3	4	5
11. Reduce the weighting of personality assessment conclusions based on limited cultural norms	☐	☐	☐	☐	☐
12. Interpret personality in the context of national differences[15,16] in mean scores	☐	☐	☐	☐	☐
13. Consider that newcomer "neuroticism" may simply reflect acculturative stress[17]	☐	☐	☐	☐	☐
14. Learn about and use indigenous personality tests, such as the CPAI-2[18]	☐	☐	☐	☐	☐
15. Discuss indigenous personality values and concepts with your participants	☐	☐	☐	☐	☐

Domain 2: Orientation to Group Work					
Section 1: Orientation to Group Therapy	1	2	3	4	5
16. Make time for a longer, more detailed orientation[2,6]	☐	☐	☐	☐	☐
17. Educate explicitly about roles and expectations in therapy/group work[2,6]	☐	☐	☐	☐	☐
18. Explain the typical course of treatment[2]	☐	☐	☐	☐	☐
19. Build rapport by emphasizing confidentiality[19]	☐	☐	☐	☐	☐
20. Discuss healthy termination to reduce dropout[2]	☐	☐	☐	☐	☐
21. Reduce stigma by articulating a holistic/biopsychosocial model that doesn't make clients feel personally blamed for their illnesses and struggles[2,4]	☐	☐	☐	☐	☐
Section 2: Meeting Client Expectations	1	2	3	4	5
22. Assess if the client may prefer a more active, problem-focused, and expert approach[19-27]	☐	☐	☐	☐	☐
23. Discuss with clients how needing extra time to acclimatize to a foreign therapeutic culture and having waited longer to seek help may slow initial therapeutic benefits[6]	☐	☐	☐	☐	☐
24. Offer the gift of a small solution early on as an example, and for motivation[5]	☐	☐	☐	☐	☐
Section 3: Establishing Goals/Structure	1	2	3	4	5
25. Emphasize co-constructing[19] group therapy/interventions	☐	☐	☐	☐	☐
26. Consider establishing frequent goals and markers of treatment progress with periodic review[6]	☐	☐	☐	☐	☐
Domain 3: Cultural Beliefs					
Section 1: Holistic, Psychoeducational Approach	1	2	3	4	5
27. Teach and utilize a biopsychosocial model of mental illness[2]	☐	☐	☐	☐	☐
28. Maintain a more systemic focus[28]	☐	☐	☐	☐	☐
29. Help resolve relational/social conflicts[4,6]	☐	☐	☐	☐	☐
30. Explore the consequences of interventions for the client's family[29]	☐	☐	☐	☐	☐
31. Simplify material, reduce learning load, consolidate complex topics[6]	☐	☐	☐	☐	☐
32. Consider increasing session length; teaching time for unfamiliar concepts[6]	☐	☐	☐	☐	☐
Section 2: Cultural Bridging Techniques	1	2	3	4	5
33. Use a traditional wellness model from the client's culture such as yin & yang[7] or the medicine wheel[30-32] to present mental health strategies	☐	☐	☐	☐	☐
34. Utilize the wheel of wellness[33]	☐	☐	☐	☐	☐
35. Learn and make use of cultural sayings to explain therapeutic concepts[2,34-36]	☐	☐	☐	☐	☐
36. Frame interventions so as to be congruent with specific cultural values[7,36]	☐	☐	☐	☐	☐

Section 3: Incorporating Cultural Beliefs, Strengths, and Resources	1	2	3	4	5
37. Increase focus on resolving relational problems[6]	☐	☐	☐	☐	☐
38. Assess social/familial/environmental contributions to illness and wellness[4]	☐	☐	☐	☐	☐
39. Emphasize collaboration over confrontation[4]	☐	☐	☐	☐	☐
40. Teach problem-solving for coping with practical environmental stressors[4]	☐	☐	☐	☐	☐
41. Present skills together with cultural context within which they will be effective[4]	☐	☐	☐	☐	☐
42. Refocus hierarchical, punitive cultural parenting styles on harmonious collectivist values[37]	☐	☐	☐	☐	☐
43. Reframe familial conflict as differences in acculturation and offer assistance as a cultural broker[38]	☐	☐	☐	☐	☐
44. Educate about acculturative family distancing and mental health[39,40]	☐	☐	☐	☐	☐
45. When acculturation conflicts occur in families, consider reframing acculturation as development of bicultural competence, not assimilation	☐	☐	☐	☐	☐
46. Emphasize help-seeking as finding solutions rather than admitting failure[41]	☐	☐	☐	☐	☐
47. Encourage culturally congruent and inexpensive self-care activities[4,2]	☐	☐	☐	☐	☐
48. Conduct a cultural strengths/assets search[4]	☐	☐	☐	☐	☐
49. Be aware of possible differences in values such as sharing vs. individual achievement, noninterference[42], dialectical/negotiated problem resolution[43,44]	☐	☐	☐	☐	☐
Section 4: Reducing Stigma	1	2	3	4	5
50. Increase collaboration with cultural healers, doctors, elders, religious leaders, and other physical/spiritual health practitioners[2]	☐	☐	☐	☐	☐
51. Increase visibility in the cultural community[45]	☐	☐	☐	☐	☐
52. Distribute materials and raise awareness where clients first seek help[45]	☐	☐	☐	☐	☐
53. Address community misconceptions about mental health services[45]	☐	☐	☐	☐	☐
54. Stress privacy and confidentiality[46]	☐	☐	☐	☐	☐
55. Decrease emphasis on changing cognitions; increase positive thinking, problem solving, and behavioral activation[4,6]	☐	☐	☐	☐	☐
56. Question the helpfulness rather than rationality of a problematic beliefs, particularly when stressors are real[4]	☐	☐	☐	☐	☐

Domain 4: Relationships					
Section 1: Developing Cultural Knowledge/Self-Awareness	1	2	3	4	5
57. Read about clients' cultural backgrounds	☐	☐	☐	☐	☐
58. Inquire directly about cultural values and influences	☐	☐	☐	☐	☐
59. Expose self to different cultures	☐	☐	☐	☐	☐
60. Explore Hofstede's cultural dimensions for a client's culture[47,48]	☐	☐	☐	☐	☐
61. Take cultural workshops, coursework, supervision, and consultation; diversify caseload[49]	☐	☐	☐	☐	☐
62. Utilize a White[50]/ethnic[14] identity model to guide own cultural development	☐	☐	☐	☐	☐
Section 2: Improve Joining	1	2	3	4	5
63. Utilize proper cultural etiquette in initial sessions[6]	☐	☐	☐	☐	☐
64. Offer tea; show concern about client's physical comfort; increase self-disclosure[6]	☐	☐	☐	☐	☐
65. Discuss/assess family and immigration history as an icebreaker[2]	☐	☐	☐	☐	☐
66. Normalize client feelings/perceptions of stigmatization[6]	☐	☐	☐	☐	☐
67. Actively provide validation, praise, emotional support, validate difficulty of sharing[6]	☐	☐	☐	☐	☐
68. Convey alignment nonverbally; e.g., moving one's chair to sit alongside a client while addressing a list of current problems[51]	☐	☐	☐	☐	☐
Section 3: Promoting Realistic Expectations	1	2	3	4	5
69. Explicitly discuss roles and expectations[6,2]	☐	☐	☐	☐	☐
70. Appear more professional; consider being more proactive with giving advice[7] if this matches client expectations	☐	☐	☐	☐	☐
71. Be aware of transference of expectations: e.g., a doctor, healer, or priest[52]	☐	☐	☐	☐	☐
72. Facilitate development of realistic expectations[2]	☐	☐	☐	☐	☐
73. Be aware that more severe problems may be possible due to delaying treatment due to cultural stigma of mental health help-seeking[2]	☐	☐	☐	☐	☐
74. Begin with easier tasks to inspire confidence[4]	☐	☐	☐	☐	☐
75. Share anecdotes or cases that normalize help-seeking, reduce feelings of isolation, or normalize initial difficulties[6]	☐	☐	☐	☐	☐
Section 4: Allying Against Racism and Prejudice	1	2	3	4	5
76. Actively broach the topic of race and racism in sessions[53]	☐	☐	☐	☐	☐
77. Anticipate mistrust[4]	☐	☐	☐	☐	☐
78. Strongly consider validating any feelings of victimization[4,53]	☐	☐	☐	☐	☐
79. Validate racial microaggressions[54,55] as real and hurtful	☐	☐	☐	☐	☐
Section 5: Cognitive Matching	1	2	3	4	5
80. Generally avoid challenging cultural beliefs unless this is a client goal[4]	☐	☐	☐	☐	☐
81. Use cognitive matching: match responses, discussions, and interventions to individual, sociocultural, or universal levels by following client language[56]	☐	☐	☐	☐	☐

Domain 5: Cultural Differences in Expression and Communication

Section 1: Differences in Communication	1	2	3	4	5
82. Consider using silence to demonstrate understanding in initial sessions[4]	☐	☐	☐	☐	☐
83. Avoid misinterpreting normal low-key, indirect communicative behavior as passivity, avoidance, or shyness, if such communication is a cultural trait[2]	☐	☐	☐	☐	☐
84. Allow Aboriginal persons ample time to finish speaking[57]	☐	☐	☐	☐	☐
85. Be aware of differences in meaning of smiles, silence, and eye contact[19,58]	☐	☐	☐	☐	☐
86. Increase self-disclosure[19,58-62], invitational body language[64]; invite questions[19]	☐	☐	☐	☐	☐
87. Employ visuals, translators, supportive friends or family members, multilingual dictionaries[64]	☐	☐	☐	☐	☐
88. Be mindful of the ethical limitations of using child translators[19]	☐	☐	☐	☐	☐
89. Apologize for the limitations of one's cultural helping style but express a willingness to understand the group participants and their situations[65]	☐	☐	☐	☐	☐
90. Utilize homework evaluation forms[66]; translated exit/feedback slips (e.g., SRS[67] and ORS[68] group versions)	☐	☐	☐	☐	☐
91. Discuss the cultural meaning of interpersonal distance[58]	☐	☐	☐	☐	☐
Section 2: Expression of Distress	1	2	3	4	5
92. Focus part of early assessment on physical symptoms[2]	☐	☐	☐	☐	☐
93. Inquire about psychosocial symptoms indirectly: "Dealing with headaches and dizziness can be quite troublesome; how are these affecting your mood, relationships, etc.?"[69]	☐	☐	☐	☐	☐
94. Help clients differentiate between thoughts and feelings during treatment[6]	☐	☐	☐	☐	☐
95. Use a nonstigmatizing procedure to make a codiagnosis with a client[7]	☐	☐	☐	☐	☐

Domain 6: Issues of Salience

Section 1: Specific Cultural Issues	1	2	3	4	5
96. Take the initiative to learn about the strengths and challenges of individual cultural groups[2]	☐	☐	☐	☐	☐
97. Adopt an expanded understanding of responsibilities as a mental health worker[70,71]	☐	☐	☐	☐	☐
98. Assist/counsel clients on meeting practical needs, overcoming structural barriers[4,68-73]	☐	☐	☐	☐	☐
99. Use the three dimensional model of multicultural counseling[70]	☐	☐	☐	☐	☐
100. Consult with the community or community leaders on adapting your counseling approach[6,7]	☐	☐	☐	☐	☐
101. Use the FMAP[6] or cultural adaptation process model[74] to incorporate community feedback into therapeutic modifications	☐	☐	☐	☐	☐

Note

Due to space limitations, the endnotes have been deleted from the inventory. The complete inventory and endnotes are available from the first author's website at www.culturedpsychology.com/.

Strengths-Based Group Supervision with Social Work Students

Mari Alschuler, Linda McArdle, & Thelma Silver

Over the last 20 years, social work intervention with client systems has moved towards models that emphasize the strengths perspective (Saleebey, 2013). In the educational arena, supervision of social work students in their field placements has also begun to emphasize models that incorporate concepts of the strengths perspective (Bransford, 2009; Lietz & Rounds, 2009). These concepts can also be applied to group supervision. The focus of this paper is to integrate theoretical models of the strengths perspective, narrative theory (Freeman, 2011; White & Epston, 1990), and reflective practice (Schön, 1983), while incorporating the techniques of parallel process (Miehls, 2010) and the Socratic method (Barsky, 2010) into group supervision of social work students. This is also a model that can incorporate the diversity of supervisors, clients, and students.

Group Supervision

Nearly all trainees in the helping professions receive supervision during their internships. Supervision of social workers dates back to the earliest days of the profession (Kadushin & Harkness, 2014). Field education of social work students has often been provided through the use of group supervision in addition to, or instead of, individual supervision (Bogo, Globerman, & Sussman, 2004).

Supervision has been divided into a tripartite schema consisting of administrative or managerial tasks, educational or clinical tasks, and supportive tasks (Kadushin & Harkness, 2014). Supervision is typically provided in individual or group formats; some agencies provide one or the other, or both. Lietz (2008) suggested that group supervision is both effective and efficient and can provide trainees with supervision in all three functions. Further, group supervision permits supervisors to view interns from a different vantage point compared to how each student presents him- or herself in individual supervision. In addition, agencies find group supervision to be more cost effective, and supervisors find it more efficient in terms of time.

Some of the advantages of group over individual supervision are that supervisees can receive multiple viewpoints about work with diverse clients, which fosters critical thinking and creative problem-solving; share common problems and insecurities about their work, alleviating anxiety and preventing nondisclosure; receive emotional support; and begin to develop a sense of professional identity (DiMino & Risler, 2012; Ellis & Douce, 1994; Kadushin & Harkness, 2014; Lietz, 2008; Milne, Sheikh, Pattison, & Wilkinson, 2011). There are also several disadvantages of group supervision (Kadushin & Harkness, 2014). The supervisor, as group leader, must juggle individual supervisee personalities, educational abilities, and emotional needs. As in all groups, there is an inherent risk of groupthink and the stifling of creativity in supervisory groups.

Further, group process needs to take center stage in group supervision, according to DiMino and Risler (2012). Supervisors have to pay close attention to group dynamics. Conflicts, competition, and rivalry between group members must be managed in order to develop intimacy and trust. The group setting is the ideal place to learn how to deal with power struggles, diverse points of view, expectations, and need for support (Kadushin & Harkness, 2014).

Balancing group-as-whole and individual issues, managing group process, and handling group dynamics are other issues which may cause some supervisors to offer only individual supervision (Ellis & Douce, 1994). Depending on the supervisor's skills and willingness to explore cultural diversity or other differences, there is a risk of ignoring such differences. DiMino and Risler (2012) further contended that the supervisor needs to attend to his or her own use of self; protect boundaries, including dual relationships with supervisees; and be willing "to take risks and become vulnerable" (p. 67).

According to Bogo and McKnight (2005), there has been a dearth of empirical research on the effectiveness of all types of supervision in the helping professions. Many of the empirical studies reviewed in their meta-analysis of articles about supervision from 1994 to 2004 examined perceptions of general aspects of the supervisory relationship; others examined supervisory process and client outcomes more specifically. Unfortunately, the authors decided to focus solely on studies conducted within the U.S. There were many other limitations to the articles they reviewed: doctoral studies; exploratory studies; convenience sampling; measurement bias; and the use of self-report measures.

Milne et al. (2011) conducted a meta-analysis of 11 controlled studies, with a goal of developing evidence-based training in clinical supervision. This review covered only individual supervision, which was a limitation. The authors concluded that "no apparent consensus exists on what constitutes effective supervisor training" (Milne et al., 2011, p. 54) and that there is limited information on how to evaluate this training.

Kadushin and Harkness (2014) described some positive results of research comparing group to individual supervision. Supervisees receiving group supervision stated they had received training in a wider variety of diverse cases, obtained direct advice and feedback from both peers and supervisors, and saw their peers as capable of providing them with valuable consultation. However, after summarizing several empirical studies since the 1970s, they concluded that individual supervision "is a preferred option when supervisees are offered a choice" (Kadushin & Harkness, 2014, p. 295) between the two modalities.

In a Canadian qualitative study, Bogo et al. (2004) looked at key factors and processes in group supervision of field students. Their pilot study relied on retrospective recall by past field group supervisees, and the actual study used an all-female sample of 18 students over two academic years in the late 1990s. Five supervisors led seven groups; all but one field instructor were also female. Both supervisees and supervisors were predominantly Euro-Canadian. Group process issues were rarely discussed openly in the groups; supervisors did not appear to facilitate these groups in a manner that allowed students to express their insecurities. Students' peer relationships appeared to have influenced how conflict, trust, cohesion, competition, and anxiety about competence were discussed or managed.

Bogo et al. (2004) pinpointed the necessity to have competent supervisors leading student groups. They described the values of modeling participation and openness, which facilitated students' risk taking; promoting group norms, which allowed the members to establish safety and a climate of trust, which further led to sharing their vulnerabilities and anxieties, reducing their fear of criticism; facilitating group dynamics, which prevented favoritism and monopolization, using direct confrontation when necessary to diffuse conflict; and giving constructive feedback, which encouraged open communication and peer-to-peer feedback. The authors summarized their study with a list of emerging themes, which they posited as recommendations for the group supervision of social work field students. The group supervisor should provide (a) clear expectations about how the group will operate, such as time per student for case presentations and the order and format of presentations (logistics); (b) a constructive learning climate by managing group member behaviors through modeling; (c) assistance to supervisees as they establish group norms; (d) active intervention should behavioral (non-normative) problems occur; (e) timely and constructive feedback; and (f) educational information on group process and group dynamics, providing members with the opportunity to enact these (Bogo et al., 2004).

Strengths-Based Group Supervision

The strengths-based model of group supervision incorporates concepts from the models of supportive supervision (Kadushin & Harkness, 2014) and cooperative supervision (Proctor & Inskipp, 2001, as cited in Ögren & Sundlin, 2009) with the concepts of empowerment (Saleebey, 2013), resilience and self-efficacy (Kearns & McArdle, 2012). In supportive supervision (Kadushin & Harkness, 2014), the supervisor is one who reaches for the strengths of the supervisees through recognition of their successes and provision of positive reinforcement of the skills and assets that are demonstrated. The supervisor motivates and provides a place of support. In group supervision, the supervisees also take on the responsibility to reach for their peers' strengths and give support.

Strengths-based supervisors assist supervisees in focusing on what is working in the present, rather than pathologizing clients or their own abilities. In strengths-based group supervision of students, skill development can occur through storytelling about cases and reflective and Socratic questioning. By training supervisees in narrative techniques such as restorying, strengths-based supervisors can assist group members' ability to remain attuned through a "not-knowing" stance (Freeman, 2011), which serves to strengthen their relationship with their clients by de-emphasizing the power differential (Bransford, 2009). By reflecting on their work during supervision, student supervisees listen to narratives and learn to move within them to co-create shared experiences with clients through parallel process.

Proctor and Inskipp (2001, as cited in Ögren & Sundlin, 2009) described training group supervision of therapists as falling into three functions. The first was authoritative and focused on the supervisory dyad; it is called "supervision in the group." The second was cooperative, which related to "supervision by the group." The third type, participative, or "supervision with the group," was placed between the other two types, as if on a continuum. In a participative group, the supervisor "focuses on the individual group members, and encourages the supervisees' active participation in the supervision" (Proctor & Inskipp, 2001, as cited in Ögren & Sundlin, 2009, p. 133).

We believe that group supervision using a strengths perspective (Saleebey, 2013) lends itself to being a cooperative type of supervision, or supervision by the group. Proctor and Inskipp (2001, as cited in Ögren & Sundlin, 2009) stated that a cooperative relationship with clients is a key concept in the strengths perspective, whereby the social worker engages collaboratively with the client to improve the client's life. Applying this concept to group supervision, the supervisor engages with the group cooperatively to enhance students' skills and abilities. The field supervisor and the group members act in partnership in setting the agenda and providing support, encouragement, and feedback to one another during supervisory groups.

Empowerment

One concept that relates to group supervision and the strengths perspective is the concept of empowerment, which means enhancing one's ability to identify and use the resources in oneself and in one's environment (Saleebey, 2013). In group supervision, the students are not only accessing their abilities to reflect on their own practice, but they are also using their abilities to assist their peers, which can be an empowering experience.

Resilience

Another concept in the strengths perspective that applies to group supervision is the concept of resilience (Saleebey, 2013). Resilience combines both mastery and flexibility, and is impacted by individual attributes, as well as by social and interpersonal factors. However, resilience relates not only to individual personality or social support of others, but also to mutuality and a shared experience. Resilience has a component of reflection which adopts a person-in-environment focus as the supervisee examines the impact of the work on her- or himself (Collins, 2007, as cited in Adamson, 2012).

Thus, resilience is a multidimensional concept and lends itself to support by others, either personally or professionally (Kearns & McArdle, 2012). Through this support, supervisees can learn task-oriented coping and problem-solving skills. Moreover, resilience is also a concept that incorporates diversity of experience, as group members share their different methods of mastery and problem solving. Kearns and McArdle (2012) considered resilience as "evaluating 'what is' against the hope of 'what could be', the balance of optimism and realism. Other themes proposed are universality in terms of a shared experiences, belief in change, and crucially, meaningful relationships with others" (p. 387). All of these components of resilience can relate well to group supervision, where students can share experiences and provide feedback to each other on balancing hope and reality in their field sites.

Self-Efficacy

Self-efficacy relates closely to the concept of resilience and is the sense individuals have that they can have an impact on the events in their lives (Bandura, 1982, as cited in Kearns & McArdle, 2012). Research has identified that high self-efficacy relates to one's ability for growth and learning, especially with emotionally challenging situations. Thus, through the support of their peers and a group supervisor, students can attain a more positive sense of self, which can then impact their openness to learning. In a small qualitative study of supervision of new social workers working in Children's Services in the United Kingdom, Kearns and McArdle (2012) reported that self-efficacy related to the quality and nature of support received from supervisors and peers. As students in supervision groups understood the impact of their interventions, their perceived self-efficacy improved.

Diversity

It is important to recognize the role of diverse membership within supervision groups (Corey, 2008). This includes the supervisees, their clients, and the supervisor. Education of the facilitator should reflect the composition of the group based on the pool of supervisees participating in the sessions. Ideally, group composition issues should be handled during the initial stages of the group formation (Barsky, 2010). Diversity factors should cover a wide range of issues, such as sexual orientation, cultural background, religion and spirituality, age, disability, gender, gender identity, and political beliefs (Ellis & Douce, 1994).

To respond to their multicultural student body in the multicultural society in Israel (Arkin, Freund, & Saltman, 1999), the faculty at the University of Haifa used a group supervision model. The Haifa model, which incorporated a group developmental perspective, used both individual and group supervision with the students. The authors concluded that this group supervision model worked well for a diverse study body. According to this model, differences are viewed as strengths that could be easily integrated with the strengths perspective (Saleebey, 2013).

Issues relevant to the work of the supervisory sessions should be considered essential in education of the supervisor as a component of the "knowing" process. This early work is particularly important because it serves to enlighten the facilitator and group members regarding the range of perspectives represented by each member's world view.

Parallel Process

The concept of parallel process, initially grounded in psychoanalytic theory, views the social worker–supervisor relationship as reflecting issues present in the client–social worker relationship (Ellis & Douce, 1994; Ganzer & Ornstein, 1999). Parallel process has since been examined from other theoretical perspectives, such as narrative theory (Miehls, 2010). Supervisors need to remember that they are role models, and just as they relate to students as partners, in a parallel way this can reflect on how students relate to their clients. Ellis and Douce (1994) suggested that material which is resolved in supervision may thus become resolved in future client sessions. Thus, supervisors need to practice what they teach (Lietz & Rounds, 2009).

With the strengths perspective (Saleebey, 2013) as a unifying model in contemporary social work and social work education, we suggest this model also can reflect the supervisory parallel process (Miehls, 2010). Similarly, as we as social workers strive to work with clients in a cooperative partnership that emphasizes their strengths and abilities, empowerment, resilience, and diversity, so, too, we need to bring these concepts into the supervisee–supervisor relationship.

Student Group Supervision Case Example

The following is a social work student group supervision case example. The concepts discussed above regarding the strengths perspective (Saleebey, 2013), partnership and cooperation, resilience, and empowerment, will then be related to this example, which also includes a technique of working with a diverse population. One of the authors of this paper was an external field supervisor for three Caucasian students who were interning at the same organization that works with delinquent youth. The students were a Bachelor of Social Work (BSW) student (E), a first year Master of Social Work (MSW) student (A), and a second year MSW student (B). This supervisory group occurred during the second semester of field for the two MSW students and the first semester of field for the BSW student.

> We sat down to begin this supervision session and MSW student (A) opened her notebook with her process recording. The other student (B) said to her that she looked ready to begin. I agreed that (A) looked ready to begin and said that if that was okay with them, it was all right with me to start with (A). (A) began her narrative of her session with an African American male youth client. (B) gave much encouragement and support to (A) as she discussed the client, because (B) had this youth as a client early the previous semester, and he had not been responsive to her. However, (A) seemed to be developing good rapport with the client, who was very active in his sessions with her. The client had a strong interest in the technology of music which (A) appreciated and understood. Then (B) pointed out to (A) that she was using one of her strengths to engage the client. (E) then became involved in this discussion of the client,

because the client had been referred to a group that she facilitated, and she provided information to (A) about her group.

This example demonstrated the type of cooperative supervision that Proctor and Inskipp (2001, as cited in Ögren & Sundlin, 2009) had described. This was supervision by the group and the field instructor acted in partnership with the students. In a similar way, the student was using her partnering with the client in her sharing of an interest in music to work with the client and to bridge some of their difference. Moreover, the statement that (B) made that (A) was able to engage with the client when (B) had been unable to do so is a very supportive statement, as was the comment that (A) was using her strengths to focus on one client's strengths. This was the type of positive feedback that could encourage resiliency and self-efficacy, and also could lead to a sense of empowerment in the supervisee (Kearns & McArdle, 2012). Thus, this case example demonstrates how a few of the concepts of the strengths perspective (Saleebey, 2013) can be applied to group supervision.

As mentioned above, conflicts and competition can arise in group supervision as conflict is a part of group process (DiMino & Risler, 2012). If, in the case example above, the students (B) and (E) were overly critical of (A) as she presented, how could the supervisor use a strengths-based approach in the group?

> As (A) began her narrative of her session with the African American male youth client, (B) seemed to become overly critical and (E) joined in on the criticism. The supervisor noted that (B) and (E) wanted to give feedback. However, feedback is more helpful when it is stated in the positive of what could be done differently. The supervisor suggested that perhaps (B) and (E) could restate their responses in regards to what was positive about (A)'s intervention and give other options of intervention.

In the hypothetical case example, the supervisor is reaching for strengths in the students who were being overly critical and encouraging them to develop more supportive and strengths-based responses. Thus, one can see from this case example how a few of the concepts of the strengths perspective (Saleebey, 2013) can be applied to group supervision. A strengths-based approach to group supervision can be demonstrated through various models. The following section focuses on using narrative methods.

Narrative Approaches to Group Supervision

Narrative Therapy and the Strengths Perspective

Narrative therapy (NT), as developed by White and Epston (1990), is a postmodern method within the paradigm of social constructionism, which posits that reality is formed through linguistic and other agreements by those living in a particular society and culture during a specific historical period (Whiting, 2007). Active listening to narratives includes hearing and observing changes in the narrator and listeners' behaviors that signal the emergence of problem-saturated narratives. NT uses techniques such as reauthoring or restorying narratives (White & Epston, 1990) in order to obtain some distance from the problem, and to begin to disconnect participants' sense of self from their problem self (Howard, 2008).

NT focuses on client empowerment through collaborative conversations. Freeman (2011) explained that a focus on strengths within narratives helps individuals to "shift from explaining" (p. 26) their lives to "overcoming those experiences, as a way of recreating themselves, and as evidence of their strengths and resilience" (p. 26). Client stories often contain images or metaphors which may be conduits for uncovering strengths. Therapists can help clients develop a strengths-based revised life narrative focused on their strengths, supports, and resources. Some stories may have never been told before due to oppression or discrimination. Narrative therapists and supervisors can help clients and supervisees break these silences and ensure that voices that have been silenced in the past are released and heard. A strengths-based approach to group supervision, then, may be demonstrated through narrative means.

Narrative Supervision

Storytelling is a selective discourse: what people choose to tell is countered by what they choose to omit; supervisees are selective in the stories they import to supervision. A client tells a story; a supervisee tells a story about the client; supervisors may even tell a story about past experiences with their own clients. What is learned in supervision is then exported back to direct practice by the supervisee in parallel process.

Narrative-based supervisors train supervisees to look at how one interprets and makes meaning of the world and the stories one tells, and to explore how one might contextualize one's identities within the wider sociocultural and political realms (Kearns & McArdle, 2012). As in clinical practice, if supervision is problem—rather than strengths-based—supervisees may be hesitant in sharing mistakes, uncertainty, or other concerns, such as fear of judgment or a personal history of oppression. By helping supervisees generate or reauthor resilient stories, they can learn to "incorporate vital and previously neglected aspects of lived experience" (Gard & Lewis, 2008, p. 31), including any prior experiences of having been silenced or negated by oppression or discrimination.

One of the goals of narrative supervision is to help the supervisee approach case material, self-awareness, and use of self in a more positive stance (Howard, 2008). Helping students unlearn or deconstruct their own self-criticism is crucial, according to Gard and Lewis (2008). If students bring in problem-saturated stories, supervisors can help them learn to externalize the problem so they do not equate themselves to the problem. Externalizing a problem helps clients and supervisees see moments when they defied or refused "to perform according to the requirements of the problem" (Gard & Lewis, 2008, p. 26) story, by which they then start identifying unique outcomes that allow them to dissolve the problem or find new solutions. The supervisor's role is to validate trainees' progress and independence, help them feel safe enough to share all of their experiences in supervision, focus on what worked, and ensure that they view their self-criticism, not themselves, as the problem (Freeman, 2011; Gard & Lewis, 2008; Kelley, 2013).

One technique that can be used within a narrative approach (White & Epston, 1990) to group supervision is to help supervisees develop a "not-knowing" stance (Bransford, 2009; Freeman, 2011). This attitude refutes the therapist role as expert and reduces the inherent power differential in both the supervisor–supervisee and the supervisee–client dyads. Bransford (2009) recommended that, after the supervisor has created a safe space, students would silently observe their own thoughts and bodily sensations while their peers described case material. The supervisor/therapist listens actively from this not-knowing stance, checking for metaphors, images, and beliefs (which may be faulty), and determining how language is uniquely used by the storyteller.

The role of the group supervisor thus becomes that of a facilitator who uses encouraging questions designed to seek understanding of client issues that may not have been previously considered (Barsky, 2010). Supervisees are encouraged to educate the facilitator, who embodies not-knowing regarding the issues the group seeks to resolve. By partnering with student supervisees in a group setting, the supervisor may use Socratic questioning as one technique to further develop the narratives. This technique is described below, followed by an example of a collaborative, interdisciplinary team conference which used a strengths-based approach, Socratic questioning, and narrative inquiry.

The Socratic Method of Inquiry

Strengths-based supervision (Saleebey, 2013) may also be facilitated through the use of pointed clinical questions during group supervision (Barsky, 2010). Socrates used this educational method as a means to stimulate debate between individuals with opposing viewpoints. Socrates realized that this dialectical technique permitted group members to ask and answer questions, ultimately resulting in heightened critical thinking. Through guided oppositional discussion aimed at pitting one point of view against the other, students are allowed to strengthen their perspectives and to think about the question before speaking.

Socratic methods can be adapted for group supervision to assist professionals who are challenged to understand difficult clinical practice issues (Barskey, 2010; Copeland, 2010; Straker, 2014). Using the Socratic method of inquiry, the group supervisor asks one or more participants a series of questions in order to help them discuss and analyze a case scenario in unique ways using different perspectives (Yassour-Borochowitz, 2004). Participants generate their own understanding, knowledge, or truths from engaging in a dialogue with the facilitator (Maxwell, 2007).

Barsky (2010) has suggested that, in order to adapt the Socratic method of inquiry to a group educational context, the facilitator may use a number of strategies linked to the first two stages of the generalist problem-solving process (p. 149). When using the process in a supervisory capacity, the process begins with the engagement stage, which introduces issues to be discussed and explains the

Socratic inquiry method. Participants are given an opportunity to raise concerns about the process at this stage. The supervisor then demonstrates empathy regarding students' concerns and suggests ground rules for a safe environment for discussion and learning (Barsky, 2010, p. 149). This process allows all participants to develop consensus regarding the issues for discussion, learning objectives, and agreed-upon ground rules.

The second stage of the process is the assessment and learning stage (Barsky, 2010). At this time, the case situation is presented, giving students an opportunity to express their initial views, restate their previously discussed views, demonstrate understanding, or invite clarification (Barsky, 2010, p. 149). Questions are then posed by the supervisor to raise doubts about the students' previously held views, allowing them the chance to look at the case from a different perspective. To heighten the critical-thinking process, the supervisor then poses a series of hypothetical questions designed to raise exceptions to current issues under discussion. The purpose of this step is to raise doubts about the participants' strongly held beliefs.

This stage of the process challenges the supervisor to "take the member's [or members'] views to an extreme" (Barsky, 2010, p. 150). This provides an opportunity for the supervisor to demonstrate an interest in learning from the students. Participants then consider what might happen if their concepts were applied to every case they encountered. This serves as an opportunity to change how they might view the issue, given the new information that they have obtained through the assessment process. The facilitator's role also involves patience and understanding as supervisees attempt to reason through their issues and thinking to find possible answers to their dilemmas.

Types of Questions Used in Socratic Inquiry

Conceptual clarification questions. These questions provide an opportunity for students to analyze what they are asking and thinking about. This type of question allows students to link the concepts that support their argument. These questions may be identified as the "tell me more" questions that assist them in probing deeper into their critical-thinking process. Typical questions include, "Can you give me an example?" or "Are you saying . . . or . . . ?"
Probing assumptions. This type of question probes unquestioned

suppositions and previously-held beliefs which are the foundation of an argument. Many times, the participant's assumptions may be based on strongly held familial belief systems which may prove difficult to change when challenged. Probing questions might include "How did you choose those assumptions?" or "What would happen if . . . ?"

Probing rationale, reasons, and evidence. When students provide a rationale for their arguments, the role of the supervisor is to probe the underlying source. The goal is to challenge participants to dig into their reasoning rather than taking it at face value. Questions that probe into rationale and require evidence include "How do you know this?" or "Can you give me an example of that?" or "What do you think causes . . . ?"

Questioning viewpoints and perspectives. Strengths-based supervisors (Saleebey, 2013) should recognize that the participants' position may be challenged using many different versions of their argument. The goal should be to challenge each student to identify his or her position and show that there are other, equally valid, viewpoints to consider. Examples might include the following: "What alternative ways of looking at this are there?" or "What are the strengths and weaknesses of . . . ?"

Probe implications and consequences. The participants' arguments may have logical implications relative to the problem or case issue. Do these arguments make sense? The role of the supervisor should be to question whether the consequences are desirable (Straker, 2014). Questions linked to implications and consequences tend to include "What are the consequences of that assumption?" or "What are the implications of . . . ?" or "How does . . . affect/fit with what you've learned before?"

According to Barksy (2010), the use of Socratic inquiry focuses primarily on the assessment and learning stage. This method provides an opportunity for understanding a situation rather than performing and planning, implementation, and follow-up stages of the problem-solving process (Barksy, 2010, p. 150). Socratic questioning may be used with other groups, as in the development of learning experiences for social work students (Corey, 2008). It may also be useful with clients who are faced with problems coping with or handling difficult ethical issues (Reamer, 2006). The ultimate goal for use of this method in the group context would be for the participants to gain a better understanding of the issues needing to be dealt with and methods to be considered when trying to resolve them.

Interdisciplinary Case Example

Students in social work, nursing, nutrition, and speech therapy formed a supervision group led by instructors in each of the four fields of practice. This group has met four times per semester and has used interdisciplinary group simulations to facilitate the development of professional case assessment and potential interventions. As an example, one of the nursing instructors role-played a client. Historically, the pre-existing problems inherent in interdisciplinary teamwork are social in nature. Based on this assumption, the supervisory team identified the significance of applying an Adlerian perspective to the interdisciplinary process. Using this approach allowed the faculty supervisors an opportunity to develop a sense of belonging and team connectedness in the group process (Corey, 2008).

Simulation scenario. Mrs. E is a 74-year-old African American woman married to her husband for 50 years. Mr. E has a history of late-stage liver cancer. Mrs. E and her husband had one son who was killed in the Gulf War. Their daughter-in-law and grandson are very supportive and assist the couple. Mrs. E's husband reported that his wife (our patient) has become increasingly forgetful and appears depressed most days. She has been fearful about his health and their potential inability to remain in their home based on their combined health concerns. Mr. E is realistic about his own prognosis and is unsure how to identify and provide appropriate care for his wife now and in the near future. Mr. and Mrs. E and their daughter-in-law have visited several local assisted living facilities, but they are unsure if Mrs. E's care would be manageable at that level. The community-based health care team, represented in the simulation by the interdisciplinary students, has been requested to analyze the case and provide recommendations.

Interdisciplinary case conference. The faculty members assumed roles as "seekers of understanding." The ground rules were that discussion about the client scenario would take place in a safe environment in which all participants could share critical thinking and their personal perspectives. Faculty members helped the students identify issues in ways they might not have previously considered, such as from a strengths perspective (Saleebey, 2013). They used a series of Socratic questions to assist the interdisciplinary students to discuss and analyze the simulation scenario (Barsky, 2010; Copeland, 2010; Straker, 2014). Faculty processed impressions about client needs, potential diagnoses for Mrs. E, opportunities for interdisciplinary collaboration, and so on. At the engagement stage (Barsky, 2010), supervisors requested students use empathy and concern for the family. During the assessment stage, after the case was presented to the students, they were invited to provide ideas, thoughts, and preliminary analyses related to Mrs. E and her family. Supervisors posed questions that sought to elucidate different points of view about possible diagnoses, such as dementia, clinical depression, or delirium. Faculty provided hypothetical questions to raise exceptions to current issues, such as the effects of Mr. E's terminal illness and impending death on Mrs. E.

During the final case analysis, group members were encouraged to share their perspectives regarding the work that had been done throughout the process with this patient. This discussion served to challenge their previously held beliefs regarding interdisciplinary team roles, personal convictions and values based on earlier learning regarding discipline-specific responsibilities, and best practices that would ultimately benefit the patient.

In conclusion, the evaluation of the experience received from the participants reflected their unanticipated insight that resulted from the interdisciplinary group interaction. The exercise challenged previously held beliefs regarding roles based on members' disparate disciplines and encouraged members to think of themselves as interdisciplinary learners. The use of questions in interdisciplinary group settings, in some cases, provided the supervisor the opportunity to focus on what the members were saying by reflecting on their subjective experiences. This method of supervision ultimately assisted in the recognition of different ways of viewing the patient's situation based on the dialogue stimulated by the interdisciplinary team during the Socratic inquiry process (Barsky, 2010).

Discussion

This paper represents a beginning theoretical conceptualization on using the strengths perspective (Saleebey, 2013) in conjunction with narrative inquiry (White & Epston, 1990), Socratic questioning (Barsky, 2010), and an awareness of the importance of parallel process (Miehls, 2010) in the supervision of interdisciplinary groups. The case examples presented relate some of the practical uses of this approach for group supervision of students.

In the above discussion we demonstrated how the strengths perspective (Saleebey, 2013), which has been used in interventions with client systems, can also be used in a parallel manner with group supervision of social work students, thus making the process more participatory. Through group supervision, students can demonstrate resilience by sharing experiences, but they can also access their diverse skills and life situations (Kearns & McArdle, 2012). By using narrative inquiry techniques (White & Epston, 1990) and Socratic questioning (Barsky, 2010), supervisors can encourage students to share details of their client work with the other group members.

A strengths-based approach (Saleebey, 2013) to supervision focuses on what is working rather than on a deficit narrative. By listening for metaphors, images, and faulty beliefs that shore up problem-saturated stories that supervisees (and clients) tell, supervisors can elicit narratives from those whose voices may have been silenced due to oppression or discrimination (Freeman, 2011; White & Epston, 1990). The supervisor can help trainees identify the importance of reflecting on their subjective reality while facilitating openness to the interprofessional group process (Corey, 2008). By stressing the importance of the supervisor enabling student participants to enter into their own subjective reality, they may become more open to collaborative teamwork without losing their own sense of identity in the group process. Using the support of the group can be empowering and can increase supervisees' sense of efficacy (Kearns & McArdle, 2012).

In conclusion, the role of the supervisor is critical in the development of student learning through the use of alternative methods of thinking and interacting in a collaborative group setting. The use of pointed clinical questions and applied case scenarios in Socratic inquiry may lead students to develop agreements and a common understanding regarding client issues (Barsky, 2010). Ultimately, strengths-based group supervision may develop increasingly professional interactions among students, leading to a mutually supportive team process.

References

Adamson, C. (2012). Supervision is not politically innocent. *Australian Social Work, 65*(2), 185–196.

Arkin, N., Freund, A., & Saltman, I. (1999). A group supervision model for broadening multiple-method skills of social work students. *Social Work Education, 18*, 49–58.

Barsky, A. E. (2010). *Ethics and values in social work: An integrative approach for a comprehensive curriculum.* New York, NY: Oxford.

Bogo, M., Globerman, J., & Sussman, T. (2004, Winter). The field instructor as groupworker: Managing trust and competition in group supervision. *Journal of Social Work Education, 40*(1), 13–26.

Bogo, M., & McKnight, K. (2005). Clinical supervision in social work: A review of the research literature. *The Clinical Supervisor, 24*(1/2), 49–67.

Bransford, C. L. (2009). Process-centered group supervision. *Clinical Social Work Journal, 37*, 119–127. doi:10.1007/s10615-009-0200-x

Copeland, M. (2010). *Socratic circles: Fostering critical and creative thinking in middle and high school.* Portland, ME: Stenhouse.

Corey, G. (2008). *Theory and practice of group counseling* (7th ed.). Belmont, CA: Thompson.

DiMino, J. L., & Risler, R. (2012). Group supervision of supervision: A relational approach for training supervisors. *Journal of College Student Psychotherapy, 26*, 61–72. doi:10.1080 /87568225.2012.633050

Ellis, M. V., & Douce, L. A. (1994, May/June). Group supervision of novice clinical supervisors: Eight recurring issues. *Journal of Counseling & Development, 72*, 520–525.

Freeman, E. M. (2011). *Narrative approaches in social work practice: A life span, culturally centered, strengths perspective.* Springfield, IL: Charles C. Thomas.

Ganzer, C., & Ornstein, E. D. (1999). Beyond parallel process: Relational perspectives on field instruction. *Clinical Social Work Journal, 27*, 231–246.

Gard, D. E., & Lewis, J. M. (2008). Building the supervisory alliance with beginning therapists. *The Clinical Supervisor, 27*(1), 39–60.

doi:10.1080/07325220802221470

Howard, F. (2008, June). Managing stress or enhancing wellbeing? Positive psychology's contributions to clinical supervision. *Australian Psychologist, 43*(2), 105–113. doi:10 .1080/005006081978647

Kadushin, A., & Harkness, D. (2014). *Supervision in social work* (5th ed.). New York, NY: Columbia Press.

Kearns, S., & McArdle, K. (2012). 'Doing it right?'—Accessing the narratives of identity of newly qualified social workers through the lens of resilience: "I am, I have, I can." *Child and Family Social Work, 17,* 385–394. doi:10.1111/j.1365-2206.2011.00792.x

Kelley, P. (2013). Narratives. *Encyclopedia of Social Work.* Retrieved from http://socialwork .oxfordre.com/view/10.1093/acrefore/978019997583

Lietz, C. A. (2008). Implementation of group supervision in child welfare: Findings from Arizona's Supervision Circle Project. *Child Welfare, 87*(6), 31–48.

Lietz, C. A., & Rounds, T. (2009). Strengths-based supervision: A child welfare supervision training project. *The Clinical Supervisor, 28,* 124–140. doi:10.100/0732522090334065

Maxwell, M. (2007). *Introduction to the Socratic method and its effect on critical thinking.* Retrieved from http://www.socraticmethod.net

Miehls, D. (2010). Contemporary trends in supervision theory: A shift from parallel process to relational and trauma theory. *Clinical Social Work Journal, 38,* 370–378.

Milne, D. L., Sheikh, A. I., Pattison, S., & Wilkinson, A. (2011). Evidence-based training for clinical supervisors: A systematic review of 11 controlled studies. *The Clinical Supervisor, 30,* 53–71. doi:10.1080/07325223.201 1.564955

Ögren, M.-L., & Sundin, E. C. (2009). Group supervision in psychotherapy: Main findings from a Swedish research project on psychotherapy supervision in a group format. *British Journal of Guidance & Counselling, 37*(2), 129–139. doi:10.1080/03069880902728614

Reamer, F. G. (2006). *Social work values and ethics* (3rd ed.). New York, NY: Columbia University Press.

Saleebey, D. (2013). *The strengths perspective in social work practice* (6th ed.). New York, NY: Pearson.

Schön, D. A. (1983). *The reflective practitioner.* New York, NY: Basic Books.

Straker, D. (2014). *Changing minds: Socratic questions.* Retrieved from http://changingminds .org/techniques/questioning/socratic_questions.htm

White, M., & Epston, D. (1990). *Narrative means to therapeutic ends.* New York, NY: W. W. Norton.

Whiting, J. B. (2007). Authors, artists, and social constructionism: A case study of narrative supervision. *The American Journal of Family Therapy, 35,* 139–150. doi:10.1080 /01926180600698434

Yassour-Borochowitz, D. (2004). Reflections on the researcher-participant relationship and the ethics of dialogue. *Ethics and Behavior, 14*(2), 175–186.

Part 4
Student Voices

A New Group Worker Learns and Practices

Samantha Swift

Beginning an internship stirred mixed feelings, excitement to put passion into practice, and nervousness about those "not enough" thoughts. I believe these to be common feelings among many students who are entering new professional roles, where the challenge is to bring a textbook to life. As a student, it is important to remember that best practices presented in textbooks are final products. Researchers, scholars, and practitioners have also learned through trial and error, so in this article I hope to highlight common stumblings that may occur among new group workers and solutions to rectify them.

Stumblings and Solutions

Parallel Learning Process

Traditional learning at colleges and universities has encouraged students to take a passive role, with little interactive, practice-based learning (Dabbour, 1997). Conversely, Hakeem (2001) found that students saw improved academic performance after participating in experiential activities compared to students who did not. Experiential activities performed in conjunction with coursework is called parallel learning. Parallel learning enables students to grow academically while they practice their burgeoning professional skills. Some social work education programs have incorporated parallel learning, enabling students the opportunity to simultaneously experience the roles of student/learner and social worker/professional. This is beneficial for social workers because it encourages the students to learn empathy, which is essential in recognizing the dignity and worth of people (National Association of Social Workers, 2008). It also helps social work students to critically evaluate their work and enriches their interactions with clients.

Need for a Group

During my first year internship at an outpatient mental health clinic, I was assigned by my field supervisor to facilitate a group on anger management. In an effort to understand how anger affected clients, I listened during intake assessments and heard stories of how clients struggled to stay out of jails and hospitals, and how aggressive behaviors had caught the attention of others (e.g., family, friends, and law enforcement) resulting in crisis interventions. Individual accounts described various factors that contributed to aggressive behaviors: paranoia, command hallucinations, and drug induced psychosis, as well as coping skills that have served to protect them from different types of abuse they received at home or work during indigency, or within abusive relationships, or when involved in a gang. After being hospitalized or incarcerated, many of the clients sought outpatient treatment, which led them to our agency.

Calm and Collected

As a novice group worker, I opted to partner with another intern to cofacilitate our group. We recruited clients through referrals from care coordinators and intake coordinators, flyers, and by word of mouth by clients at the clinic. Membership was open to new members and held in "The Clubhouse," a common area for all clients at the clinic. Deciding on a curriculum and materials for group sessions was critical, especially considering our inexperience coordinating group work. When researching evidenced-based sources online, I came across a 12-week curriculum specifically targeted towards anger management and mental health. The sessions were a combination of psychoeducation and experiential activities to help members apply and explore triggers, family dynamics, emotions, and positive coping skills (Reilly, Shopshire, Durazzo, & Campbell, 2002). Knight (2014) explained a valuable role manuals can provide students: they familiarize new group workers with common themes. We reviewed the plan and received approval on the curriculum from our field supervisor.

As the group evolved, members who attended were usually waiting for an appointment or happened to be hanging out in the Clubhouse.

Despite our recruitment efforts to attract members who would benefit from the group purpose, our group was instead attended by members who stated they did not have anger issues. During our facilitator debriefings, we discussed these incongruities and eventually found that we lacked important input from group members: we realized that the group's purpose came from staff, so we re-evaluated. We discovered that a majority of the members said they wanted self-esteem building groups. They provided feedback about the structure and stated they enjoyed the activities and open discussions.

We used group member feedback to create new group topics related to mindfulness, spirituality, and mental health, and asked members how they felt about incorporating these themes into sessions. Most were enthusiastic about incorporating some meditative and self-esteem building elements. Soliciting feedback from the group enabled members to contribute in ways we had not expected. For example, one member shared a technique for anger management: she had been taught to hold sand in her hands and allow it to slip through her fingers, falling back into the earth, as the sand symbolized anger. Another member reported that sitting quietly with her eyes closed actually made her auditory hallucinations worsen. As members shared personal and cultural coping skills during sessions, other members appeared to become more open and interested in the diversity of the group members. Additionally, allowing members to share personal experiences and strengths found through their religions and spirituality helped to solidify the bridge of external resources to work within the group.

Navigating Taboos

During our first session, a member began to share about familial stressors with his mother and increasing auditory hallucinations. In his culture (ethnic Chinese), spirituality was the preferred treatment for mental health issues, which contradicted the recommendations of providers he had been seeing. The difference in cultural values created family discord and eventually manifested into him having homicidal thoughts towards his mother. This session led us to a discussion on establishing rules related to "taboo topics" and how to ensure safety within the group. After receiving mixed feedback from other group workers, we believed "taboo" topics were important for members to talk about and could help them to begin to see that they were not alone (add mutual aid). These topics were common and significantly impacted their lives, often isolating them from family, friends, and communities who did not share the same struggles. Enabling members to share about these topics helped to foster group cohesion, an important principle of group work practice (Toseland & Rivas, 2005).

Redefining Group Purpose

Another ethical dilemma was the lack of input from group members in developing the group purpose. It was not until after the group had begun that I learned about group work ethics and the democratic process that characterizes group work. This also negatively impacted self-determination and created barriers to identifying goals, which conflicts with a core value of social work in the United States (National Association of Social Workers, 2008). The challenge as a new group worker was learning late in the group's development that group members' involvement was essential in every stage of the group, including the planning stage. Additionally, because the members lacked goals, we did not have any metric to measure or use for an evaluation. According to the International Association of Social Work With Groups (IASWG; 2010), evaluation of the group's progress is an essential practice in group work to ensure that members' concerns are being addressed.

Conclusion

One of the greatest lessons that the parallel process taught me was to stay adaptable. My agenda and discussion topic were not always directly relevant to the immediate needs of group members, and we had to adjust along the way. The IASWG (2010) Standards for Social Work Practice With Groups call for creativity in group work and flexibility to tend to current needs. Unique to group work is that the focus of the work is on the process rather than attainment of goals and accomplishments (Cohen & Olshever, 2013). A group member described her recovery experience as "peeling back layers of an onion," meaning that changes occurred subtly and in small increments. As a new group worker I can relate; developing skills to empower members and cultivate feelings of ownership of the group took months. When the focus of my efforts as a facilitator shifted from trying to teach members how to manage anger and stress to facilitating a conversation among all members to share their experiences, strengths, and hope, I began to see the essence of group work.

References

Cohen, C. S., & Olshever, A. (2013). IASWG standards for social work practice with groups: Development, application, and evolution. *Social Work With Groups, 36*(2/3), 111–129. doi:10.1080/01609513.2012.763107

Dabbour, K. S. (1997, May). Applying active learning methods to the design of library instructions for a freshman seminar. *College and Research Libraries, 58*, 299–308.

Hakeem, S. (2001). Effect of experiential learning in business statistics. *Journal of Education for Business, 77*(2), 95.

International Association of Social Work With Groups. (2010). *Standards for social work practice with groups* (2nd ed.). Retrieved from http://www. iaswg.org/docs /AASWG_Standards_for_Social_Work_Practice_with_ Groups2010.pdf

Knight, C. (2014). Teaching group work in the BSW generalist social work curriculum: Core content. *Social Work With Groups, 37*(1), 23–35. doi:1 0.1080/01609513.2013.816918

National Association of Social Workers. (2008). *Code of ethics of the National Association of Social Workers*. Retrieved from http://www.socialworkers. org/pubs/code/code.asp

Reilly, P. M., Shopshire, M. S., Durazzo, T. C., & Campbell, T. A. (2002). *Anger management for substance abuse and mental health clients: Participant workbook*. Rockville, MD: Center for Substance Abuse Treatment, Substance Abuse and Mental Health Services Administration. Retrieved from http://162.99.3.213/products/manuals/pdfs /angrmngmnt_part_ wb_08r.pdf

Toseland, R. W., & Rivas, R. F. (2005). *An introduction to group work practice* (5th ed.). Boston, MA: Allyn and Bacon.

Psychoeducational Groups: Do They Meet the Diverse Needs of Women Who Have Been Abused by a Partner?

Stephanie L. Baird

Psychoeducational groups are a common social work intervention provided to survivors of intimate partner violence (IPV; Feder, Wathen, & MacMillian, 2013). However, despite the frequency of the provision of this intervention, there are many questions to consider related to whether they meet the diverse needs of IPV survivors. After providing a brief definition and overview of IPV, along with a description of psychoeducational groups, I outline my literature review findings. I then pose key remaining questions about the provision of this service to clients with diverse needs, including the needs of IPV survivors experiencing trauma. Finally, I offer conclusions for ensuring effective therapeutic group services for all survivors of IPV.

Background

The World Health Organization (WHO; 2013) has defined IPV as "behaviour by an intimate partner that causes physical, sexual or psychological harm, including acts of physical aggression, sexual coercion, psychological abuse and controlling behaviours" (p. vii). Unfortunately, IPV continues to be a significant issue, with Statistics Canada (2011) having stated that 17% of Canadians have reported an experience of emotional or financial abuse in a current or previous relationship. While IPV occurs to both males and females, the lifetime prevalence for women is particularly high, cited between 20 to 25% (Howard et al., 2010). Globally, the WHO has found that 13 to 61% of women between the ages of 15 and 49 have reported being physically abused by an intimate partner at least once (García-

Moreno, Jansen, Ellsberg, Heise, & Watts, 2005). Therefore, due to the high prevalence of IPV for women, I focus this discussion specifically on women.

IPV can have devastating consequences, such as depression, posttraumatic stress disorder (PTSD), physical injuries, health problems, increased risk of suicide, and even fatalities (DeJonghe, Bogat, Levendosky, & von Eye, 2008; Iverson, Shenk, & Fruzzetti, 2009). Given the high prevalence of IPV and the many negative consequences, it is essential that survivors receive effective therapeutic services. Frequently, these services are provided in the form of psychoeducational support groups, which have been described as the most common intervention for survivors of IPV (Feder et al., 2013). Psychoeducational groups tend to focus on providing information, empowerment, and advocacy to survivors of IPV, in order to promote healing (Tutty, Bidgood, & Rothery, 1993). Although the number of sessions and structures of these groups can vary, most tend to provide information on topics such as abuse and self-esteem, provide community resources, and offer support to group members.

As a social worker who has provided individual and group counselling services to IPV survivors for many years, I have observed positive impacts from psychoeducational groups. These positive effects include improved self-esteem, reduced stress, and reduced social isolation for group members (Allen & Wozniak, 2011; Tutty et al., 1993). However, I have also observed that some women stop attending these groups, and I have questioned the reasons for ceased attendance. The issue of attendance in groups for survivors of IPV has also been discussed in a study by Martinez and Wong (2009), who focused on using techniques such as reminder calls to increase attendance. As I began to pay attention to this issue, I noticed that service providers tend to individualize the reasons women stop attending these groups, assuming that women have stopped attending because they have returned to abusive relationships or they were not ready for a group experience (Pollack, 2004). While these reasons may be true for some women, these assumptions do not allow space for thinking critically about the services that are provided or for asking questions about possible problems with the services themselves.

Literature Review

A detailed literature review has shown many gaps in information about the effectiveness of groups for IPV survivors. In particular, there are few empirical studies of interventions for survivors of IPV. Barner and Carney (2011) stated that "further research into intervention policy and practice is needed to determine further courses of action in IPV intervention and treatment" (p. 240). Another gap was identified in specifying which kind of intervention is most helpful in which situation, rather than using similar IPV interventions for all situations (Stover, Meadows, & Kaufman, 2009).

One empirical study of 12 support groups for battered women in Waterloo Region, Ontario, was conducted by Tutty et al. (1993), with favourable results. The study described support groups as "the treatment of choice for battered women by most practitioners" (Tutty et al., 1993, p. 325). What is most interesting about this study, however, is that the services being offered to IPV survivors in Waterloo Region in 1993 were markedly similar to the services offered in 2014, more than 20 years later. This trend has also been observed in a review by Barner and Carney (2011), who found that "shelters for victims of IPV have maintained a steady state, providing a similar array of services for victims in 2009 as they did at the onset of the Battered Women's movement" (p. 240).

Pyles and Postmus (2003) reflected on this trend in the literature as well, discussing how the diversity in the communities and populations social workers serve has not been adequately reflected in the IPV literature. Pyles and Postmus also discussed the disquieting lack of literature reflecting the needs of women who have experienced abuse within a same-sex relationship or who have a disability. These findings reflect a further need to explore how psychoeducational services for IPV reflect the diverse experiences and needs of all IPV survivors. Perhaps the positive results found by Fuchsel and Hysjulien (2013), who employed a culturally specific group format for immigrant Mexican women who had experienced IPV, can provide an impetus for considering the use of culturally relevant interventions for IPV survivors.

Key Questions From Critical Theories

Critical theories, which include antioppressive practices (AOPs) and structural theory, offer an important lens through which to explore key questions about offering psychoeducational groups to survivors of IPV. Critical theories focus on the "analysis of power, privilege, inequity, discrimination and domination along identities of race, gender, class, sexual orientation, religion, age, and dis/ability" (Wong, 2004, p. 2). Structural theory emphasizes the importance of considering the impact of the structures themselves and ensures that the structures of agencies, intake processes, and groups do not create any barriers or discriminate "on the basis of class, race, gender, ability, sexual orientation, age, [or] religion" (Weinberg, 2008, p. 2). In particular, service providers need to ask questions related to whether these structures themselves contribute to women's reasons for ceased attendance at groups.

Although it has been noted that IPV occurs across all cultures, age groups, socioeconomic levels, and religious groups, women who are from multiple oppressed groups have been identified as being at increased risk due to additional power inequalities and less access to resources (McLeod, Hays, & Chang, 2010; Walker, 2013). For this reason, using AOPs, IPV must be viewed within the larger context of systemic oppression (Bograd, 1999; Sakamoto & Pitner, 2005; Strier, 2007). Key questions service providers need to ask are related to whether the group experience creates any additional experience of oppression by excluding women who have been marginalized in multiple ways, by providing an experience where the facilitator is framed as the "expert," or by furthering oppression through the power differentials between group facilitators and group members (Pollack, 2004; Sakamoto & Pitner, 2005).

Trauma and Overstimulation

There are also important questions to consider related to how women experiencing characteristics of trauma are impacted by group settings. One study by Kubany et al. (1995) identified that rates of

PTSD in shelters were as high as 45% to 84% for survivors of IPV. A study of helpful and harmful therapeutic interventions by Stenius and Veysey (2005) described the most harmful effects as occurring when "treatment providers do not take into consideration a woman's trauma history" (p. 1165). For trauma survivors, there is a potential that exposure to certain group information and traumatic stories from other women in the group may trigger the participants' own traumatic memories in harmful ways. Courtois and Ford (2013) specifically cautioned against group therapy for trauma, warning that because groups can "potentiate clients' feelings in ways that easily result in overstimulation, it is imperative for therapists to involve their clients only in groups that are in their range of tolerance" (p. 194). Unfortunately, most psychoeducational group programs for IPV that I have observed do not screen specifically for trauma, which means that facilitators have no way to identify these possible risks to clients. Thus, another important question to consider is whether the group experience can be overstimulating or retraumatizing for women who are experiencing trauma. While some group therapists have discussed the use of containment strategies to help clients to process traumatic events in group settings in safe and healthy ways (Doran & Punter, 2009), it is not known how often these approaches are implemented in psychoeducational groups for IPV.

Conclusion

While psychoeducational group services provide many survivors of IPV with helpful, supportive, and therapeutic services, more research is needed to determine if they truly meet the diverse needs of all IPV survivors. As identified in the review by Stover et al. (2009), for survivors of IPV, specific research is needed into which treatment is best for whom. In the meantime, service providers need to ask more questions about the groups they are offering, about the experiences of women who stop attending groups for IPV, and about the structures of their agencies, processes, and groups. As well, service providers need to continue to ask questions about the power dynamics between group facilitators and group members, in order to ensure that the group experience is not one that provides further experiences of oppression.

References

Allen, K. N., & Wozniak, D. F. (2011). The language of healing: Women's voices in healing and recovering from domestic violence. *Social Work in Mental Health, 9*(1), 37–55.

Barner, J. R., & Carney, M. M. (2011). Interventions for intimate partner violence: A historical review. *Journal of Family Violence, 26*(3), 235–244.

Bograd, M. (1999). Strengthening domestic violence theories: Intersections of race, class, sexual orientation, and gender. *Journal of Marital and Family Therapy, 25*(3), 275–289.

Courtois, C. A., & Ford, J. D. (2013). *Treatment of complex trauma: A sequenced, relationship based approach.* New York, NY: The Guilford Press.

DeJonghe, E. S., Bogat, G. A., Levendosky, A. A., & von Eye, A. (2008). Women survivors of intimate partner violence and post-traumatic stress disorder: Prediction and prevention. *Journal of Postgraduate Medicine, 54*(4), 294–300.

Doran, M., & Punter, J. (2009). Childhood sexual abuse: Trauma and healing in groups through the symbolic presence of the mother and the phallus. *Group Analysis, 42*(3), 233–245. doi:10.1177/0533316409339560

Feder, G., Wathen, C. N., & MacMillan, H. L. (2013). An evidence-based response to intimate partner violence: WHO guidelines. *JAMA, 310*(5), 479–480.

Fuchsel, C. L. M., & Hysjulien, B. (2013). Exploring a domestic violence intervention curriculum for immigrant Mexican women in a group setting: A pilot study. *Social Work With Groups, 36*(4), 304–320.

García-Moreno, C., Jansen, H. A. F. M., Ellsberg, M., Heise, L., & Watts, C. (2005). *WHO multi-country study on women's health and domestic violence against women: Initial results on prevalence, health outcomes and women's responses.* Geneva, Switzerland: World Health Organization. Retreived from http://www.who.int/gender/violence / who_multicountry_study/en/

Howard, L. M., Trevillion, K., Khalifeh, H., Woodall, A., Agnew-Davies, R., & Feder, G. (2010). Domestic violence and severe psychiatric disorders: Prevalence and interventions. *Psychological Medicine, 40*, 881–893. doi:10.1017/S0033291709991589

Iverson, K. M., Shenk, C., & Fruzzetti, A. E. (2009). Dialectical behavior therapy for women victims of domestic violence: A pilot study. *Professional Psychology: Research and Practice, 40*(3), 242–248.

Kubany, E. S., Abueg, F. R., Owens, J. A., Brennan, J. M., Kaplan, A., & Watson, S. (1995). Initial examination of a multidimensional model of guilt: Applications to combat veterans and battered women. *Journal of Psychopathology and Behavioral Assessment, 17,* 353–376.

Martinez, K., & Wong, S. (2009). Using prompts to increase attendance at groups for survivors of domestic violence. *Research on Social Work Practice, 19*(4), 460–463. doi:10.1177 /1049731508329384

McLeod, A. L., Hays, D. G., & Chang, C. C. (2010, Summer). Female intimate partner violence survivors' experiences with accessing resources. *Journal of Counseling & Development, 88,* 303–310.

Pollack, S. (2004). Anti-oppressive social work practice with women in prison: Discursive reconstructions and alternative practices. *British Journal of Social Work, 34,* 693–707.

Pyles, L., & Postmus, J. L. (2004). Addressing the problem of domestic violence: How far have we come? *Affilia, 19*(4), 376–388.

Sakamoto, I., & Pitner, R. O. (2005). Use of critical consciousness in anti-oppressive social work practice: Disentangling power dynamics at personal and structural levels. *British Journal of Social Work, 35,* 435–452.

Statistics Canada. (2011). *Family violence in Canada: A statistical profile, 2009.* Retrieved from http://www.statcan.gc.ca/pub/85-224-x/85-224-x2010000-eng.pdf

Stenius, V., & Veysey, B. (2005). "It's the little things." *Journal of Interpersonal Violence, 20*(10), 1155–1174. doi:10.1177/0886260505278533

Stover, C. S., Meadows, A. L., & Kaufman, J. (2009). Interventions for intimate partner violence: Review and implications for evidence-based practice. *Professional Psychology: Research and Practice, 40*(3), 223–233.

Strier, R. (2007). Anti-oppressive research in social work: A preliminary definition. *British Journal of Social Work, 37*(5), 857–871.

Tutty, L. M., Bidgood, B. A., Rothery, M. A. (1993). Support groups for battered women: Research on their efficacy. *Journal of Family Violence, 8*(4), 325–342.

Walker, T. (2013). Voices from the group: Violent women's experiences of intervention. *Journal of Family Violence, 28*(4), 419–426.

Weinberg, M. (2008). Structural social work: A moral compass for ethics in practice. *Critical Social Work, 9*(1). Retrieved from http://www.uwindsor.ca/criticalsocialwork/structural-social-work-a-moral-compass-for-ethics-in-practice

Wong, Y.-L., R. (2004). Knowing through discomfort: A mindfulness-based critical social work pedagogy. *Critical Social Work, 4*(1). Retrieved from http://www1.uwindsor.ca /criticalsocialwork/knowing-through-

discomfort-a-mindfulness-based-critical-social-work-pedagogy
World Health Organization. (2013). *Responding to intimate partner violence and sexual violence against women: WHO clinical and policy guidelines.* Geneva, Switzerland: WHO Press. Retreived from http://www.who.int/reproductivehealth/publications/violence /9789241548595/en/

Group Dynamics in the Classroom: Comparing the Applicability of Group Stage Models

Kyle McGee

Research has shown that groups have a course of stages they go through from beginning formation to ending separation (Caple, 1978; Garland, Jones, & Kolodny, 1973; Tuckman, 1965). Much study has been done regarding group phase development in treatment and support groups, but there is still much to be learned about how these phases relate to a classroom group. This article briefly explores how two prominent group models, the Boston model (Garland et al., 1973) and the relational model (Schiller, 1995, 1997), can help social work educators to further understand group dynamics in the classroom and thus provide a way to enhance their students' learning. I use a teaching experience of mine as a case study example.

The Class as Group

The concept of the class group is not new to social work educators. Schwartz (1964) was first to acknowledge that a parallel process often exists for social work students in the classroom that mirrors their experience in fieldwork. His work highlighted that the teacher as facilitator of this process is an important element in student learning. Shulman (1987) also presented situational experiences from teaching in social work education and offered a conceptual frame regarding the nature of group dynamics and their impact to the learning process in the classroom. Shulman's main premise was that learning occurs via the intersection of both content and process of the educational experience. He argued that educators often have a tendency to think of content and process as dichotomous rather than integrated. Other social work educators have developed these ideas over time and proposed ways to enhance student learning through use of class group activities and assignments that encourage learning through process of experience (Cramer, Ryosho & Nguyen, 2013; Holley & Steiner, 2005; Quiros, Kay & Montijo, 2012).

Comparing Two Group Stage Models

Group stage models help explain the developmental processes that occur during the life of a group. They serve as a frame to identify patterns of behavior in both members and the group as a whole, and offer a useful guide to group workers in deciding on courses of action to facilitate the successful achievement of each stage in development (Ciardello, 2007). Experienced instructors will often say that they have encountered situations where tensions and disputes have surfaced between students in class. The ways that instructors address these issues can have a direct impact on their ability to create a successful learning environment. Comparing elements of the Boston model (Garland et al., 1973) and the relational model (Schiller, 1995, 1997) can offer some insight for instructors to better understand group dynamics that occur in a classroom, especially with respect to interpreting and managing ruptures in process.

The Boston model and relational model both maintain that a group's development occurs in five linear stages from beginning formation to ending termination. A pivotal area where these models differ, however, is in the stage where conflict occurs in the development of a group. The Boston model indicates that conflict within a group is related to power and control issues and precedes a group's ability to develop intimacy (Garland et al., 1973). Conversely, the relational model suggests that intimacy in groups, particularly those with women, occurs prior to dealing with conflict and power issues (Schiller, 1995, 1997). Both models lead to a similar destination, but they have different means of sequence to this end. Comparing each of these models in relation to class group process thus offers a broader conceptual framework for educators to consider when conflict arises in a class group.

The following case study describes a social work class I taught and highlights the comparison of these two group stage models. The considerations I present are meant to be a starting point for further conceptual exploration and research; they are not meant to provide answers, but rather to help teachers increase their focus on the questions needing to be asked.

A Case Example for Study

Some years ago I taught a foundations of social work practice course where a rupture in group process took place. The course duration was an entire academic year (two semesters) and as one could imagine, as an instructor, I was able to get to know my student group fairly well. The composition of the class was quite diverse in regards to race, religion, socioeconomic status, and sexual orientation; however, a significant area of homogeneity in the class was gender, as the class was predominantly women. Approximately two weeks into the first semester, an email was circulated by the public safety department of the school that explicitly directed social work students on how to travel safely to and from school in the particular neighborhood in which it was located. The school was situated in a major city of the northeast U.S. and had recently relocated to a new area after residing for years in a more affluent one. The reaction from students about this safety notification was mixed, and the idea that it highlighted elements of racial and class division between the school and its surrounding community was questioned. While some students felt relieved to know the school was aware that they were at some risk, others felt strongly that it implied a message of the school's "separateness" from the community.

A particularly emotional encounter took place in class where a student of color became upset as she explained her own experience of growing up in a poor neighborhood where the encroachment of a major university had also taken place. This experience was very hurtful, and the student acknowledged feeling that the actions of our university had openly conveyed a similar message: that members of her community were seen as dangerous. The class was visibly moved by this personal story however; a response made soon afterward by another female student (not of color) expressed support and validation for the security alert on the grounds of its particular importance for the safety of female students at the school. The dialogue between students about this became very conflicted, and a palpable sense of uncertainty and distrust continued in the class throughout much of the year, particularly when discussion took place about issues of race and oppression in social work practice.

Considerations for Practice

Taking the class group example and applying the Boston model and relational model raises interesting considerations. If one were to use the Boston Model to analyze the class conflict, then the focus would center on working through issues of power and control within the group (Garland et al., 1973). However, use of the relational model would suggest that a process of developing connection and relationship between students would be the focus area of attention (Schiller, 1995, 1997). Both models suggest that a need for trust is necessary although the means to get to that trust is rooted in two different paths of conceptual interpretation.

Another point of interest in this analysis is that the class was made up of predominantly women. Examining gender composition is highly relevant to the extent of how each stage model may apply, particularly with the stages associated with the relational model. From my experience, over recent decades, there has been an increasing proportion of female students in social work classes. Does this support a need for more attention toward factors associated with the relational model in teaching? It is beyond the scope of this article to fully explore this question, but it is certainly worthy of more attention.

The use of group stage models can help instructors enhance their ability to create successful learning environments. Although a task group by nature, a classroom environment demonstrates characteristics of sequential development that can be enhanced by comparisons of group stage models. The Boston model and the relational model are both widely known in the field of social group work and their contributions can be applicable to understanding classroom groups. As suggested in a teaching example, there appears to be a growing trend of an increasing proportion of female students in schools of social work, which may support an increased attention to the relational model.

References

Caple, R. (1978). The sequential stages of group development. *Small Group Behavior, 9*(4), 470–476.

Ciardello, S. (2007). *Worker perception of group development: Testing the applicability of the Boston model for the stages of group development* (Unpublished doctoral dissertation). Wurzweiler School of Social Work, Yeshiva University, New York.

Cramer, E. P., Ryosho, N,. & Nguyen, P. V. (2013). Using experiential exercises to teach about diversity, oppression, and social justice. *Journal of Teaching in Social Work, 32*, 1–13.

Garland, J., Jones, H., & Kolodny, R. (1973). A model for stages of development in social work groups. In S. Bernstein (Ed.), *Explorations in group work* (pp. 17–71). Boston, MA: Milford House.

Holley, L. C., & Steiner, S. (2005). Safe space: Students' perspectives of classroom environments. *Journal of Social Work Education, 41*(1), 49–64.

Horejsi, C. (1977). "Homemade" simulations: Two examples from the social work classroom. *Journal of Education for Social Work, 13*, 76–82.

Quiros, L, Kay, L. & Montijo, A. M. (2012). Creating emotional safety in the classroom and in the field. *Reflections: Narratives of Professional Helping, 18*(2), 42–47.

Schiller, L. Y. (1995). Stages of development in women's groups: A relational model. In R. Kurland & R. Salmon (Eds.), *Group work practice in a troubled society* (pp. 117–138). New York, NY: The Haworth Press.

Schiller, L. Y. (1997). Rethinking stages of development in women's groups: Implications for practice. *Social Work With Groups, 20*(3), 3–19.

Schwartz, W. (1964). *The classroom teaching of social work with groups: A conceptual framework for the teaching of the social group work method.* New York, NY: Council of Social Work Education.

Shulman, L. (1987). The hidden group in the classroom: The use of group process in teaching group work practice. *Journal of Teaching in Social Work, 1*(2), 3–31.

Tuckman, B. (1965). Developmental sequence in small groups. *Psychological Bulletin, 63*, 384–399.

The Chrysalis Model: Mutual Aid in "Peer Juries," School-Based Restorative Justice Groups

Rebecca Witheridge

Peer juries are group-based restorative justice interventions used in schools to address student wrongdoing (Illinois Balanced and Restorative Justice [IBARJ] Project, 2014). Referred students meet with a group of their peers to discuss their case, make amends, and avoid punishment. I coordinated a peer jury for one academic year at a large suburban Midwestern high school and discovered that the most powerful part of the program actually occurred after the cases were complete—when referred students were invited to become jurors themselves. In this role reversal, I recognized a unique opportunity for mutual aid.

In this article I provide a brief overview of restorative justice, mutual aid, and peer jury programming. I outline the Chrysalis model of peer jury program design, which deliberately harnesses the power of mutual aid and transforms referred students into jurors, giving them an important role, a respected voice, and the ability to positively impact other referred students. Finally, gaps in the literature and recommendations for research are identified.

Relevant Concepts

Restorative Justice

Restorative justice embodies "a process where those primarily affected by an incident of wrongdoing come together to share their feelings, describe how they were affected and develop a plan to repair the harm done or prevent a recurrence" (Wachtel & McCold, 2001, p. 121).

Unlike punitive approaches of discipline, restorative justice focuses on the "spirit and intent, rather than the letter, of the law" (Stinchcomb, Bazemore, & Riestenberg, 2006, p. 125). Restorative justice argues that "crime is a violation of people and of interpersonal relationships[,] violations create obligations[, and] the central obligation is to put right the wrongs" (Zehr & Gohar, 2003, p. 17). Research has demonstrated that restorative practices effectively decrease offender recidivism and are associated with high levels of satisfaction for victims and offenders (Latimer, Dowden, & Muise, 2005).

Mutual Aid in Group Work

Mutual aid, "the healing power of receiving help while simultaneously helping others" (Gitterman, 2010, p. 7), is central to group work. It refers to "people helping one another as they think things through, [and] . . . relies on spontaneous communication and interaction" (Steinberg, 2004, p. 3) within groups. Unlike individual therapy, in which the clinician is the primary source of change, mutual aid systems require decentralized authority "as a vehicle for helping members exchange their skills and strengths" (Steinberg, 1999, p. 108). Mutual aid is what makes social work with groups unique (Steinberg, 1999).

Mutual Aid in Peer Jury Programming

Peer juries are group-based restorative justice interventions found in schools and are designed and run in a variety of ways (Burke, 2013; IBARJ Project, 2014). In the peer jury program at the school where I worked (called Peer Jury), student offenders facing suspension were referred to a confidential meeting with the student victim and a few of their peers. The group engaged in a dialogue to learn about the harm that was done, how it affected each party, and what motivated the behavior. After the referred student admitted to wrongdoing, the whole group determined a nonpunitive way that he or she could repair the harm. A written agreement was created listing specific, attainable, and measurable reparations. After they were completed, the case was closed, and the referred student's suspension was eliminated.

Peer jury sessions include all of the components needed for mutual aid, including problem solving, sharing information, and mutual support (Steinberg, 2004, p. 194). Jurors help referred students to process and learn from their misconduct while also gaining valuable skills and experiences. Referred students gain from the process (their suspensions are eliminated, they are listened to nonjudgmentally, etc.), and sessions also benefit victims, the school, and the community. The victims help the referred students to learn from their mistakes.

The Chrysalis Model:
Referred Students Become Jurors

At the school where I worked, the formal peer jury process was often followed with one seemingly small, but enormously powerful, addition: at the conclusion of each case, referred students were encouraged to become jurors themselves for other students' cases. This invitation was extended solely for recruitment purposes, but I saw that this role reversal also created a rich opportunity for mutual aid. Because referred students were often considered troublemakers by school staff, they were far more accustomed to being chastised than acting as role models. The idea that they could contribute positively to their peers and their school community was novel. For some of these students, Peer Jury was the first extracurricular activity in which they had ever participated. Not all referred students accepted the invitation, but I saw that those who did seemed to benefit and became invested members of Peer Jury.

One student, Shannon, was referred for kicking out a door and leaving school premises without permission. For the terms of her agreement, Shannon wrote a letter of apology to the janitors and created a poster encouraging her peers to stay in school. Shannon found her experience so meaningful that she decided to join Peer Jury, and soon began to volunteer as a juror multiple times a week. Not only did her participation in Peer Jury keep Shannon engaged in school, but it also provided her with a chance to share the wisdom of her own experiences with her peers. Shannon was not the only referred student who demonstrated such eagerness to help others—by the end of the school year, about one third of the volunteer juror pool consisted of previously referred students who had become invested in the program of their own accord.

To combine the strengths of restorative justice and mutual aid, I propose the Chrysalis model of peer jury. Named for its transformative nature, this model would formalize the invitation process already occurring at the school discussed in this article. As opposed to having the program end after reparations are made, each referred student would also be required to act as a juror for another referred student's case. Only after acting as juror in at least one other case would that referred student's own case be completed, and his or her suspension eliminated. With the deliberate inclusion of this invitation, Peer Jury would become truly restorative, in that it would simultaneously confront and disapprove of wrongdoing "while supporting and acknowledging the intrinsic worth of the wrongdoer" (Wachtel & McCold, 2001, p. 121). This connects directly with mutual aid in group work, which requires the involvement and acceptance of the whole person, "not just their needy or problematic parts" (Steinberg, 2010, p. 56), in order for participants to move beyond helping themselves to also helping others.

Conclusion

The Chrysalis model is a simple yet potentially transformative model of peer jury. The impact of mutual aid on participants has not yet been demonstrated in this model, suggesting the need for further study of this aspect of the model. Additionally, the impact of peer juries on recidivism needs to be investigated. Research has indicated that criminal offenders who help others by sharing their stories may be less likely to reoffend (Kenemore & Roldan, 2006; LeBel, 2007); it seems logical that referred students would experience similar benefits. Some peer jury programs in Illinois are already reintegrating offenders into the community by making them jurors (IBARJ Project, 2014), although I could find no formalized program structure reflecting this process. Further research needs to be conducted on the intersection of restorative justice practices and mutual aid in group work, as few resources currently exist.

Restorative approaches such as Peer Jury "ask not what a person's deficits are, but rather what positive contribution the person can make" (Maruna & LeBel, 2003, p. 97). Group workers aim to "devise ways of creating more helpers" (Riessman, 1965, p. 28). Giving previously referred students the chance to act as jurors for others in need is one small but mighty way of bringing these philosophies to life. Like caterpillars becoming butterflies, referred students can be transformed by mutual aid when they become helpers and not simply recipients of help.

References

Burke, K. S. (2013). *An inventory and examination of restorative justice practices for youth in Illinois*. Chicago, IL: Illinois Criminal Justice Information Authority.

Gitterman, A. (2010). Mutual aid: Back to basics. In D. M. Steinberg (Ed.), *Orchestrating the power of groups: Beginnings, middles, and endings (overture, movements, and finales)* (pp. 1–16). London, England: Whiting & Birch.

Illinois Balanced and Restorative Justice Project. (2014). *Restorative practices in schools.* Retrieved from http://www.ibarji.org/peerjuries.asp

Kenemore, T. K., & Roldan, I. (2006). Staying straight: Lessons from ex-offenders. *Clinical Social Work Journal, 34*(1), 5–21. doi:10.1007/s10615-005-0003-7

Latimer, J., Dowden, C., & Muise, D. (2005). The effectiveness of restorative justice practices: A meta-analysis. *The Prison Journal, 85*(2), 127–144. doi:10.1177/0032885505276969

LeBel, T. P. (2007). An examination of the impact of formerly incarcerated persons helping others. *Journal of Offender Rehabilitation, 46*(1/2), 1–24. doi:10.1080 /10509670802071485

Maruna, S., & LeBel, T. P. (2003). Welcome home? Examining the "reentry court" concept from a strengths-based perspective. *Western Criminology Review, 4*(2), 91–107.

Riessman, F. (1965). The "helper" therapy principle. *Social Work, 10*(2), 27–32.

Steinberg, D. M. (1999). The impact of time and place on mutual-aid practice with short-term groups. *Social Work With Groups, 22*(2/3), 101–118. doi:10.1300/J009v22n02_07

Steinberg, D. M. (2004). *The mutual-aid approach to working with groups: Helping people help one other* (2nd ed.). Binghamton, NY: The Haworth Press.

Steinberg, D. M. (2010). Mutual aid: A contribution to best-practice social work. *Social Work With Groups, 33,* 53–68. doi:10.1080/01609510903316389

Stinchcomb, J. B., Bazemore, G., & Riestenberg, N. (2006). Beyond zero tolerance: Restoring justice in secondary schools. *Youth Violence and Juvenile Justice, 4*(2), 123–147. doi:10 .1177/1541204006286287

Wachtel, T., & McCold, P. (2001). Restorative justice in everyday life. In H. Strang & J. Braithwaite (Eds.), *Restorative justice and civil society* (pp. 114–129). New York, NY: Cambridge University Press.

Zehr, H., & Gohar, A. (2003). *The little book of restorative justice.* Intercourse, PA: Good Books.

The Mind–Body Connection and Group Therapy

Rachel Seed

A growing body of recent literature and clinical interest has focused on mindfulness as a promising clinical intervention both for clients and practitioner. Mindfulness promotes the awareness and importance of the mind–body connection in the moment and emphasizes the conscious understanding of one's internal workings that may contribute to one's distress (Newsome, Waldo, & Gruszka, 2012). Although the goal of mindfulness is to increase awareness of the physical and mental self in the present moment, the foundation of the experience reduces stress and promotes relaxation. The use of mindfulness practice has been associated with higher levels of psychological wellness (Dunn, Callahan, & Swift, 2013).

Mindfulness-based theory was founded in both spiritual and neurobiological ideologies. The theory was transformed from Buddhist meditative practices and ideals. The focus is on understanding the source of internal suffering and using self-soothing coping skills to bring awareness to any source of distress and distraction. The unique approach seeks to encourage a better understanding of self to reduce anguish and promote happiness (Rejeski, 2008). Mindfulness based therapies focus on self-care, which encourages the participant to actively observe and bring awareness to the self in the moment.

Mindfulness-based practice, though grounded in spiritual foundations, has important neurobiological benefits. Practices developed from mindfulness-based theory promote the human capacity for neuroplasticity, lower emotional reactivity, and improve affect regulation (Grossman, Niemann, Schmidt, & Walach, 2004). Further neurobiological benefits include the ability to assist with balancing and rebalancing the nervous system. Humans are hardwired to fluctuate between a state of arousal (sympathetic nervous system) and a state of calmness (parasympathetic nervous system). Occasionally, however, one may find his or her self too high or too low. Practices that emphasize moment-to-moment awareness and internal regulation promote appropriate recognition of exaggerated nervous system states and assist in rebalance.

Mindfulness can be effectively learned in a group setting (Newsome et al., 2012). Group work practices and principles—the creation of a safe environment, mutual aid, and the therapeutic factors of the group process—can form the fundamentals for effectively learning, experiencing, and practicing mindfulness. Developing mindfulness techniques in a group setting allows clients to increase skills learned from others, eases anxiety, and promotes relaxation (Allen, Chambers, Knight, & Melbourne Academic Mindfulness Interest Group, 2006). Mindfulness-based group work creates a safe space that focuses on enhancing emotional processing, decreasing emotional reactivity, increasing self care, and promoting active engagement in present life.

The primary focus of a mindfulness-oriented group is to improve coping skills, increase awareness, and learn functional skills to promote relaxation. Using a group work setting, as opposed to an individual mindfulness-based session, provides participants with advantages such as peer support (universality) and mutual aid. "Group delivery mindfulness techniques provide the participants with advantages such as learning from others' insights, increased motivation to practice through peer support, and assistance with the isolation common with many illnesses" (Allen et al., 2006, p. 292).

Informal mindfulness techniques, which were used in the workshop at the XXXVI Annual Symposium of the International Association for Social Work With Groups, emphasized group work that focused on breathing, gentle movement, and visualization exercises. The combined movements—instruction in gentle stretching and breath awareness—provided participants with examples of how the skills could benefit consumers and practitioners in various settings. Participants were verbally guided through such techniques and the various practices require little to moderate mobility depending on the desired population.

A mindfulness-based group, which was presented during the workshop at the symposium, was developed for caregivers and patients and implemented at a large urban hospital. The group emphasized the neurobiological and spiritual foundations and benefits. The group involved guiding participants through 15 minutes of informal mindfulness-based techniques. The techniques consisted primarily of seated gentle movement and breathing exercises. Participants reported on an anonymous, qualitative evaluation that the group provided participants with time to "step back" and meet others in similar situations, and that they were able to become more aware of their own current emotions. The survey used a narrative response and was voluntary. The benefits of the group consisted of not only the group dynamic advantages, but also a brief period for participants to focus on self-care and learn practical skills that can be implemented into one's daily routine. The use of informal techniques in a brief period of time allows the group to be easily accessible by the busy participants in the hospital setting, and the techniques are both welcoming and user friendly.

User-friendly techniques that may be used in a time-limited group setting and were presented during the workshop included gentle stretching, standing or seated, that allowed the facilitator to guide participants to synchronize their breath with movement. This technique emphasizes simple movement in the group setting where participants focus on using breath as an anchor for movement. A body scan is another mindfulness-based technique that emphasizes the focus on each area of the body to increase awareness and relaxation. The body scan promotes both general and specific focus of attention. The guided practice brings the attention down the body to specific areas of the figure. Self-massage is a technique the further emphasizes the body scan. The self-massage technique allows participants to self-indulge and provides special attention to any noticeably tense or tight areas in the body.

Each of these skills can be learned in a time limited setting, such as the group discussed, and may be implemented in a variety of settings either standing, sitting, or laying down. Guiding members through these practices in a group setting allows participants to aid one another in their journey to relaxation and ease any anxiety that may arise during the movements and practice. Mindfulness-based practices in group delivery settings are cost and time efficient, and they allow the group to engage in motivational and mutual cathartic experiences. Mindfulness training can be a simple approach to decrease stress and potentially increase functional skills and quality of life (Zeller & Lamb, 2011).

Mindfulness-based practice has both cultural and spiritual foundations. These foundations promote the use of the approach to be used with diverse populations and settings. I plan to implement and further study the benefits of mindfulness-based group work in a long-term care setting. Goals for future clinical application include enhancing understanding of such informal mindfulness techniques with a population with undeveloped coping skills and decreased insight. Such techniques have been observed to be beneficial in geriatric populations: "Mindfulness based interventions that focus on reconnecting the mind and body around the theme of acceptance have particular therapeutic value for older adults, because physical symptoms, deteriorating biological systems, chronic disease, caregiving, and suffering are inevitable" (Rejeski, 2008, p. 140).

This foundational understanding of mindfulness-based theory and group practice offers participants a chance to observe ruminating thoughts and avoid the general inobservance many experience in daily life and stresses. The primary goal is for participants to use a brief group setting to promote self-awareness and bring attention to the present reality of any given situation or time. Continued research is recommended to further understand mindfulness-based groups and the associated benefits in various populations and settings.

References

Allen, N. B., Chambers, R., Knight, W., & Melbourne Academic Mindfulness Interest Group. (2006). Mindfulness-based psychotherapies: A review of conceptual foundations, empirical evidence and practical considerations. *The Australian and New Zealand Journal of Psychiatry*, 40(4), 285–294.

Dunn, R., Callahan, J. L., & Swift, J. K. (2013). Mindfulness as a transtheoretical clinical process. *Psychotherapy*, 50(3), 312–315.

Grossman, P., Niemann, L., Schmidt, S., & Walach, H. (2004). Mindfulness-based stress reduction and health benefits: A meta-analysis. *Journal of Psychosomatic Research*, 57(1), 35–43.

Newsome, S., Waldo, M., & Gruszka, C. (2012). Mindfulness group work: Preventing stress and increasing self-compassion among helping professionals in training. *Journal for Specialists in Group Work*, 37(4), 297–311.

Rejeski, W. J. (2008). Mindfulness: Reconnecting the body and mind in geriatric medicine and gerontology. *The Gerontologist*, 48(2), 135–141.

Zeller, J. M., & Lamb, K. (2011). Mindfulness meditation to improve care quality and quality of life in long-term care settings. *Geriatric Nursing*, 32, 2.

Index

context and method 70–1
liberatory education 70–1
overview 69–70
see also Pechakucha
social work
as change agency 38
worldview 70–1
social work education, responsibilities 89
social work practice, implications of sacred circles 38
social workers, challenges and stressors 123
socialisation 146–8
adoptive parents 196
Socratic method 231–2, 236
types of questions 232–4
South Africa 4, 5, 13–14
Special Projects Application Review Committee (SPARC) project 18–19
spirit 27
connection with 29–30
spiritual well-being 129–30
spiritual wellness 123–5
spirituality 124–5
caregivers 125
cultural relevance 145–6
and dreams 126–7
mindfulness 269
substance abuse 125
stages, of groups 62, 256
Standards for Groupwork 5–6, 8
Standing Senate Committee on Social Affairs, Science and Technology
111
status, of group work 198
Steinberg, D.M. 44, 49, 50, 166, 264
Stenius, V. 252
Stevens, K. 188
stewardship 33
stigma, and cultural relevance 149
Stinchcomb, J.B. 262
stories and storytelling, organizations 66–7
stories of timelessness 33–5
story-telling
collective discoveries 80–1
supervision 229–31
Stover, C.S. 250, 252

Lightning Source UK Ltd.
Milton Keynes UK
UKOW06f0041221015

261143UK00001B/44/P

9 781861 771384